Teaching With
Documents

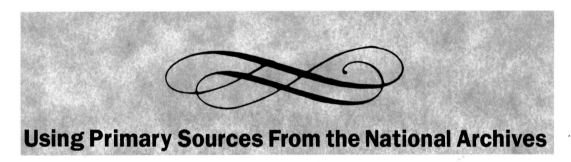

Using Primary Sources From the National Archives

National Archives and Records Administration
and
National Council for the Social Studies
Washington, DC

PUBLISHED FOR THE
NATIONAL ARCHIVES AND RECORDS ADMINISTRATION
BY THE NATIONAL ARCHIVES TRUST FUND BOARD
1989

Library of Congress Cataloging-in-Publication Data

United States. National Archives and Records Administration.
    Teaching with documents: using primary sources from the National
Archives.
      p.   cm.
   ISBN 0-911333-79-7
  1. United States — History — Study and teaching (Secondary)
  2. United States — History — Sources.   I. Title.
  E175.8.U55   1989
  973'.071'2 — dc20   89-12602

Designed by Janet Morgan Stoeke, Alexandria, VA.
Composed by General Typographers, Washington, DC.
Printed by Automated Graphic Systems, Inc., White Plains, MD.

Table of Contents

Foreword

In 1977, the National Archives began a collaboration with the National Council for the Social Studies that has been applauded ever since by classroom teachers and administrators, as well as by the two institutions themselves. Among the products of this collaboration has been a feature article in *Social Education*, the journal of NCSS, which was originally titled "Document of the Month" and is now called "Teaching with Documents." Highlighting one National Archives document in each article, "Teaching with Documents" also provides practical suggestions for using the document in several classroom settings. It has proved to be one of the journal's most popular departments.

That popularity is due, no doubt, to the enthusiasm and skillfulness of teachers who have become increasingly aware of the educational worth and the excitement of using documents in the classroom, where students can examine and comment on a letter, a report, a photograph, or a map created by someone who has participated in a significant moment of history. This interest has been one of our great satisfactions at the National Archives. It was therefore a natural step to compile these articles into one publication, convenient for teachers to use wherever they are.

DON W. WILSON
Archivist of the United States

Acknowledgments

We wish to thank those archivists, educators, and editors who helped us to produce this department. Many National Archives staff members aided us. Without their help, the search for records would have been far more time consuming and difficult. The comments and reactions of educators who have written and spoken to us have shaped and improved the document selection and the teaching exercises over the years. We have been fortunate, too, to have so many editors at the National Archives and National Council for the Social Studies who have reviewed so ably our manuscripts.

Special thanks go to the contributors who have researched and written "Document of the Month" and "Teaching With Documents." Most of the writers have been affiliated in the past or at present with the Education Branch, Office of Public Programs, National Archives and Records Administration. Mary Alexander, Walter S. Bodle, Ce Ce Byers, Marilyn Childress, Elsie T. Freeman (Freivogel), Kathryn Gent, Leslie Gray, Jean West Mueller, Wynell Burroughs Schamel, Linda Simmons, Nadine Smith, John Vernon, and J. Samuel Walker wrote with consistent clarity and attention to pedagogical and historical detail. Several classroom educators have also contributed superb articles: Patricia Baars, Marshall High School, Portland, OR; Stan Beck, Alpena High School, Alpena, MI; Jean Preer, The Catholic University of America and the National Archives Volunteer Association, Washington, DC; and Jan D. Schultz, Montgomery County Public Schools, MD. The uniform excellence of the department is a tribute to all who have been associated with it in the decade of its publication.

Introduction

Documents — reports, maps, photographs, letters, drawings, and memoirs — created by those who participated in or witnessed the events of the past tell us something that even the best written article or book cannot convey. The use of primary sources exposes students to important historical concepts. First, students become aware that all written history reflects an author's interpretation of past events. Therefore, as students read a historical account, they can recognize its subjective nature. Second, through primary sources the students directly touch the lives of people in the past. Further, as students use primary sources, they develop important analytical skills.

To many students, history is seen as a series of facts, dates, and events usually packaged as a textbook. The use of primary sources can change this view. As students use primary sources they begin to view their textbook as only one historical interpretation and its author as an interpreter of evidence, not as a purveyor of truth. For example, as students read personal letters from distressed farmers to President Franklin D. Roosevelt, as they look at WPA administrators' reports on economic conditions in Pennsylvania and Oregon, or as they listen to recordings of government-produced radio dramas, they weigh the significance of these sources against such generalizations as: "The most urgent task that Roosevelt faced when he took office was to provide food, clothing, and shelter for millions of jobless, hungry, cold, despairing Americans."[1] Students begin to understand that such generalizations represent an interpretation of past events, but not necessarily the only interpretation. They become aware that the text has a point of view that does not make it incorrect but that does render it subject to question. Primary sources force

students to realize that any account of an event, no matter how impartially presented it appears to be, is essentially subjective.

As students read eyewitness accounts of events at Little Big Horn or letters to Congressmen expressing concern about women's suffrage, or look at photographs from the Civil War and then attempt to summarize their findings, they become aware of the subjective nature of their conclusions. The disagreements among students in interpreting these documents are not unlike those among historians. Through primary sources students confront two essential facts in studying history. First, the record of historical events reflects the personal, social, political, or economic points of view of the participants. Second, students bring to the sources their own biases, created by their own personal situations and the social environments in which they live. As students use these sources, they realize that history exists through interpretation — and tentative interpretation at that.

Primary sources fascinate students because they are real and they are personal; history is humanized through them. Using original sources, students touch the lives of the people about whom history is written. They participate in human emotions and in the values and attitudes of the past. By reading a series of public opinion surveys from World War II, for example, students confront the language of the person interviewed and his or her fears about shortages, as well as the interviewer's reactions recorded after the interview. These human expressions provide history with color and excitement and link students directly to its cast of characters.

Interpreting historical sources helps students to analyze and evaluate contemporary sources — newspaper reports, television and radio programs, and advertising. D. J. Steel and L. Taylor state it well in *Family History*

---

[1] Lewis Paul Todd and Merle Curti, *Rise of the American Nation* (New York, 1966), p. 667.

in Schools: "[History] trains the child in gathering, sifting and evaluation of evidence, Such a training was never more necessary than in a society in which mass media can make children and adults the passive recipients of the carefully manipulated thought-packed politicians, advertisers, planners and bureaucrats."[2] By using primary sources, students learn to recognize how a point of view and a bias affect evidence, what contradictions and other limitations exist within a given source, and to what extent sources are reliable. Essential among these skills is the ability to understand and make appropriate use of many sources of information. Development of these skills is important not only to historical research but also to a citizenship where people are able to evaluate the information needed to maintain a free society.

Perhaps best of all, by using primary sources students will participate in the process of history. They will debate with teachers and classmates about the interpretation of the sources. They will challenge others' conclusions and seek out evidence to support their own. The classroom will become a lively arena in which students can test and apply important analytical skills.

Primary Sources and Where To Find Them: Suggestions for Teachers

To introduce your students to primary sources, you might begin with materials that they themselves possess, such as birth certificates, social security cards, passports, or drivers' licenses. What do these sources tell us about the individuals and the society in which they live? How might these sources be used by historians? Consider how school, employment, medical, and family records could be used to develop generalizations about twentieth-century student life.

Beyond personal records, there are a variety of other sources available. Where can you locate documentation on your neighborhood or community? Your sources can

be both governmental and private: Federal census figures, newspapers, local government files, personal diaries, and interviews with longtime residents. In most cities and towns, local historical groups, preservation societies, and museums serve as excellent starting points for classes locating documentary materials about local communities. On the state level, historical societies, archives, and museums are valuable depositories for useful primary materials. Many of these agencies offer specific programs for high school students, and many would welcome suggestions for joint projects.

The Education Branch of the National Archives promotes teaching with primary sources in a variety of ways. Through "Teaching with Documents" (formerly called "Document of the Month"), a regular feature in *Social Education,* it provides source materials from the National Archives with suggestions for using these documents in the classroom.

Through a series of units, the Education Branch also offers classroom teaching materials to supplement secondary-level social studies curriculums. Each of these units includes from 35 to 50 reproductions of documents from the National Archives and a teacher's guide containing suggested teaching activities. Titles in this series are *The Civil War: Soldiers and Civilians; The Progressive Years, 1889-1917; World War I: The Home Front; The 1920s; The Great Depression and New Deal; World War II: The Home Front; The Constitution: Evolution of a Government; The Truman Years: 1945-1953; Peace and Prosperity: 1953-1961;* and *The Bill of Rights: Evolution of Personal Liberties.*

To further assist you in developing your own materials from National Archives sources, the Education Branch offers an annual summer workshop: "Primary Teaching: Original Documents and Classroom Strategies." In this eight-day workshop, teachers, using National Archives material, develop units of their own choosing and design. Some of the units developed by teachers in past workshops have included a study of presidential entertaining as a cere-

---

[2]D. J. Steel and L. Taylor, *Family History in Schools* (London, 1973), p. 2.

mony, a creative writing lesson using letters from farmers to President Roosevelt during the 1930s, and a look at military discipline during the War of 1812. Before attending the workshop, teachers select topics about which appropriate materials can be located in the National Archives. During the workshop, participants review and select documents and create their own classroom approaches to them. For information on these programs write Education Branch, Office of Public Programs, National Archives, Washington, DC 20408, or call 202-523-3347.

You need not take a course to use primary sources in your classroom, however. You can collect them around a topic; or, better yet, you can ask students to find them; or, in the case of oral histories, you can create them. The returns in terms of skills development are great, and your students will begin to sense the exciting and changing nature of history.

This introduction was adapted from an article written by Mary Alexander, CeCe Byers, and Elsie Freeman.

The World Economy: An Early Problem for Young America

Although the Treaty of Paris formally ended the American Revolution on September 3, 1783, tensions between the former warring nations remained. The leaders of the former colonies faced the tasks of creating a new government and, at the same time, establishing a presence in the world. Their relations with old antagonists like the British caused special problems.

The British felt no need to cooperate with their former colonies; on the contrary, they pressured the insolvent new government to honor its treaty obligations, which included compensating Loyalists who had suffered financial losses. Pending satisfaction of those debts, British garrisons remained encamped on the western frontier. To add insult to injury, British merchants viewed the new nation as an ideal market for their goods. After the interruption of trade by the Revolution, British merchants flooded U.S. seaports with inexpensive and much-desired goods.

U.S. merchants reacted to this British competition with anger, echoing cries of earlier years. The threat to the healthy markets they had enjoyed during the military hostilities added to their ire. They petitioned their state legislators and the Congress to regulate trade between the new states and international commerce. As before the Revolution, the Massachusetts merchants voiced their concern with great force. By June 1785, under pressure from the merchants, the Massachusetts legislature formally acted to assume responsibility for regulating trade between the state and

other nations. The Massachusetts act admonished the Congress to take up the matter and to provide leadership in controlling international commerce for all the states.

The four years between the Treaty of Paris and the Constitutional Convention exposed several weaknesses of the government as established by the Articles of Confederation. In addition to the problem of maintaining a simple quorum at meetings, the Congress balanced precariously between lack of leadership and the ever-increasing demands of the states. The regulation of commerce languished as one of the issues awaiting action.

A meeting in Annapolis, Md., in 1786, was initially called to resolve differences between Maryland and Virginia over control of the Potomac River. It evolved to include representatives from five states. The experienced politicians in Annapolis quickly recognized that the problems of trade, both internal and international, were clear evidence of the inadequacies of the confederation. The Annapolis Convention adjourned without resolving the trade issues, but with a call for a convention to reform the governing system established by the Articles of Confederation. Within a year, the meeting called for in Annapolis convened in Philadelphia to revise the Articles of Confederation. Article 1, section 8, of the new U.S. Constitution created by the convention placed control of commerce squarely in the hands of the federal government. The demands of the Massachusetts merchants, as illustrated here, were finally resolved.

The Minds of the People being greatly and juftly agitated by the apparent Intention of the Government and the Merchants of Great-Britain to deprive the induftrious Trader of every Benefit of our Commerce, by the entire Monopoly of the fame to themfelves ; and this Apprehenfion being increafed by authentic Advices received by the laft Ships---A numerous and refpectable Meeting of the Merchants, Traders, and others, convened at Faneuil-Hall, on Saturday the 16th Inft. to confider the alarming State of our Trade and Navigation, the following Votes were unanimoufly agreed to :---

WHEREAS no commercial treaty is at prefent eftablifhed between thefe United States and Great-Britain : and whereas certain Britifh merchants, factors, and agents, from England, are now refiding in this town, who have received large quantities of Englifh goods, and are in expectation of receiving farther fupplies, imported in Britifh bottoms, or otherways, greatly to the hindrance of freight in all American veffels ; and as many more fuch perfons are daily expected to arrive among us, which threatens an entire monopoly of all Britifh importations in the hands of all fuch merchants, agents, or factors, which cannot but operate to the effential prejudice of the intereft of this country :

THEREFORE, to prevent, as far as poffible, the evil tendency of fuch perfons continuing among us (excepting thofe of them who fhall be approbated by the Selectmen) and to difcourage the fale of their merchandize—WE the merchants, traders, and others, of the town of Bofton, DO AGREE,

THAT a committee be appointed to draft a petition to Congrefs, reprefenting the embarrafments under which the trade now labours, and the ftill greater to which it is expofed ; and that the faid committee be empowered and directed to write to the merchants in the feveral fea-ports in this State, requefting them to join with the merchants in this town in a fimilar application to Congrefs, immediately to regulate the trade of the United States, agreeably to the powers vefted in them by the government of this Commonwealth ; and alfo to obtain inftructions to their reprefentatives at the next General Court, to call the attention of their delegates in Congrefs, to the importance of bringing forward fuch regulations as fhall place our commerce on a footing of equality.

VOTED, That the faid committee be requefted to write to the merchants in the feveral fea-ports of the other United States, earneftly recommending to them an immediate application to the Legiflatures of their refpective States, to veft fuch powers in Congrefs (if not already done) as fhall be competent to the interefting purpofes aforefaid ; and alfo to petition Congrefs, to make fuch regulations as fhall have the defired effect.

VOTED, That we do pledge our honor, that we will not directly, or indirectly, purchafe any goods of, or have any commercial connections whatever with, fuch Britifh merchants, factors, or agents, as are now refiding among us, or may hereafter arrive either from England, or any part of the Britifh dominions (except fuch perfons as fhall be approved as aforefaid)—and we will do all in our power to prevent all perfons acting under us, from having any commercial intercourfe with them until the falutary purpofes of thefe refolutions fhall have been accomplifhed.

VOTED, That we will not let or fell any warehoufe, fhop, houfe, or any other place for the fale of fuch goods, nor will we employ any perfons who will affift faid merchants, factors or agents by trucks, carts, barrows or labor (except in the refhipment of their merchandize) but will DISCOUNTENANCE all fuch perfons who fhall in any way advife, aid, or in the leaft degree, help or fupport fuch merchants, factors or agents, in the profecution of their bufinefs, as we conceive all fuch Britifh importations are calculated to drain us of our currency, and have a direct tendency to impoverifh this country.

VOTED, That a committee be appointed to wait on thofe perfons who have already let any warehoufe, fhop, houfe, or any other place, for the difpofal of the merchandize of fuch merchants, agents, or factors, and inform them of the refolutions of this meeting.

VOTED, That we will encourage, all in our power, the manufactures and produce of this country, and will, in all cafes, endeavour to promote them.

VOTED, That a committee be appointed to make immediate application to the Governor and Council of this Commonwealth, requefting them, if they think proper, to direct the feveral Naval-Officers in this State, to grant no permit for the landing of goods from the dominions of Great-Britain configned to, or the property of perfons of the aforefaid defcription, until the meeting of the Legiflature.

VOTED, That copies of thefe refolutions be printed and difperfed among the inhabitants, that they may be adopted and carried into execution, with that temper which is confiftent with the character of good citizens.

☞ ON our public virtue muft depend the fuccefs of the meafures propofed ; and relying on that zeal for the public fafety, which has been fo often and effectually exercifed by this town, they cannot fail of meeting the warm and unanimous approbation of the State in general, and of all thofe who are well-wifhers to the profperity and lafting happinefs of America.

The document is from the Papers of the Continental Congress, 1774-1789, item 42, volume 1, page 350, Record Group 360. Thanks go to James Schweiger, Dover High School, Dover, Del., for identifying this document as one of interest to students and of use to teachers.

Teaching Activities

Some 18th Century language and printing styles may confuse students. We suggest that you review this document with students before making any assignment. Be sure to point out the archaic use of "f" as "s" in the text.

1. The word puzzle on the previous page is designed to encourage students to read the document carefully. You may want to use the puzzle as a homework assignment before you discuss the document.

2. To help students understand the document, ask them to answer each of the following questions. Who developed the broadside? Where? When? In a sentence, state the main idea of the document. List the seven actions agreed to by the group. What does the broadside tell you about trade in Massachusetts after the Revolution?

3. One of the actions voted by the Boston merchants outlines a boycott of English goods. Discuss with students the concept of a boycott and direct them to develop a list of international boycotts initiated by the United States in recent years. Consider with students whether or not an international boycott is an effective diplomatic tool.

4. "Isolationism," "interdependence," "free trade," "multinational corporations," "imperialism," "post-industrial," and "monetarism" all describe aspects of the world economy today. Direct students to define these terms and to explain whether or not they can be applied to the world economic situation of the 18th Century.

5. The actions proposed by the Boston merchants directly relate to several events described in most textbooks — the naviga-tion acts, Shay's rebellion, and the Annapolis Convention. Assign students to read about one of these events and to explain how the document relates to it.

6. Broadsides such as this served to inform and to persuade citizens in the United States before the widespread use of newspapers. Direct students to develop a broadside of their own design to alert others to an injustice or an issue of special interest. Be sure to encourage students to think about the elements that make up a broadside (e.g., patriotic slogans, visuals, and logical arguments).

Word Puzzle

```
A  S  U  B  R  O  A  D  S  I  D  E
T  I  O  N  A  F  I  N  D  E  A  B
S  U  T  B  A  Y  O  W  R  T  U  O
M  O  S  F  R  I  D  O  P  D  X  Y
B  O  M  O  N  O  P  O  L  Y  U  C
D  O  M  I  S  R  T  A  F  G  H  O
E  R  M  A  F  T  N  A  R  S  I  T
X  O  S  T  H  D  O  G  F  N  M  T
D  F  A  N  E  U  I  L  H  A  L  L
```

Student directions: In the word puzzle find and circle the five words listed below.
The words may appear vertically, horizontally, or diagonally.

Boycott
Broadside
Dominions
Faneuil Hall
Monopoly

Explain in a sentence how each of the terms relates to the document.

The Ratification of the Constitution

On September 17, 1787, a majority of the delegates to the Constitutional Convention approved the document over which they had labored since May. After a farewell banquet, delegates swiftly returned to their homes to organize support, most for but some against the proposed charter. Before the Constitution could become the law of the land, it would have to withstand public scrutiny and debate. The document was "laid before the United States in Congress assembled" on September 20. For 2 days, September 26 and 27, Congress debated whether to censure the delegates to the Constitutional Convention for exceeding their authority by creating a new form of government instead of simply revising the Articles of Confederation. They decided to drop the matter. Instead, on September 28, Congress directed the state legislatures to call ratification conventions in each state. Article 7 stipulated that nine states had to ratify the Constitution for it to go into effect.

Beyond the legal requirements for ratification, the state conventions fulfilled other purposes. The Constitution had been produced in strictest secrecy during the Philadelphia convention. The ratifying conventions served the necessary function of informing the public of the provisions of the proposed new government. They also served as forums for proponents and opponents to articulate their ideas before the citizenry. Significantly, state conventions, not Congress, were the agents of ratification. This approach insured that the Constitution's authority came from representatives of the people specifically elected for the purpose of approving or disapproving the charter, resulting in a more accurate reflection of the will of the electorate. Also, by bypassing debate in the state legislatures, the Constitution avoided disabing amendments that states, jealous of yielding authority to a national government, would likely have attached.

Ratification was not a foregone conclusion. Able, articulate men used newspapers, pamphlets, and public meetings to debate ratification of the Constitution. Those known as Antifederalists opposed the Constitution for a variety of reasons. Some continued to argue that the delegates in Philadelphia had exceeded their congressional authority by replacing the Articles of Confederation with an illegal new document. Others complained that the delegates in Philadelphia represented only the well-born few and consequently had crafted a document that served their special interests and reserved the franchise for the propertied classes. Another frequent objection was that the Constitution gave too much power to the central government at the expense of the states and that representative government could not manage a republic this large. The most serious criticism was that the Constitutional Convention had failed to adopt a bill of rights proposed by George Mason. In New York, Governor George Clinton expressed these Antifederalist concerns in several published newspaper essays under the pen name Cato, while Patrick Henry and James Monroe led the opposition in Virginia.

Those who favored ratification, the Federalists, fought back, convinced that rejection of the Constitution would result in anarchy and civil strife. Alexander Hamilton, James Madison, and John Jay responded to Clinton under the name of Publius. Beginning in October 1787, these three penned

85 essays for New York newspapers and later collected them into 2 volumes entitled *The Federalist,* which analyzed the Constitution, detailed the thinking of the framers, and responded to the Antifederalist critics.

They successfully countered most criticism. As for the lack of a bill of rights, Federalists argued that a catalogued list might be incomplete and that the national government was so constrained by the Constitution that it posed no threat to the rights of citizens. Ultimately, during the ratification debate in Virginia, Madison conceded that a bill of rights was needed, and the Federalists assured the public that the first step of the new government would be to adopt a bill of rights.

It took 10 months for the first nine states to approve the Constitution. The first state to ratify was Delaware, on December 7, 1787, by a unanimous vote, 30-0. The featured document is an endorsed ratification of the federal Constitution by the Delaware convention. The names of the state deputies are listed, probably in the hand of a clerk. The signature of the president of Delaware's convention, Thomas Collins, attests to the validity of the document, which also carries the state seal in its left margin. Delaware's speediness thwarted Pennsylvania's attempt to be first to ratify in the hope of securing the seat of the national government in Pennsylvania.

The first real test for ratification occurred in Massachusetts, where the fully recorded debates reveal that the recommendation for a bill of rights proved to be a remedy for the logjam in the ratifying convention. New Hampshire became the ninth state to approve the Constitution, in June, but the key states of Virginia and New York were locked in bitter debates. Their failure to ratify would reduce the new union by two large, populated, wealthy states, and would geographically splinter it. The Federalists prevailed, however, and Virginia and New York narrowly approved the Constitution. When a bill of rights was proposed in Congress in 1789, North Carolina ratified the Constitution. Finally, Rhode Island, which

had rejected the Constitution in March 1788 by popular referendum, called a ratifying convention in 1790 as specified by the Constitutional Convention. Faced with threatened treatment as a foreign government, it ratified the Constitution by the narrowest margin, two votes, on May 29, 1790.

The Delaware ratification is taken from RG 11, the General Records of the U.S. Government.

Teaching Activities

1. Prepare students to work with a 200-year-old document by discussing such unique qualities as handwriting, spelling, formation of the letter "s," vocabulary, style, and the use of parchment and iron-based ink (which bleeds through in time). Distribute copies of the document. Read aloud the first two lines of the transcription as the students read the document silently. As a group activity, the students should continue reading the document aloud. You may help them if they stumble. Discuss the advantages and disadvantages of working with a handwritten original source.

2. Provide a copy of the Constitution for each student. Ask students to consult articles 5 and 7 along with the Delaware ratification document and compare point by point the procedures for ratifying the Constitution with the procedures for ratifying amendments to the Constitution.

3. Instruct the students to research the arguments of the debate over ratification. You could share the information in this article with your class. Ask the students to list the arguments of the Antifederalists and the counterarguments of the Federalists and then write a paragraph in response to these questions: What has been the outcome of these arguments? Are the arguments significant today?

4. Consider the Constitution as a framework of government. On the chalkboard make a list with your students of practical steps needed to activate the Constitution and institute a government, beginning with

We the Deputies of the People of the Delaware State, in Convention met, having taken into our serious consideration the Federal Constitution proposed and agreed upon by the Deputies of the United States in a General Convention held at the City of Philadelphia on the seventeenth day of September in the year of our Lord one thousand seven hundred and eighty seven, Have approved, assented to, ratified, and confirmed, and by these Presents, Do in virtue of the Power and Authority to us given for that purpose, for and in behalf of ourselves and our Constituents fully, freely, and entirely approve of, assent to, ratify, and confirm the said Constitution.

Done in Convention at Dover the seventh day of December in the year aforesaid and in the year of the Independence of the United States of America the twelfth. In Testimony whereof we have hereunto subscribed our Names—

[certification paragraph]
... to all whom these Presents shall come Greeting, I Thomas ... Collins President of the Delaware State do hereby certify that the above instrument of writing is a true copy of the original ratification of the Federal Constitution by the Convention of the Delaware State, which original ratification ... now on my ... to affix. In Testimony whereof I have caused the seal of the Delaware State to be hereunto affixed.

Tho Collins

New Castle County	Kent County	Sussex County
Gunning Bedford	Nicholas Ridgely	John Ingram
Jacob Broom	Richard Smith	John Jones
Gunning Bedford Jun	George Truitt	William Moore
Richard Bassett	Richard Bassett	William Hall
James Sykes		Thomas Laws
Allen McLane		Isaac Cooper
Daniel Cummins Senr		Woodman Stockly
Joseph Barker		John Laws
Nicholas Way		Thomas Evans
Thomas Duff		Israel Holland
Edward White		
George Manlove		
Gunning Bedford Jun		

the ratification procedures, election of the President, selection of a capital site, etc. The resolution of the Constitutional Convention on September 17, 1787, sometimes referred to as the fifth page of the Constitution, is a good resource for this activity. In a discussion of these steps, lead your students to recognize the difference between the theory in a document written to describe a government and the reality of putting a government into action.

5. Assign your students to research the ratification story in specific states (their own home states and states selected as case studies). Set up a story-telling day in which each student tells the best stories they found in their research.

6. The delegates of the Delaware convention whose names appear on the ratification document provide an interesting sociological study. Ask your students to look carefully at the names and describe the patterns or categories they recognize. Note: Your students should observe the emerging patterns of ethnic groups, the sex, and the origin of the names listed.

Order	State	Date	Votes for	Votes Against
1	Delaware	December 7, 1787	30	0
2	Pennsylvania	December 12, 1787	46	23
3	New Jersey	December 18, 1787	38	0
4	Georgia	January 2, 1788	26	0
5	Connecticut	January 9, 1788	128	40
6	Massachusetts	February 6, 1788	187	168
7	Maryland	April 28, 1788	63	11
8	South Carolina	May 23, 1788	149	73
9	New Hampshire	June 21, 1788	57	47
10	Virginia	June 25, 1788	89	79
11	New York	July 26, 1788	30	27
12	North Carolina	November 21, 1789	194	77
13	Rhode Island	May 29, 1790	34	32

Text of the Document

We the Deputies of the People of Delaware State in Convention met having taken into our serious consideration the Federal Constitution proposed and agreed upon by the Deputies of the United States in a General Convention held at the City of Philadelphia on the seventeenth day of September in the year of our Lord one thousand seven hundred and eighty seven, Have approved, assented to, ratified, and confirmed and by these Presents, Do, in virtue of the Power and Authority to us given for the purpose for and in behalf of ourselves and our Constituents, fully, freely, and entirely approve of, assent to, ratify, and confirm the said Constitution.

Done in Convention at Dover this seventh day of December in the year aforesaid and in the year of the Independence of the United States of America the twelfth. In Testimony whereof we have hereunto subscribed our Names

To all whom these Presents shall come Greeting. I Thomas Collins President of the Delaware State do hereby certify that the above instrument of writing is a true copy of the original ratification of the Federal Constitution by the Convention of the Delaware State which original ratification is now in my possession. In Testimony whereof I have caused the seal of the Delaware State to be hereunto anexed.

Tho.⁵ Collins

Sussex County
John Ingram
John Jones
William Moore
William Hall
Thomas Laws
Isaac Cooper
Woodman Storkly
John Laws
Thomas Evans
Israel Holland

Kent County
Nicholas Ridgely
Richard Smith
George Truitt
Richard Bassett
James Sykes
Allen McLane
Daniel Cummins, Sr.
Joseph Barker
Edward White
George Manlove

New Castle County
Ja.ˢ Latimer, President
James Black
Jn.ᵃ James
Gunning Bedford, Sr.
Kensey Johns
Thomas Watson
Solomon Maxwell
Nicholas Way
Thomas Duff
Gunn.ᵍ Bedford, Jr.

Maps Using Hachure and Contour Methods

Map makers have traditionally used various means to represent the three dimensions of the earth in two-dimensional images. Prior to the nineteenth century, for example, the most common device for indicating relief on a map was through variations of light and shade.

As the use of shading became systematized during the eighteenth and nineteenth centuries, French cartographers referred to these shading lines as "hachures." Hachures represent the slope of the land — the more gentle the slope, the fewer the lines — and the absence of line indicates flat terrain. The illustration on the right side of the document is an example of this system.

The use of contour lines to visually represent different elevations of land came into general use toward the end of the nineteenth century. An early version of a contour map is seen on the left. Simply speaking, a single contour line corresponds to a single elevation of the land. Because the contour line defines a curved surface (the earth), each line encloses a more or less circular area. The total effect is a pattern of concentric lines. The "base" line or *datum* for most contour maps is sea level, with each line on the map representing a standard distance above or below the base line. As each line signifies an increase or decrease in the land elevation (in this map, 3 feet), one can accurately calculate height by simply counting the lines from the base line (the water's edge in this instance). The slope of any change in the landscape relief can also be determined by noting the proximity of the contour lines to one another. A high concentration of lines tells the map user that the elevation changes sharply, while widely spaced lines indicate a gradual slope.

The two maps of Salem Neck, Massachusetts, surveyed by George W. Whistler (father of artist James A. McNeill Whistler) and William G. McNeill, topographical engineers for the United States Army, were created for a study conducted in 1822 of fortifications in the area. When the Office of Chief of Engineers decided in 1861 to study the feasibility of reconditioning the forts, they referred to these maps and the reports accompanying them.

This document is part of the records of the Office of the Chief of Engineers, United States Army (Record Group 77, Fortifications file, drawer 18, sheet 11).

Suggestions for Teaching

In order for students to answer the following questions, they must (a) examine the maps closely, (b) familiarize themselves with the scale and accompanying note (located at the bottom center of the document), and (c) understand contour and hachure methods of mapping. (The exercises can be adjusted to meet the needs of your students.)

Maps as Maps — Basic Map Skills:

1. What evidence is there in this document that tells you that the land area is not an island?

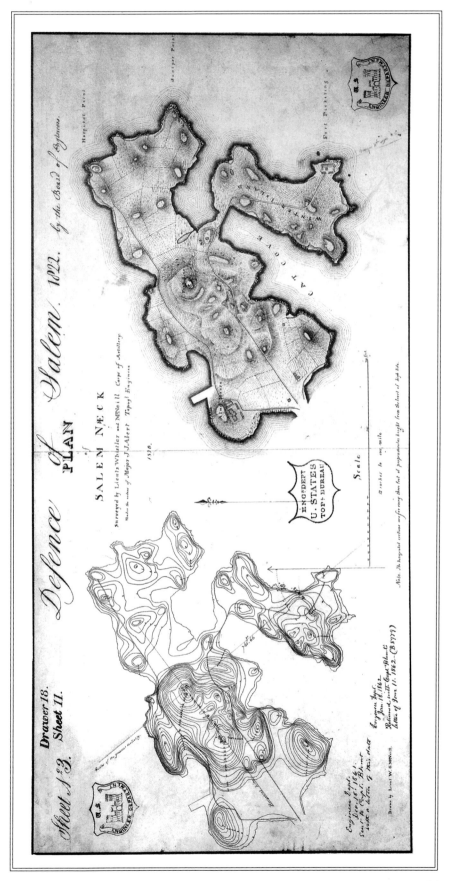

11

2. What descriptive information contained in the map on the right side of the illustration is omitted on the left?

3. Calculate the length and width of Salem Neck in miles.

4. How are points of elevation represented on each of these maps?

5. Using both maps, try to calculate the height of the area where the Alms House is located. Which of the two maps is preferable? Why?

Maps as Historical Documents:

1. What does this document tell you about mapping techniques in 1822?

2. Is there evidence in the document that the map was used after 1822?

3. How might this document have been useful to historians and/or cartographers in the past? How and why might it be used today?

4. Can you find Salem Neck on a contemporary map? Why or why not?

Census of Cherokees in the Limits of Georgia in 1835

The year 1835 marked the end of an era for 16,542 Cherokee Indians living in parts of North and South Carolina, Kentucky, Tennessee, Alabama, and Georgia. Under pressure from state and federal authorities, a small group of Cherokee signed the Treaty of New Echota with the United States government; it ceded their eastern lands. Under terms of the treaty, the tribe received designated lands west of the Mississippi River and was ordered to relocate within two years. Most Cherokee had to be forced to leave their lands under military escort in 1838 and 1839.

In 1835 the United States government directed the Office of Indian Affairs to take a federal census of the Cherokee. This census served to record the number of Cherokee and to establish the value of their lands. The 66-page tabulation reveals much about nineteenth-century Cherokee lifestyle.

Census statistics indicate that by 1835 the Cherokee had adapted to the encroaching white culture. Unlike many other tribes, the Cherokee engaged in farming, rather than hunting, as a primary means of subsistence. Of 2,668 families registered in this census, 2,495 (about 93 percent) had at least one farm. The Cherokee economic structure also included black slaves. In 1824, the Cherokee owned more than 1,000 slaves; by the time of this census, the number had increased to 1,500. Light industry was another aspect of white influence on the Cherokee economy. Indian spinsters and weavers manufactured cloth and clothing. Census records of sawmills and gristmills provide further evidence of industries, similar to neighboring white culture.

Perhaps the most striking feature of eastern Cherokee culture was the development of a written language. The 1835 census documents a small, but significant, percentage of literacy among the Cherokee. Sequoya had invented a Cherokee syllabary of 86 characters by 1821; by 1828, the first copy of a newspaper printed in Cherokee and English, the *Cherokee Phoenix*, was in circulation.

The document reproduced here is a portion of page 49 from the 1835 census of the Cherokee. Thirty-eight columns of information fill two pages (numbered page 49). Information is filled in under the following column headings: Heads of Families, Indians, Half-breeds, Quadroons, and Whites; Residence, State and County, and Watercourse; Males, Under 18 years; Males, Over 18 years; Females, Under 16 years; Females, Over 16 years; Total Cherokees; Slaves, Males; Slaves, Females; Total Slaves; Whites connected by marriage; Farms; Acres in cultivation; Houses; Bushels wheat raised; Bushels corn raised; Bushels corn sold; For how much; Bushels corn bought; For how much; Mills; Ferry boats; Farmers over 18 years; Mechanics over 18 years; Readers in English; Readers in Cherokee; Half-breeds; Quadroons; Full-blooded; Mixed Catawbys; Mixed Span-

CENSUS OF CHEROKEES in the limits of *Georgia* in 1835,

HEADS OF FAMILIES, INDIANS, HALF-BREEDS, QUADROONS, AND WHITES.	RESIDENCE, STATE AND COUNTY, AND WATERCOURSE.	MALES.		FEMALES.		TOTAL CHEROKEES.	SLAVES.			Whites connected by marriage.	Farms.	Acres in cultivation.	Houses.	Bushels wheat raised.	Bushels corn raised.	Bushels wheat sold.		For how much.	Bushels corn bought.	For how much.
		Under 18 years.	Over 18 years.	Under 16 years.	Over 16 years.		Males.	Females.	Total Slaves.											
	Floyd County Ga.																			
Eulaulanah	Etowee River	6	1	2	3	12					1	6	2		10	31			30	12
The Spirit	"		1	6	2	10					1	5	1		1				25	125
Nancy Harris	"		1	4	3	2	10				1	2	3		30				12	12
John Fields	"	3	3	3	1	10	1		1		1	30	7		100					
Mills	"	3	1	1	1	6					1	5	2		100	30		15		
Stitch	"	1	2	3	4	10					1	5	3		100					
Sucking	"		1		1	2					1	2	1		30					
Soobin	"		1		1	2					1	2	2		10					
Tahtayle	"	4	1		1	6					1	13	4		100	10		5		
Peggy	"		1	1	2	4														
Don't do it	"	1	5	4	6	16					1	18	7		300	30		125		
George	"	2	1	1	1	5					1	12	3		200					
Cininiah tahtakee	"	4	2	1	2	9					1	12	6		200	40		20		
Cudon the Roost	"	3	1	2	1	7					1	5	3		50	10		5		
Buffalo Fish	"	3	2	1	4	10	2	1	3		1	30	7		300	100		50		
Water Hunter	"		1	1	1	3		1	1		1	10	4		100	30		15		
Owing Snake	"		1		4	5					1	3	1		75	20		10		
Quiney Vann	"	5	1	1	1	8	1	1	2		1	30	6		30					
Jacob West	"	2	3	1	1	7	8	5	13	1	1	100	15	11	2000	400		700		
Foggs	"	2	1	2	2	7							2							
David Vann	Ceader Ck.	3	1		2	6	7	6	13		1	200	17		2500	1000		300		
John	"		1	1	1	3					1	2	2		30					
David Harris	Ballplay Ck.		1			1														
Little Meat	Ceader Ck.	2			1	3					1	1			20	8		4		
Roasting Fox	Coosa River	2	2	1	1	6					1	12	5		15					
Samuel	"		3	4	2	9					1	5	2		50					
Kahnenah	"		2	1	1	4					1	7	4		60	6		6		
Jim Foster	"	1	1	6	3	11					1	3			30					
Ootalie	"				1	1					1	6	1		40					
Tooewskee	"	1	2	2	3	8					1	6	1		30					
Sam Spring	"	1	2		2	5					1				30				5	112
Ahkechy	Beach Creek	1	1	4	1	7					1	5	2		40					
Cuyyooskee	"	2	1	4	2	9					1	10	3		200	15		114		
Samuel Mills	Coosa River	2	1	1	2	6					1	30	7		100				10	5
Sweet Rail	"	2	1	3	1	7					1	4	2		30				4	2
Cabbon Smith	"	1	1		1	3	4	1	5		1	40	11		20	50		50		
Homony Smith	Chattooga Riv.		1	2	1	4					1		2							
Ned Lee	Coosa River	2	1	4	1	8					2	8	3		6				10	5
Tuttle	"	4	2	2	2	10					1	2			0				1	14
Main Crow	Chattooga Riv.	3	2	1	3	9		3	3	1	1	14	4		200	50		25	5	4
Robbin McGear	"		1	1	1	3					1	1	1		2					
Bread Cutter	"		1	1	1	3					1	3	2		20	10		6		
Arch Sallee	"	1	2	2	1	6					2	15	1		100	300		170		
Jim Saccullee	"	1	1	1	1	4					1	10	2		300	70		30		
Tom Saccullee	"	1		2	2	11				1	1	25	2		20	150		72		
		70	68	76	78	292	22	19	41	3	42	767	173	11	7038	3460			102	574

iards; Mixed Negroes; Weavers; Spinsters; Reservees; Descendants of Reservees; Total; and Remarks.

The 18 headings on the right of page 49, not reproduced here, reveal that of the 292 Cherokee listed, there were: 18 who read English, 38 who read Cherokee, 51 weavers, 72 spinsters, 4 mechanics, 169 fullblooded Cherokee, 12 half-breeds, and 9 quadroons. There were also three gold mines on the property of Roasting Fox, Burnt Rail, and Tovesuskee. There were no ferry boats or mills.

This document is from the Census of Cherokees in the limits of Tennessee, Alabama, North Carolina, and Georgia in 1835, Entry 219, Records of the Bureau of Indian Affairs, Record Group 75.

Suggestions for Teaching

1. *Motivator:* Provide each student with a copy of the Cherokee census and the puzzle. Each answer builds on the answer to the previous question. The answers are: (1) 292, (2) 3, (3) 876 (4) 16, (5) 892, (6) 2, (7) 1784, (8) 41, (9) 1,825, (10) 10, (11) 1,835, (12) the final answer is 1835.

2. *What's in a Name?* Direct students to choose for themselves descriptive names to reflect their personalities, interests, or objects important to them. Collect the names in a list and read each name to the class. Ask students to try to match the descriptive names with the persons who selected those names.

3. *Testing a Generalization:* The worksheet below lists ten generalizations relating to Cherokee Indians in 1835. Students are directed to weigh the validity of those generalizations by using the document. Reproduce and distribute a copy of the document and worksheet for each student. Once the worksheets are completed, review student responses.

4. *Map Skills.* Direct students to an atlas of the United States and ask them to locate the Cherokee tribe in 1835 by using the geographical information provided in the census. Ask students to answer the following questions:
    a. In what area of Georgia did the Cherokee in this census reside?
    b. What major city is in this area today?
    c. Estimate the number of miles that the Cherokee had to travel to reach the Mississippi River.

5. *Creative Writing.* Direct students to assume the role of one of the Cherokee recorded on the census list. Ask them to compose a letter to the federal government or to a fellow Cherokee that describes their feelings after learning of the Treaty of New Echota. Ask students to include in their letters how they think life would be different and what they would miss most.

6. *Synthesis:* Ask students to write a short paragraph describing the lifestyle of the Cherokee based on the information provided in the 1835 census. Students might include such topics as work, family, slaves, and crops.

Cherokee Census: A Puzzle

(1) _____ Find the total number of Cherokee recorded in this census. Indicate this number on the line to the left.

(2) _____ Locate the number of Indians connected by marriage to whites.

(3) _____ *Multiply* answer #1 by answer #2.

(4) _____ How many Cherokee lived near Beach Creek?

(5) _____ *Add* answer #4 to answer #3.

(6) _____ How many persons owned 10 or more slaves?

(7) _____ *Multiply* answer #5 by answer #6.

(8) _____ What is the total number of slaves owned by all the Cherokee?

(9) _____ *Add* answer #8 to answer #7.

(10) _____ How many bushels of corn did Roasting Fox raise?

(11) _____ *Add* answer #10 to answer #9.

(12) [_____] Enter your final answer here.

Worksheet

Instructions for Students: Below are ten statements about the Cherokee Indians in 1835. Using the census page, decide whether or not the document supports the statement and mark your answer in one of the columns to the left. If you are uncertain, mark the "Need More Information" column.

Yes	No	Need More Information	
____	____	____	1. Most Cherokee were farmers.
____	____	____	2. The Cherokee tribe was nomadic.
____	____	____	3. The Cherokee sold most of the corn they raised.
____	____	____	4. The federal government only recognized males as the heads of households.
____	____	____	5. The government identified Cherokee residences by the closest body of water.
____	____	____	6. The Cherokee were slaveholders.
____	____	____	7. Floyd County, Georgia, was a good place to grow corn.
____	____	____	8. Very few Cherokee intermarried with whites.
____	____	____	9. Animals were important to the Cherokee.
____	____	____	10. Some Cherokee could read English.

A Ship's Manifest, 1847

Between 1820 and 1874, the captains or masters of all vessels arriving in United States ports from foreign countries were required to submit a list of passengers, known as the *manifest,* to the Collector of Customs in the district in which the ship arrived. These reports included information regarding the age, sex, occupation, nationality, and destination of the aliens. The District Collector of Customs sent quarterly reports with copies of the manifests to the Secretary of State, who submitted this information to Congress. By 1874, only statistical reports to the Treasury Department were required of the customs collectors. In 1891, the Office of Superintendent of Immigration was created under the Treasury Department to further centralize control over immigration.

The ship's manifest presented here is the first page of the passenger list of the brig *Acadian* for May 14, 1847, the year in which 234,968 alien passengers arrived at ports in the United States. Irish immigration peaked between 1841 and 1850, with 49% of the aliens entering the United States coming from Ireland.

This manifest is part of the records of the Bureau of Customs (Record Group 36). The complete manifest is available on microfilm at the National Archives, or through your nearest regional Archives. The microfilm number is M277, roll 22.

Suggestions for Teaching

Duplicate copies of the manifest for your class to use in small groups or individually. Review the arrangement of the manifest with the class, and make note of the column headings. These headings will be essential to the students' understanding of the document.

Questions and Activities for Students:

1. What kinds of information about the passengers can be found in the manifest? Consider the following:
    a. What is the nationality of most passengers?
    b. What are the occupations of the passengers?
    c. What are the final destinations of the passengers?
    d. Note that some of the passengers have the same surnames. What might this tell you about them?
    e. Why would the government want or need to collect information about these passengers?

2. Describe in writing four passengers, or groups of passengers, on the *Acadian.* For example: Ann Brogin was a 20-year-old servant from Ireland traveling to the United States. (This exercise is designed to help students begin to identify and organize the information found in the document. It is necessary for students to be able to do this before they begin to deal with matters of interpretation.)

3. Make a list of possible reasons why you think many of the passengers might be traveling to North America. (Consider the date of the manifest and relevant European events.)

4. What conclusions, if any, about immigration might be drawn from this manifest? (Make sure your conclusions are based on information found within the document.)

5. How might this document, and others like it, be used in a family history project? (Consider the ethnic population of Boston today.)

COPY of Report and List of the Passengers taken on board the *Brig Aradian* of *Boston* whereof *Thos Y Mood* is Master, burthen *137* tons, and 00ths of a ton, bound from the Port of *Halifax* for *New York.*

NAMES.	AGE.	SEX.	Occupation, Trade, or Profession.	Country to which they severally belong.	Country of which they intend to become inhabitants.	Remarks relative to any who may have died or left the vessel during the voyage.
Miss Jordan McLane	30	Female		Nova Scotia	Nova Scotia	
Miss Charlotte McDougall	18	"		Newfoundland		
Louisa J Kennett	10	"				
Wm H O Graham	36	Male	Merchant	Nova Scotia	Congress No States	
Wm Howard Rd	25	"	Carpenter	Scotland		
Revd Peter Ross	38	"		No State		
Robt McMurdock	20	Female		Nova Scotia		
" Dunn	40	"	Servant			
" Henry	51	"	"			
" McIvoth	17	"	Dry Maker			
" Ann Gough	32	"	"		Ireland	
Ellen Finny	53	"	Servant			
Mary Mackery	45	"				
Sarah McBrady	13	"				
Ann McElwary	7	"				
Bridget McElwary	10	"	Servant			
Ann McElwany	20	"				
Mary Brogin	21	"				
Catharine Dolin	14 Mo	"	Trader	No States		
Mrs Dolin	30	Male	Mechanic			
Patk Murphy	30	"	Farmer			
John H McCoy	40	"	Mayor			
Danl McCoy	40	"	"			
Edward O'Brien	40	"	Laborer			
Michael Edward	32	"				

Lincoln's Spot Resolutions

Tension has existed between the legislative and the executive branches of the U.S. government over war powers since the Constitution simultaneously vested Congress with the power to declare war and the president with the power of commander in chief.

Although Jefferson insisted on congressional approval before sending troops into combat, later presidents have not felt bound by this precedent. Their alternate view was boosted by the Supreme Court in 1827 in the case *Martin* v. *Mott.* The Court ruled that it was constitutional for Congress to vest the president with the discretionary authority to decide whether an emergency had arisen and to raise a militia to meet such a threat of invasion or civil insurrection. Nonetheless, in the winter of 1845-46, as relations between the United States and Mexico deteriorated, there was no express delineation of powers between the two branches.

Prior to Texas's independence, the Neuces River was recognized as the northern boundary of Mexico. Spain had fixed the Neuces as a border in 1816, and the United States ratified it in the 1819 treaty by which the United States had purchased Florida and renounced claims to Texas.

Even following Mexico's independence from Spain, American and European cartographers fixed the Texas border at the Neuces. When Texas declared its independence, however, it claimed as its territory an additional 150 miles of land, to the Rio Grande. With the annexation of Texas in 1845, the United States adopted Texas's position and claimed the Rio Grande as the border.

Mexico broke diplomatic relations with the United States and refused to recognize either the Texas annexation or the Rio Grande border. President James Polk sent a special envoy, John L. Slidell, to propose cancellation of Mexico's debt to United States citizens who had incurred damages during the Mexican Revolution, provided Mexico would formally recognize the Rio Grande boundary. Slidell was also authorized to offer the Mexican government up to $30 million for California and New Mexico.

Between Slidell's arrival on December 6, 1845, and his departure in March 1846, the regime of President Jose Herrara was overthrown and a fervently nationalistic government under General Mariano Paredes seized power. Neither leader would speak to Slidell. When Paredes publicly reaffirmed Mexico's claim to all of Texas, Slidell left in a temper, convinced that Mexico should be "chastised."

Zachary Taylor

The agent for chastisement was already in place. On January 13, 1846, more than 3,500 troops commanded by General Zachary Taylor moved south under President Polk's order, from Corpus Christi on the Neuces River to a location on the north bank of the Rio Grande. Advancing on March 8 to Point Isabel, the U.S. troops found that the settlement had been burned by fleeing Mexicans. By March 28, the troops were near the mouth of the Rio Grande across from the Mexican town of Matamoros.

Polk claimed the move was a defensive measure, and expansionists and Democratic newspapers in the United States applauded his action. Whig newspapers said that the movement was an invasion of Mexico rather than a defense of Texas. While newspapers in Mexico called for war, General Pedro de Ampudia warned, "If you insist in remaining upon the soil of the department of Tamaulipas, it will clearly result that arms, and arms alone, must decide the question."

General Ampudia's prediction came true on April 25 when Mexican cavalry crossed the Rio Grande and attacked a mounted American patrol, killing five, wounding eleven, and capturing forty-seven.

President Polk

In Washington, President Polk, although unaware of the developments, had drafted a message asking Congress to declare war on Mexico on the basis of Mexico's failure to pay U.S. damage claims and refusal to meet with Slidell. At a cabinet meeting on May 9, he notified his cabinet that he would ask for war in a few days. Only Secretary of the Navy George Bancroft counseled for delay, waiting for a Mexican attack.

On that evening, Polk received Taylor's account of the April 25 skirmish. Polk revised his war message, then sent it to Congress on May 11 asserting, "Mexico has passed the boundary of the United States, has invaded our territory and shed American blood upon America's soil." On May 13, Congress declared war, with a vote of 40-2 in the Senate and 174-14 in the House.

Although Congress had declared war, it was not without reservation. An amendment was proposed, although defeated, to indicate that Congress did not approve of Polk's order to move troops into disputed territory. Sixty-seven Whig representatives voted against mobilization and appropriations for a war.

Ohio Senator Tom Corwin accused Polk of involving the United States in a war of aggression. Senator John C. Calhoun of South Carolina abstained from voting, correctly foreseeing that the war would aggravate sectional strife. Massachusetts Senator

Daniel Webster voiced doubts about the constitutionality of Polk's actions, believing that Polk had failed to consult adequately with Congress. As the war deepened, "Conscience" Whigs denied Polk had tried to avoid war.

A freshman Whig congressman from Illinois, Abraham Lincoln, questioned whether the "spot" where blood had been shed was really U.S. soil. On December 22, 1847, he introduced the "Spot Resolutions," of which the second and third pages of Lincoln's handwritten copy are shown. One of several congressional resolutions opposing the war, it was never acted upon by the full Congress. Lincoln's action temporarily earned him a derisive nickname, "spotty Lincoln," coined by one Illinois newspaper.

Other citizens shared their legislators' concern, particularly those in the Northeast who saw the war as a ploy to extend slavery. The most celebrated was Henry David Thoreau, who refused to pay his $1 Massachusetts poll tax because he believed the war an immoral advancement of slavery.

Acerbic former president John Quincy Adams described the war as a southern expedition to find "bigger pens to cram with slaves." Regional writer James R. Lowell, author of the *Biglow Papers,* had his Yankee farmer Hosea Biglow scorn fighting to bring in new slave states. Charles Sumner, a noted abolitionist, also condemned the war from pacifist principles. Philadelphian Joseph Sill's diary records widespread public disapproval for the war by October 1847. The Massachusetts state legislature resolved the war an unconstitutional action because it was initiated by order of the president with the "triple object of extending slavery, of strengthening the slave power and of obtaining the control of the free states."

Concern that Taylor's order sending troops into the disputed territory provoked the clash was foremost in an October 1847 article in one Whig newspaper, *The American Review:* "The Constitution contemplates that before deliberate hostilities shall

Resolved by the House of Representatives, that the President of the United States be respectfully requested to inform this House—

First: Whether the spot of soil on which the blood of our citizens was shed, as in his messages declared, was, or was not, within the territories of Spain, at least from the treaty of 1819 until the Mexican revolution

Second: Whether that spot is, or is not, within the territory which was wrested from Spain, by the Mexican revolution—

Third: Whether that spot is, or is not, within a settlement of people, which settlement had existed ever since long before the Texas revolution, until its inhabitants fled from the approach of the U.S. Army—

Fourth: Whether that settlement is, or is not, isolated from any and all other settlements, by the Gulf of Mexico, and the Rio Grande, on the South and West, and by wide uninhabited regions on the North and East—

Fifth: Whether the People of that settlement, or a majority of them, or any of them, had ever, previous to the bloodshed, mentioned in his messages, submitted themselves to the government or laws of Texas, or of the United States, by consent, or by compulsion, either by accepting office, or voting at elections, or paying taxes, or serving on juries, or having process served upon them, or in any other way—

Sixth: Whether the People of that settlement, did, or did not, leaving unprotected their homes and their growing crops, flee from the approach of the United States Army, before the blood was shed, as in his messages stated; and whether the first blood so shed, was, or was not shed, within the enclosure of the People, or some of them, who had thus fled from it—

Seventh: Whether our citizens, whose blood was shed, as in his messages declared, were, or were not, at that time, armed officers, and soldiers, sent into that settlement, by the military order of the President through the Secretary of War— and

Eighth: Whether the military force of the United States, including those citizens, was, or was not, so sent into that settlement, after Genl. Taylor had, more than once, intimated to the War Department that, in his opinion, no such movement was necessary to the defence or protection of Texas—

be undertaken in any case, a declaration of war shall be made; but in this case a hostile aggressive move was made under the personal orders of the President."

Ironically, when Lincoln became president, he extended the war powers of the executive, action he had criticized as a congressman. Following the firing on Fort Sumter, he declared a naval blockade on his own authority. The capture and condemnation of four runners led to a case that went to the Supreme Court. In 1863 the Court affirmed Lincoln's actions in the *Prize Cases*, 2 Black 635.

The "Spot Resolutions" are kept in the Records of the U.S. House of Representatives, RG 233, HR 30 A-B 3. A reproduction of the first page of the resolutions is available upon request from the Education Branch, NEEE, National Archives, Washington, DC 20408.

Teaching Suggestions

Interpreting the Document
1. Students should review information in their textbooks about the U.S. entry into the Mexican War and opposition to that war. Supplement the text with information from the note to the teacher.

2. Ask students to locate on a map or in an atlas the following geographical features: the Neuces River, the Rio Grande, Corpus Christi, Point Isabel, Matamoros.

3. Ask students to read the document, either aloud as a class or silently. Then ask them to summarize each of the eight resolutions in their own words.
   a. Using the text and teacher's note, ask students to answer each of Lincoln's points.
   b. Using Polk's war message, ask students to answer each of the points.
   c. Ask students to compile a list of secondary sources where they might find information to resolve the discrepancies between the two versions of the events.
   d. Ask students to compile a list of primary sources that they could examine to resolve the discrepancies between the two versions.

Public Opinion
1. Most students are aware that television influences public opinion from politics to fashion, but they are less sensitive to the impact of other forms of communication. As a class, discuss the following questions.
   a. Apart from television, how do they get information about current events?
   b. Apart from television, what sources do they turn to for information upon which to base an opinion? (For example, consumer, book, movie, record, or fashion reviews, and editorials?)
   c. Can they tell what side of an issue their local newspaper favors? Opposes? How?
   d. Apart from articles on the editorial page, what other decisions made by newspaper editors influence public opinion and knowledge?
   e. What impact would political party newspapers have had in the 1840s, an era before television or radio?

2. Antiwar protesters did not just appear with the Vietnam War, as some students believe. Time permitting, you may wish to assign students to read Thoreau's essay "Civil Disobedience," or the play based on his incarceration, *The Night Thoreau Spent in Jail*, or James R. Lowell's *Biglow Papers*, or other examples of opposition to the Mexican War. Students should report to the class the issues raised and tactics used by these earlier protesters.

3. Direct students to look into earlier and later antiwar material, from Aristophanes' *Lysistrata* to Holly Near's songs about the conflict in Central America. Ask students to conduct research and prepare written or oral reports or to write an editorial on one of the following topics:
   a. Protesters of conscience against wars other than the Mexican War,
   b. Moral issues raised by conscientious objectors at different periods in history,
   c. Tactics used by antiwar protesters over time and how these tactics have changed.

Lincoln's Letter to Siam

Historical Background
(Note: Siam became Thailand in 1939.)

Very early in our nation's history, foreign nations began to offer gifts to the President and other high-ranking officials. Article 1, section 9, of the Constitution clearly sets forth the United States government's position on gift offers from heads of foreign governments to federal officials. The specific clause reads: "No Person holding any Office of Profit or Trust under them [the United States], shall, without the Consent of Congress, accept of any present, Emolument, Office, or Title, of any kind whatever, from any King, Prince, or foreign State." When consulted, however, Congress has often allowed United States diplomats to accept relatively inexpensive foreign gifts, especially when refusal of a token gift might be construed as an insult.

Most Presidents accepted gifts only on behalf of the American people, and they deposited them in governmental archives. Usually the State Department received these gifts in the President's name and Congress assumed responsibility for their ultimate disposition. Congress formalized this policy in 1881. But, as the actions of subsequent administrations indicated, the 1881 gift law did not sufficiently address a number of significant questions: Could the President keep gifts personally intended for him as opposed to those officially tendered to him as head of his government? Could the State Department turn over gifts it had received during his term to the President when he left office? Could official gifts be housed somewhere other than with State Department archives — for example, in a Presidential Library? Since 1881, various interpretations of these questions have prompted Congress to draft additional legislation to clarify its position toward foreign gifts.

Lincoln's Response to a Royal Proffer

From 1851 to 1868, Maha Mongkut (Rama IV) ruled Siam. Like the kings that preceded him, King Rama IV wished to resist Western imperialist designs upon Siam, but, unlike them, he so admired certain Western practices, particularly in education, that he sought contacts in the West. His unique melding of Eastern and Western ways has been fancifully characterized in the movie "The King and I." His letters to the United States Presidents of his day are among the treasures of the National Archives.

The two letters to which Lincoln replied demonstrate King Rama IV's knowledge of the United States, or at least its government. One letter recognized that the President could accept royal gifts only as "the common property of the Nation"; the other noted the United States military experiment to introduce camels into the American Southwest and suggested that, in the same spirit, elephants be imported from Siam to perform heavy labor.

In his reply to this offer by King Rama IV, Lincoln graciously accepts three gifts — a daguerreotype portrait of King Rama IV and his favorite daughter (right), a sword, and elephant tusks. However, he courteously declines the proffered elephants.

Further Details
• The Salutation "Great and Good Friend" used in the President's letter to the King was commonly used for addressing mem-

Word Puzzle

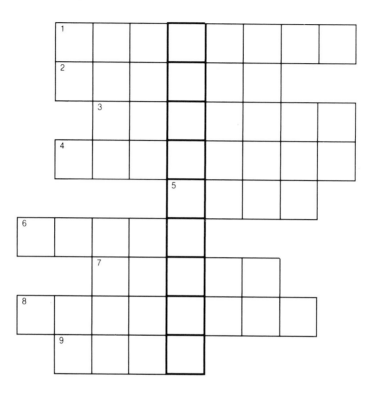

Directions:
To solve the puzzle, use information from the document to fill in the horizontal spaces. When the puzzle is completed, the word that will appear in the vertical ruled box is one that is significant to the document.

Clues:
1. According to Lincoln, gifts offered in peace are more honorable than _____ of war.
2. Last name of the Secretary of State in 1862.
3. Lincoln considered the Siamese gifts as tokens of peace. What word in the documents means peaceful?
4. The U.S. government would place the King's gifts here.
5. Approximate length of time between the date of the King's letters and the date of Lincoln's reply.
6. One of the gifts from Siam was a _____ of fine quality.
7. The most efficient energy form for land and water transportation in the 1860s.
8. Lincoln informed this legislative group about the Siamese gifts.
9. The name of this country today is Thailand.

Great and Good Friend:

I have received Your Majesty's two letters of the date of February 14th, 1861.

I have also received in good condition the royal gifts which accompanied those letters, — namely, a sword of costly materials and exquisite workmanship; a photographic likeness of Your Majesty and of Your Majesty's beloved daughter; and also two elephants' tusks of length and magnitude such as indicate that they could have belonged only to an animal which was a native of Siam.

Your Majesty's letters show an understanding that our laws forbid the President from receiving these rich presents as personal treasures. They are therefore accepted in accordance with Your Majesty's desire as tokens of your good will and friendship for the American People. Congress being now in session at this capital, I have had great pleasure in making known to them this manifestation of Your Majesty's munificence and kind consideration.

Under their directions the gifts will be placed among the archives of the Government, where they will remain perpetually as tokens of mutual esteem and pacific dispositions more honorable to both nations than any trophies of conquest could be.

I appreciate most highly Your Majesty's tender of good offices in forwarding to this Government a stock from which a supply of elephants might be raised on our own soil. This Government would not hesitate to avail itself of so generous an offer if the object were one which could be made practically useful in the present condition of the United States.

Our political jurisdiction, however, does not reach a latitude so low as to favor the multiplication of the elephant, and steam on land, as well as on water, has been our best and most efficient agent of transportation in internal commerce.

bers of royalty.

• Several words in the document appear to substitute an "f" character for the first of two consecutive "s"s. Actually, the "f" is what is called a "long s" and was a common writing practice in the 17th and 18th centuries.

The letter reproduced here is from Volume 3 (1856-1864) of the "Communications to Foreign Sovereigns and Heads of States" Series, General Records of the Department of State, Record Group 59. It is in a clerk's hand, not that of President Lincoln.

Suggestions for Teaching

The following suggestions are ideas for class discussions or for independent student projects. They are organized by course subject.

For Geography classes: The gifts offered to President Lincoln by the King of Siam reflect some of the natural resources and cultural values of Siam. Direct students to do research on one country and to select several products or items that might be representative gifts from that country. The following are suggested countries: Belgium, Colombia, Sierra Leone, Pakistan, and New Zealand. Place a map of the world on a bulletin board and ask students to locate their countries and explain to the class the reasons for selecting these particular gifts.

For American History and Government classes: American Presidents are prohibited from accepting gifts from foreign governments without Congressional permission. Discuss this policy with students. Consider these issues: What motivates a head of state to send expensive gifts to the leader of another country? Does the value of a gift affect whether it should be accepted?

For World History classes: What gifts do you think would have been appropriate for the President to have sent to the King? Would the same gifts be appropriate today? What was the nature of the relationship between the United States and Siam in 1861? What is that relationship today?

For American Studies classes: King Rama IV is characterized in the novel *Anna and the King of Siam* (and later in the movie, "The King and I"). Many other fictionalized books are based on historical incidents. Assign students to read one of these works and to describe to the class how it reflects the historical period: *The Confessions of Nat Turner, The Red Badge of Courage, In Cold Blood, Northwest Passage,* and *The Winds of War.*

Here is a simple puzzle designed to stimulate interest in the document. We suggest that you post the document on the bulletin board and reproduce copies of the puzzle for interested students.

Answer Key

1	T	R	O	**P**	H	I	E	S
2	S	E	W	**A**	R	D		
3		P	A	**C**	I	F	I	C
4	A	R	C	**H**	I	V	E	S
5				**Y**	E	A	R	
6	S	W	O	R	**D**			
7		S	T	E	**A**	M		
8	C	O	N	G	R	E	S	S
9		S	I	A	**M**			

I shall have occasion at no distant day to transmit to Your Majesty some token of indication of the high sense which this Government entertains of Your Majesty's friendship.

Meantime, wishing for Your Majesty a long and happy life, and for the generous and emulous People of Siam the highest possible prosperity, I commend both to the blessing of Almighty God.

Your Good Friend,
Abraham Lincoln.

Washington, February 3, 1862.
By the President:
William H. Seward,
Secretary of State.

Abraham Lincoln,
President of the United States of America.

To Her Majesty Doña Isabel II,
By the Grace of God and the Constitution
of the Spanish Monarchy Queen of Spain,
&c., &c.

Great and Good Friend:

I have received the letter which Your Majesty was pleased to address to me on the 28th of October, last, announcing that Her Royal Highness the Infanta Doña Maria Christina, spouse of His Royal Highness the Infante Don Sebastian Gabriel, had on the 20th of the preceding August safely given birth to a Prince upon whom, at the baptismal font had been bestowed the names of Francisco Maria Isabel Gabriel Pedro.

I participate in the satisfaction which this happy event has afforded to Your Majesty's Royal Family, and offer my sincere

29

Surgeon General's Office

When news of the outbreak of the Civil War reached Dorothea Dix, she immediately headed for Washington to volunteer her services. Miss Dix was already well known for her efforts to secure humane treatment for the mentally ill, and Secretary of War Simon Cameron gladly accepted her offer to organize women nurses for the Union cause.

In her rented quarters, Miss Dix became a one-woman bureaucracy, organizing and dispatching nurses as the tides of battle changed. On June 10, 1861, she was officially commissioned the nation's first Superintendent of Women Nurses.

In the early days of the war, confusion reigned. Lack of coordinated action and shortages of supplies, along with an abundance of willing but untrained volunteers, presented enormous challenges. Some way was needed to select volunteers who could withstand the rigors of wartime nursing. Miss Dix wanted particularly to discourage women whom she suspected of wishing only to be near husbands or sweethearts on the battlefield.

The featured document, Circular Order No. 8 of July 14, 1862, was intended as much to limit volunteers as to recruit them. It reflected Miss Dix's own preference for simplicity and stoutheartedness. It emphasized plain looks, plain manner, and maturity. Ability to care for the wounded was one desirable qualification, but, strangely, not the foremost one. In the early 1860s, nursing was not yet a profession for which women formally trained.

All inquiries about nursing service and all women seeking to volunteer were re-ferred by the Surgeon General's Office to Dorothea Dix.

The letter books of the Surgeon General at the National Archives contain handwritten copies of these letters as well as requests that Miss Dix locate and dispatch supplies and nurses immediately to new scenes of action. Some women who failed to pass her scrutiny sneaked aboard troop trains and served gallantly on the front lines. Others, like Clara Barton, acted on their own.

One of Miss Dix's best-known nursing recruits was Louisa May Alcott, later the famous author of *Little Women*. Miss Alcott had only served briefly in a converted Washington hotel when she became seriously ill. Dorothea Dix helped nurse her back to health, and Miss Alcott thanked her in "Hospital Sketches," a series of newspaper articles describing her Civil War experience, later published in book form.

Ironically, Dorothea Dix could not have met the standards she outlined in her circular order. At the start of the Civil War she was already 60 years old. Born in 1802, she had grown up in Massachusetts, taught school, and written a number of popular books for children. Despite chronic ill health, she had then spent two decades traveling all over the country visiting the mentally ill, publicizing their plight, and persuading state legislatures to furnish money to build clean, modern, restful institutions for the insane.

A major figure in the period of antebellum reform, she is credited with prompting the establishment of more than 20 state hospitals. Although she had strong views on

Circular No. 8.

WASHINGTON, D. C., *July 14, 1862,*

No candidate for service in the Women's Department for nursing in the Military Hospitals of the United States, will be received below the age of thirty-five years, nor above fifty.

Only women of strong health, not subjects of chronic disease, nor liable to sudden illnesses, need apply. The duties of the station make large and continued demands on strength.

Matronly persons of experience, good conduct, or superior education and serious disposition, will always have preference; habits of neatness, order, sobriety, and industry, are prerequisites.

All applicants must present certificates of qualification and good character from at least two persons of trust, testifying to morality, integrity, seriousness, and capacity for care of the sick.

Obedience to rules of the service, and conformity to special regulations, will be required and enforced.

Compensation, as regulated by act of Congress, forty cents a day and subsistence. Transportation furnished to and from the place of service.

Amount of luggage limited within small compass.

Dress plain, (colors brown, grey, or black,) and while connected with the service without ornaments of any sort.

No applicants accepted for less than three months' service: those for longer periods always have preference.

D. L. DIX.

Approved,
WILLIAM A. HAMMOND,
Surgeon General.

the other reform issues of her day — temperance, slavery, and votes for women — she did not speak on them publicly for fear of distracting attention from the cause of better care for the mentally ill.

The Civil War presented Dorothea Dix with a new opportunity for service, as it did for many women. Although she lacked nursing experience or training, she knew a great deal about hospitals and had high standards for patient care. She found it hard to adjust those standards to the difficult conditions of wartime and was often frustrated by inevitable delays and inefficiency. She clashed with doctors who resented her interference and her surprise inspections. By the war's end she retained her title but little of her once absolute authority over women nurses.

With characteristic dedication, she had labored for years without a day off. She remained in Washington after the war to secure a suitable memorial for Union soldiers buried in the National Cemetery at Fort Monroe, Virginia. She refused all honors and compensation, asking only for the flag of the nation she had served so long.

Secretary of War Edwin Stanton responded with a set of flags and a letter praising her work. Among her bequests, Miss Dix left the flags to Harvard College and $100 to Hampton Institute, located near the site of the Union soldiers' memorial.

The featured document is found in the Records of the Surgeon General's Office, Record Group 112, Volume 1, Circulars and circular letters, 1861-85.

Teaching Activities

1. Ask your students to discuss what qualifications are necessary for a nurse today. How do these compare with the requirements set out by Dorothea Dix in Circular Order No. 8? Consider what factors might account for the differences.

2. Women writing to the Surgeon General about service as a nursing volunteer were advised to contact Miss Dorothea Dix at 505 12th Street, Washington, D.C. Today's volunteers for emergency services (firefighting, nursing service, rescue squad) must be prepared to convince professionals of their suitability for service. Ask your students to draft a letter either to Miss Dix or a contemporary figure, describing their qualifications and reasons for wanting to serve.

3. Dorothea Dix interviewed all women who came to Washington to volunteer before approving them for service as nurses for the Union army. Volunteers for emergency services today must also go through interviews. Ask students to dramatize such an interview, either in a contemporary situation or between Miss Dix and an eager nursing recruit (using the information provided in the article and in the circular).

4. Ask students to locate evidence to support or to disprove the following statement: The Civil War was the bloodiest war in American history because the technology to kill was on the threshold of the 20th century while medicine was still in the Middle Ages.

5. Following the Civil War, Dorothea Dix raised money to complete a memorial to Union soldiers who had died in the conflict. She personally selected items for a time capsule sealed in the base of the monument at Fort Monroe, including Civil War mementos, pictures of U.S. presidents, coins, maps, a Bible, and a copy of the Constitution. Discuss with your class what they would put in a time capsule today.

Compile a list of items or gather together things in a two-foot square box to be used as a time capsule to show what is noteworthy about American life in the late 1980s.

A Letter to Giuseppe Garibaldi

Background

During the early years of the Civil War, the Union Army solicited the aid of experienced foreign officers to lead the untrained, newly recruited troops. The intent was to have these men play much the same role that General Lafayette played during the American Revolution. One such man whom the Union sought was Giuseppe Garibaldi of Italy.

Garibaldi was born July 4, 1807, in Nice, Italy (now a part of France). At a young age he joined the revolutionary forces to fight for the unification of the Italian states and their freedom from Austria. Garibaldi quickly proved himself to be a capable, charismatic leader.

In 1850, after suffering defeat at the hands of the French, Garibaldi fled to America. He was hailed by some Americans as the "Washington of Italy." He returned to Italy in 1854 and rejoined the fight for Italian independence in 1859.

Because of Garibaldi's ability and persistence as a leader, Secretary of State William H. Seward offered him command of a Union force in 1861. An American diplomat assured Garibaldi that "thousands" of Italian and Hungarian immigrants would be willing to serve under him. In fact, only 17,157 Italians and 3,737 Hungarians lived in the United States at the time. Garibaldi refused the Union offer at first because he thought his military expertise would be needed soon at home. However, the King of Italy, Victor Emmanuel II, gave him permission to go to America if he chose. Garibaldi indicated that he would join the Union Army if he were named Commander in Chief and if the Union would adopt the abolition of slavery as a war goal. The United States would not comply; Lincoln was still hopeful that the Union might be reunited without abolishing slavery. Garibaldi, therefore, refused the offer of a commission.

Garibaldi lived to see Italy united and freed from Austrian rule. He joined the French in their fight against the Prussians in 1870. He retired to his home on the Island of Caprera, in the Tyrrhenian Sea, where he died on June 2, 1882.

Teaching Activities

These activities are varied according to ability levels. Activity 1 is designed for use with students of average to below average reading abilities. It would also be suitable for some junior high students. The worksheet in Activity 1 will help these students achieve success in gathering factual information from a document. Activities 2, 3, and 4 are alternative teaching strategies for students with average to above average reading ability. Any of these activities can be used to build upon Activity 1.

Activity 1: Garibaldi Letter and Worksheet

(Information gathering, reading skills, and copying skills)
1. Make copies of the document (or a transparency for an overhead projector) and of the worksheet, "Letter to Garibaldi," for each student. (This document should reproduce clearly as a Thermofax master.)

2. Provide each student with a copy of the document or project the transparency.

Antwerp, June 8th 1861.

General Garibaldi:

The papers report that you are going to the United States, to join the army of the North in the conflict of my country. If you do, the name of LaFayette will not surpass yours. There are thousands of Italians and Hungarians who will rush to your ranks, and there thousands and tens of thousands of American citizens who will glory to be under the command of the "Washington of Italy."

I would thank you to let me know if this is really your intention. If it be, I will resign my position here as Consul and join you in the support of a Government formed by such names as Washington, Franklin, Jefferson, and their compatriots, whose names it is not necessary for me to mention to you.

I sincerely regret the death of Cavour. He was a great statesman. But you were right in demanding for your officers and soldiers what you did; for they had fought bravely under your command and deserved your highest thought.

With assurances of my profound regard,

Yours &c.

(Signed) J. W. Quiggle.

To Gen. Garibaldi,
Caprera; Italy.

Worksheet for Activity 1
Letter to Garibaldi

[1] _____ , June 8th,[2] _____ .

General[3] _____ :

    The papers report that you are going to the[4] _____
to join the[5] _____ of the[6] _____ in the
conflict of my country. If you do, the name of[7] _____
will not surpass yours. There are thousands of[8] _____
and[9] _____ who will rush to your ranks, and there [are]
thousands of American citizens who will glory to be under the command of the
[10] " _____ ."

    I would thank you to let me know if this is really your intention. If it be, I will
[11] _____ my position here as[12] _____ and join
you in the support of a[13] _____ formed by such
men as [14] _____ , [15] _____ ,
[16] _____ , and their compatriots whose names it is
not necessary for me to mention to you.

    I sincerely regret the death of[17] _____ . He was a great
[18] _____ . But you were right in demanding for your
officers and soldiers what you did; for they had fought bravely under your
command and deserved your highest thought.

    With assurances of my profound regard.

        Yours yet,

            (Signed)[19] _____

            To General[20] _____

            Caprera[21] _____ .

3. Ask a student volunteer to read the letter to the class while other students follow silently.

4. Give each student a copy of the worksheet to complete by using the information in the document. Provide a copy of the document for each student as an exercise in near-point (close) copying, or use a transparency on the overhead projector to practice far-point (distance) copying skills.

Activity 2:
Garibaldi's Job Description

(Oral and written communication skills, creative expression)
1. Tell students to imagine themselves in the following situation:

You are Lincoln's Secretary of State, William H. Seward, and you have offered Garibaldi a position of leadership with the Union Army. Garibaldi informs you by letter that he is giving serious consideration to the offer. Before making his decision, however, he requests a detailed job description of his duties.

2. Write a job description for Garibaldi. Encourage students to be creative in their job descriptions and to include as many details as they can. You may wish to have your class work in pairs or small groups.

Activity 3: You Were There

(Comparing and contrasting points of view)
1. Begin this activity by discussing with the class the following questions: Would all Union leaders want the aid of an Italian military leader in the Civil War? What factors might shape their points of view?

2. Place the following names on the board: Abraham Lincoln, President of the United States; General George McClellan, Commander of the Union Army; Antonio Enrico, 21-year-old Italian-American draftee.

3. Ask the class to imagine that the year is 1861 and the war has just begun. Ask each student to assume the role of one of the above personalities. Then direct the students to list three reasons why they would or would not support a Union policy of enlisting the aid of foreign leaders in the cause of the North. Later, ask students to compare and contrast the viewpoints of each person on this issue.

Activity 4:
Garibaldi's Motivation

(Critical thinking)
1. Use the following list to begin a discussion of factors that might have motivated Garibaldi or some other important foreign leader to support the Union cause. (As an alternative approach, ask students to develop their own list of motivations.)

    a. To enhance the leader's glory.
    b. To aid an ally in need.
    c. To enhance the glory of his or her country in the world's eyes.
    d. To increase personal wealth.
    e. To gain support from a country that could help the leader's country if assistance were needed at a future time.
    f. To help eliminate oppression within another country.
    g. To gain land or colonies as a reward.
    h. To support emigrants from the leader's country who have settled in the warring country.
    i. To increase the leader's influence in his own country.
    j. To gain military experience.

2. Ask the class to rank the reasons in order of the importance they may have had in Garibaldi's decision on whether to enter the Union cause. Encourage students to justify the order of choices, keeping in mind Garibaldi's various roles as a national leader, a military leader, and an individual. You may want to raise these additional questions: Is there enough evidence available to analyze Garibaldi's motivations? What other information would be helpful in making a careful assessment?

The letter reproduced here is enclosed in Despatch 20, Quiggle to Secretary of State, July 5, 1861, Despatches from United States Consuls in Antwerp, 1802-1906, Volume 5, General Records of the Department of State, Record Group 59.

Civil Rights Mini-Unit

During the 1960s and 1970s, a number of Federal and State programs were set up to provide educational opportunities for minorities and women. These included Head Start, special admissions programs to institutions of higher learning, and affirmative action plans. In 1974 Allan Bakke, a white male seeking admission to the University of California Medical School at Davis, challenged as discriminatory the university's special admissions program. Subsequently, the California State Supreme Court ruled in favor of Bakke. The Regents of the University of California challenged this decision before the U.S. Supreme Court. The Court's decision raises questions about the future of affirmative action programs specifically and about the rights of minorities generally. The issues surrounding this case make it a most relevant topic for discussion in the social studies.

This mini-unit provides you with a selection of historical documents that serves as background for studying the recent U.S. Supreme Court decision in the case of the Regents of the University of California v. Bakke. The documents relate to the 14th Amendment: *Plessy* v. *Ferguson, Brown* v. *the Board of Education,* and the Bakke case. Accompanying the documents are suggested activities for use in the classroom. The first activity focuses on each document individually, while the second uses all the documents with a data retrieval chart. The mini-unit also contains a time line of major events relating to the history of civil rights in the United States; it will be helpful to you and your students as you work with the documents.

We recommend that you introduce your students to primary sources by examining a selected document for factual information. This examination will underscore the significance of such information in the development of conclusions and generalizations.

In the first activity, students select a single document and review a series of related questions. Two sets of questions are included with each document. The first set of questions requires students to review the document for factual information, thus reinforcing the importance of reading documents with care. Once students have read the document, a second set of questions provides the basis for a broader discussion of the individual documents in their historical context.

In the second activity, students should carefully review all the documents as background for a general discussion of broad issues that relate to all of the documents. The discussion will encourage students to develop their own conclusions and generalizations based on factual information. The data retrieval chart will guide students in extracting factual information from the documents. Once students understand the information, they can discuss at length one or several of the following general issues. These issues are only examples. You may wish to develop your own general topics for discussion.

TIME LINE

This is a selective list of events leading to the present legal and judicial positions on civil rights in the United States. It is intended to be used as background for the documents in this mini-unit, and not as a definitive list.

Vocabulary

amendment
equal protection of the laws
franchise
monopoly
public accommodation
Reconstruction
invalid
stipulation
segregate
doctrine
grandfather clause
disfranchise
executive order
NAACP
discrimination
U.S. Court of Appeals
nullify
stay

Date: 1865
Focus: The Bureau of Refugees, Freedmen, and Abandoned Lands
Action: This Bureau was established in the War Department to help freed slaves adjust to living as free persons and to overcome the disabilities of slavery. It worked also to assist displaced whites and to administer land confiscated from the Confederacy.
Impact: The Bureau represented the Federal Government's first major attempt at social welfare. Perhaps the most important aspect of the Bureau's work was its system of public education.

Date: 1866
Focus: 14th Amendment
Action: This amendment was designed principally to provide citizenship rights to former slaves.
Impact: It guaranteed that all citizens were to receive equal protection before the law.

Date: 1866
Focus: Civil Rights Act of 1866
Action: This act provided that persons born in the United States and not subject to foreign powers were citizens of the United States.
Impact: It gave the Federal Government legal authority to deal with violators of the civil liberties of individuals.

Date: 1870
Focus: 15th Amendment
Action: This amendment was largely designed to give full voting rights to black males. It also reinforced the citizenship guarantees of the 14th Amendment.
Impact: More than 700,000 former slaves registered to vote.

Date: 1872
Focus: Bureau of Refugees, Freedmen, and Abandoned Lands
Action: The Bureau was abolished.
Impact: Blacks found themselves without Federal protection and provisions in former Confederate States unwilling to continue the work begun by the Bureau.

Date: 1873
Focus: United States Supreme Court, *Slaughter House Cases.* The State of Louisiana granted one corporation a 25-year exclusive franchise to conduct all butchering business in three of the state's parishes. The monopoly prompted a lawsuit by rival slaughterhouses, which claimed that 1,000 butchers had been denied the right to earn a living.
Action: The Court held that there were two categories of citizens — national and state — and that the privileges and immunities clause of the 14th Amendment protected only those rights derived from national citizenship.
Impact: This ruling in effect weakened the 14th Amendment because it gave State governments authority over the protection of citizenship rights.

Date: 1875
Focus: Civil Rights Act of 1875
Action: This act prohibited discrimination in places of public accommodation, excluding churches, cemeteries, and public schools.
Impact: It represented the Federal Government's last attempt to secure civil rights for blacks before Reconstruction ended in 1877.

Date: 1883
Focus: U.S. Supreme Court, Civil Rights Cases
Action: The Court ruled in five separate cases that the 14th Amendment prohibited States, not individuals, from violating civil rights.
Impact: These rulings reversed the Civil Rights Act of 1875 and undermined the effect of the 14th and 15th Amendments.

Date: 1890
Focus: Second Morrill Act (the First Morrill Act, 1862, provided Federal support for higher education in the form of land-grant colleges). These colleges usually concentrated on agricultural and mechanical subjects.
Action: One of the stipulations of the Second Morrill Act provided that annual grants be withheld from States that segregated blacks without providing separate agricultural or mechanical colleges for them.
Impact: Seventeen colleges for blacks were established. These were mainly non-degree-granting agricultural, mechanical, and industrial schools.

Date: 1896
Focus: U.S. Supreme Court, *Plessy* v. *Ferguson*
Action: The Court upheld a Louisiana law requiring segregated railroad facilities, maintaining that as long as accommodations were equal, blacks were not deprived of equal protection granted under the 14th Amendment.
Impact: This ruling established the doctrine of separate but equal.

Date: 1908
Focus: U.S. Supreme Court, *Berea College* v. *Kentucky*
Action: The Court upheld a Kentucky law that banned private schools from admitting black and white students to the same campus.
Impact: This case was interpreted to mean that States could outlaw bi-racial contacts.

Date: 1915
Focus: U.S. Supreme Court, *Guinn and Beal* v. *United States*
Action: The Court declared the Oklahoma "grandfather clause" unconstitutional because it violated the 15th Amendment by disenfranchising blacks.
Impact: The 15th Amendment was used to overturn a State law.

Date: 1938
Focus: U.S. Supreme Court, *Missouri ex rel. Gaines* v. *Canada*
Action: The Court ruled that Missouri must provide legal education for Lloyd Gaines, a black, within its boundaries.
Impact: The ruling required States to make equal provisions for blacks or admit them to State-supported universities for whites.

Date: 1941
Focus: Executive Order 8802
Action: The Order established the Committee on Fair Employment Practices to investigate complaints of discrimination against companies with Government defense contracts.
Impact: The Order paved the way for blacks to be freely hired in defense plants.

Date: 1946
Focus: Executive Order 9808
Action: The Order created the Presidential Committee on Civil Rights. The Committee issued a major report, *To Secure These Rights,* which condemned racial segregation and the denial of civil rights to blacks.
Impact: The report was seen as a landmark statement of the Federal Government's intentions in the field of civil rights.

Date: 1948
Focus: U.S. Supreme Court, *Sipuel* v. *Board of Regents of the University of Oklahoma*
Action: The Court ruled that denial of the applicant's admission to the university violated the equal protection clause of the 14th Amendment.
Impact: The NAACP played a major role in the case. This case represented its first real victory in the campaign against segregated facilities.

Date: 1948
Focus: Executive Order 9981

Action: "There shall be equality of treatment and opportunity for all persons in the Armed Services without regard to race. . . ."
Impact: The Order represented the first step toward elimination of segregation in one of the country's largest institutions, the Armed Forces. Executive Orders 9808 and 9981 recognized and began the attack on discriminatory practices.

Date: 1950
Focus: U.S. Supreme Court, *Sweatt* v. *Painter* (Texas)
Action: The Court held that the black law school at the University of Texas did not provide "a truly equal education in law." It concluded that Sweatt's exclusion from the white law school at the university violated the equal protection clause of the 14th Amendment.
Impact: The decision gave support to the admission of blacks to previously all-white graduate or professional schools.

Date: 1954
Focus: U.S. Supreme Court, *Brown* v. *Board of Education, Topeka, Kansas*
Action: This case was consolidated with the District of Columbia case of *Bolling* v. *Sharpe,* the Delaware case of *Gebhart* v. *Belton,* and the Virginia case of *Davis* v. *County School Board of Prince Edward County.* The Court decided unanimously in all these cases that school segregation violated the Constitution.
Impact: In May 1955 the Court issued its school desegregation enforcement order to admit, "with all deliberate speed," the parties involved to public schools on a racially non-discriminatory basis. The ruling was widely understood to mean that the concept of separate but equal established in *Plessy* v. *Ferguson* was overturned.

Date: 1956
Focus: U.S. Supreme Court, *Gayle* v. *Browder*
Action: The Court referred to the *Brown* v. *Board of Education, Topeka, Kansas* case to strike down segregated bus facilities in Montgomery, Alabama.
Impact: In this case, the Court officially declared that segregation, particularly in public facilities, was unconstitutional.

Date: 1957
Focus: Civil Rights Act

Action: This act prohibited interference in the exercise of voting rights; simplified the system for Federal Government involvement in voting rights violations; and established a national Commission on Civil Rights.
Impact: The act increased Federal involvement in ensuring voting rights.

Date: 1958
Focus: U.S. Supreme Court, *Cooper* v. *Aaron* (Little Rock, Arkansas)
Action: The Court upheld the U.S. Court of Appeals reversal of a stay against integration, saying that "the constitutional rights of children regardless of race can neither be nullified openly and directly by state legislators or state executive officials nor nullified by them by evasive schemes for segregation."
Impact: This action resulted from racial turmoil that erupted in Little Rock, Arkansas, when an attempt at desegregating the schools was made.

Date: 1961
Focus: Executive Order 10925
Action: The Order established the President's Committee on Equal Employment Opportunity.
Impact: The Committee had responsibility for ending discrimination by Government contractors as well as by the Federal Government itself.

Date: 1963
Focus: March on Washington
Action: Over 200,000 people gathered in Washington, D.C., to protest inequality and to ask for a remedy.
Impact: The march demonstrated wide support for the enactment of civil rights legislation.

Date: 1964
Focus: U.S. Supreme Court, *Griffin* v. *County School Board of Prince Edward County, Va.*
Action: The Court ruled that State aid to white children attending all-white private schools was unconstitutional.
Impact: Such attempts were viewed as blatant efforts to circumvent desegregation. School boards were mandated to develop "workable desegregation plans."

Date: 1964
Focus: Civil Rights Act of 1964

Action: This is the most comprehensive civil rights measure passed by Congress to date. It prohibited discrimination in public accommodations; banned the use of literacy tests as a requirement for voting, unless written tests were given to everyone; provided for Federal assistance in desegregating school systems; and banned discrimination in Federally assisted programs. The Act also provided for equal employment opportunity by declaring discrimination based on race, color, religion, sex, or national origin an unlawful employment practice. This section was to be implemented over a three-year period. It was for this purpose that the Equal Employment Opportunity Commission was created, with enforcement to be carried out by the Attorney General.
Impact: The Act abolished legal segregation and guaranteed a more favorable climate for later civil rights legislation dealing with such issues as housing discrimination and voting rights.

Date: 1964
Focus: U.S. Supreme Court, *Heart of Atlanta Motel* v. *United States and Katzenbach* v. *McClung*
Action: In these two cases involving a motel and restaurant, the proprietors based their rights to refuse accommodation to blacks on the grounds that their businesses were intrastate, not interstate. The Court ruled that each of the establishments was involved in interstate business and therefore subject to the conditions of the Civil Rights Act of 1964.
Impact: The interpretation of interstate commerce was expanded to include restaurants, motels, and other privately owned facilities that served the public.

Date: 1965
Focus: Executive Order 11246
Action: This Order was amended by Executive Orders 11375 of October 1967, and 11478 of August 1969. It established the Government's nondiscrimination compliance program. The Order is implemented by Office of Federal Contract Compliance regulations which exist in two parts: (a) obligations of contractors and subcontractors not to discriminate, and (b) contractors' obligations to develop an affirmative action program.
Impact: The Order gives the Federal Government a device for deterring discrimination in employment practices in private

institutions.

Date: 1965
Focus: Voting Rights Act of 1965
Action: This act abolished all remaining deterrents to exercising the franchise and authorized Federal supervision of voter registration where necessary.
Impact: This act closed loopholes in the 1964 measure.

Date: 1968
Focus: Civil Rights Act of 1968
Action: This Civil Rights Act, passed one week after the assassination of Dr. Martin Luther King, Jr., focused on eradicating discrimination in housing and on protecting the right of blacks to vote.
Impact: The act provided additional force to the Civil Rights Act of 1964.

Date: 1968
Focus: U.S. Supreme Court, *Jones* v. *Mayer Co.*
Action: This ruling based on the 1866 Civil Rights Act barred all racial discrimination in the sale or rental of property.
Impact: This ruling closed the loophole in the open housing section of the 1968 Civil Rights Act, which excluded owner-sold single housing and units of four or fewer owner-occupied apartments.

Date: 1972
Focus: Equal Employment Opportunity Act
Action: Public and private education institutions, State and local governments, and employees and unions with eight or more workers were covered by Federal legislation barring discrimination and were brought under the Equal Employment Opportunity Commission (EEOC).
Impact: The Commission was given authority to have its decisions enforced in the courts, but Congress did not provide the Commission with "cease and desist" power.

Data Retrieval Chart

Date	Author(s)	Recipient(s)	Main Subject(s)	For What Purpose Was the Document Written?	Unanswered or Outstanding Questions

Eight Key Documents on Civil Rights

Document 1: 14th Amendment

Article XIV.

Section 1. All persons born or naturalized in the United States, and subject to the jurisdiction thereof, are citizens of the United States and of the State wherein they reside. No State shall make or enforce any law which shall abridge the privileges or immunities of citizens of the United States; nor shall any State deprive any person of life, liberty, or property, without due process of law; nor deny to any person within its jurisdiction the equal protection of the laws.

Section 2. Representatives shall be apportioned among the several States according to their respective numbers, counting the whole number of persons in each State, excluding Indians not taxed. But when the right to vote at any election for the choice of electors for President and Vice President of the United States, Representatives in Congress, the Executive and Judicial officers of a State, or the members of the Legislature thereof, is denied to any of the male inhabitants of such State, being twenty-one years of age, and citizens of the United States, or in any way abridged, except for participation in rebellion, or other crime, the basis of representation therein shall be reduced in the proportion which the

Vocabulary: naturalized, jurisdiction, abridge, privileges, immunities, apportioned, electors, insurrection, validity, bounties, emancipation.

Questions for Students

1. Review and discuss the meaning of each section of the amendment.

2. What do the terms "privileges and immunities" and "equal protection" mean?

Discussion Questions

1. Why do you think this amendment to the Constitution was necessary?

2. The 15th Amendment specifically prohibits the disenfranchisement of citizens based on race, color, or previous condition of servitude. If the 14th Amendment protects the privileges and immunities of citizens, why was the 15th Amendment necessary? Consider also why many people feel an equal rights amendment is needed despite the fact that the 14th Amendment appears to guarantee the rights of women.

number of such male citizens shall bear to the whole number of male citizens twenty-one years of age in such State.

Section 3. No person shall be a Senator or Representative in Congress, or elector of President and Vice President, or hold any office, civil or military, under the United States, or under any State, who, having previously taken an oath, as a member of Congress, or as an officer of the United States, or as a member of any State legislature, or as an executive or judicial officer of any State, to support the Constitution of the United States, shall have engaged in insurrection or rebellion against the same, or given aid or comfort to the enemies thereof. But Congress may by a vote of two-thirds of each House, remove such disability.

Section 4. The validity of the public debt of the United States, authorized by law, including debts incurred for payment of pensions and bounties for services in suppressing insurrection or rebellion, shall not be questioned. But neither the United States nor any State shall assume or pay any debt or obligation incurred in aid of insurrection or rebellion against the United States, or any claim for the loss or emancipation of any slave; but all such debts, obligations and claims shall be held illegal and void.

Section 5. The Congress shall have power to enforce, by appropriate legislation, the provisions of this article.

Attest.

Edw. McPherson.
Clerk of the House of Representatives.

J. W. Forney
Secretary of the Senate.

Schuyler Colfax
Speaker of the House of Representatives.

La Fayette S. Foster
President of the Senate pro tempore.

Document 2: Interstate Commerce Commission Order

At a general session of the INTERSTATE COMMERCE COMMISSION, held at its office in Washington on the *third* day of *December*, A. D. 1887:

Present:

Hon. THOMAS M. COOLEY, *Chairman,*
Hon. WILLIAM R. MORRISON,
Hon. AUGUSTUS SCHOONMAKER, } *Commissioners.*
Hon. ALDACE F. WALKER,
Hon. WALTER L. BRAGG,

IN THE MATTER OF THE PETITION OF

William H. Councill

against

The Western & Atlantic Railroad Company.

This case being at issue upon complaint and answer on file, and having been duly assigned for hearing on the *22nd* day of *July*_____, 188*7*, and a hearing having been had upon the pleadings, proofs, and arguments of counsel, and the Report and Opinion of the Commission having been made and filed; *wherein it is found upon such investigation, so made, that the defendant has the legal right to separate its white and colored passengers paying the same fare. by providing separate cars for each which are equally safe and comfortable; that this separation may be carried out*

Questions for Students

1. Review the report of the ICC to ascertain these facts: a. Who is the defendant? b. Who is the complainant? c. Who heard the case? When? d. When was the final decision on this case issued?

2. What was the outcome of the case?

Discussion Questions

1. Discuss the concept of separate but equal. Consider in your discussion the question of inherent inequality.

2. This case was heard before the ICC nine years before *Plessy* v. *Ferguson*. Discuss the development of precedents and their role in lawmaking.

Vocabulary: petition, complaint, cease and desist.

Note: When he was denied a seat in a first-class railroad car after paying first-class fare, William H. Councill, principal of the State Colored Normal and Industrial School in Huntsville, Alabama, filed a complaint with the Interstate Commerce Commission (ICC) against the Western and Atlantic Railroad Company. The ICC, created in 1887, the same year in which this case was filed, was charged with protecting the public in matters relating to transportation and commerce between States. Councill alleged that by his removal to the Jim Crow car he was subjected to "unreasonable prejudice and unjust discrimination." He sought from the ICC $25,000 in damages and $1,500 in legal costs.

on railroad trains without unjust preference, or undue prejudice and disadvantage to either race, provided it be done on fair and reasonable terms. And it is further found, upon said investigation, that in denying to complainant equal accommodations furnished the other passengers, paying the same fare, the defendant railroad company subjected him to undue prejudice and unreasonable disadvantage in violation of the provisions of the Act of Congress entitled an "Act to regulate Commerce," approved February 4th, 1887.

NOW IT IS ORDERED AND ADJUDGED that the defendant, The Western and Atlantic Railroad Company, be and it hereby is notified and required to cease and desist from subjecting colored persons to undue and unreasonable prejudice and disadvantage in violation of section three of the Act to regulate Commerce, and from furnishing to colored persons purchasing first-class tickets on its road accommodations which are not equally safe and comfortable with those furnished other first-class passengers.

And it is further ORDERED that a notice embodying this order be forthwith sent to the defendant corporation, together with a copy of the Report and Opinion of the Commission herein, in conformity with the provisions of the fifteenth section of the act to regulate Commerce.

Secretary.

Document 3: Hale County, Alabama, Resolution

Hon. T.H.Aldrich

Washington

D.C.

Sir:-
        Our rights as citizens of the United States being practi
cably denied us,we the undersigned citizens of Beat No 12 Hale
County,Alabama,respectfully ask that the Congress of the United
States relieve us of all the duties incumbent upon us as citizens of the United States. We think is unjust to us to require
of us the duties of a citizen of the United States without
granting to us all the privileges of citizenship and without
guaranteeing us all the rights of a citizen. We ask that a law
be passed relieving us of all military duty in case of a war
with any foreign country.
        And your petitioners will ever pray.

P H Green   1 Daniel Banks   27
T. S. Green   2 Heywood Wilson   28
Isaac Owens   3 John McConico   29
M. S. Green   4 Mathew Silver   30
Watson Bell   5 Joseph Bell   31
Arthur Jones   6 Crous Gray   32
Bolton Sander   7 Alex Gray   33
H.C. White   8 William Dobbins   34
F.C. Owens   9 William Turner   35
J. H. Green   10 Daniel Bester   36
William Anderson   11 Sam Bester   37
Handy Amos   12 Lewis Peters   38
Austin Silver   13 Silver Bell   39
S S Smith   14 W. M. Bowdin   40
Robt. Hardaway   15 Ed Clemons   41
George Patton   16 S Charleston   42
Judge William   17 Lewis Oller   43
Lewis Shorter   18 Charl Oller   44
Holman James   19 Jacob Owens   45
Abraham James   20 Joseph Richard   46
Alfred James   21 Willis Kenedy   47
Paul James   22 Simon Witherspoon   48
William Thomas   23 Green Sample   49
John McCrackin   24 H. C. Brown   50
Andrew Laroughan   25 A W Brown   51
Steven Turner   26 Jack Evins   52

Note: Truman H. Aldrich was the Congressman from the 9th District of Alabama. This resolution was received by the Committee on the Judiciary on March 1, 1897.

"Beat No. 12" refers to the election precinct or supervisory district of the writers of the resolution.

Vocabulary: incumbent, resolution, petitioners.

Questions for Students
1. To whom are the black citizens addressing their petition?

2. What are they requesting?

Discussion Questions
1. What are the duties and privileges of citizenship?

2. Why do you think the petitioners are concerned with military duty? What do you think they are trying to accomplish by their petition? Are their requests realistic or rhetorical? Consider in your discussion the role of blacks in the military.

3. Compare and contrast the sentiments expressed in this resolution with those of the Baptist Ministers' Union Resolution (page 576). How might you explain their differences or similarities?

Document 4: Photograph: "Separate But Equal"

"SEPARATE BUT EQUAL" SCHOOLS

Above, Public School for White Children, Macon County, Ga.

Below, Public School for Negro Children, Macon County, Ga.

Photographs from "Preface to Peasantry" by Arthur Raper, University of North Carolina Press, 1936.

Questions for Students

1. Review the time line from 1866 to 1915. What does it tell you about black educational facilities in Macon, Georgia, in 1936? What questions does this information raise?

2. What are the obvious differences between the two schools as evidenced in the photographs?

Discussion Questions

1. What can you infer from this photograph about the quality of education provided by each school? Consider how you are defining quality and make only those inferences that can safely be drawn.

2. This photograph is part of a file that includes materials from the National Association for the Advancement of Colored People. Why do you think this photo was used by the organization? Why do you think it is in Federal records?

Document 5: Baptist Ministers' Union of Southern California Resolution

The Baptist Ministers' Union of Southern Cali...

To his _____
_____
Washington.D.C.

Box.II5. Duarte.Califor...
May.27th.1954.

Dear Sir:
The enclosed Resolution was submitted to the Baptist Ministers Union of
Southern California,at its last meeting held on Tuesday.May.25th.19.. by
Dr:A.Wendell Ross.
........RESOLUTION............

WHEREAS ,The Supreme Court of the United States of America,under the
leadership of Chief Justice.Earl Warren,in its recent ruling
against segregation in the American Schools,is an outstanding
contribution to the full citizenship of all peoples of our nation;
as well; as a continuation of Americanism in the world.

WHEREAS,this decision is a vital blow to Communism,and the toll of the
bell to second class citizenship of Negro peoples of America
North and South;moving in a legal way to blot out physical
psychological inferiority customs and laws against the most loyal
group of citizens in the nation.

WHEREAS,this constitutional and God given right has come after 85 years
since the emancipation of slavery by President Abraham Lincoln.

WHEREAS,This educational liberty along with the emancipation are worth-
while Spiritual advances,which after all are the onlytrue values
that are eternal;which were enunciated by our Lord and Saviour
Jesus Christ.

THEREFORE BE IT RESOLVED,that the Baptist Ministers Union of Southern
California,send this Resolution as a vote of thanks and appreciation
representing the true leadership of the Negro Race,and the
Preachers of the Gospel of Jesus Christ,to the Supreme Court of
the United States.The Hon:Earl Warren.Chief Justice of the Supreme
Court.To His Excellency.Dwight D.Eisenhower.President of the United
States,and to other leading diplomats in the RepublicanParty.
And that we urge our people North and South to be obedient to this
law;which is in their favor,as much as they have been obedient
to laws that have been against them,and their Constitutional rights.

Rev: B.B.Charles. President.

Rev:John A.Davis.Secretary.

Vocabulary: resolution, psychological inferiority, emancipation.

Questions for Students
1. To whom is the resolution addressed? Why?

2. What is the U.S. Supreme Court decision that prompted this resolution, and how did the Court rule?

3. Can you determine the race of the writers from the evidence in the document?

4. Why do you think this resolution was written?

5. The last lines of the resolution read: "And that we urge our people North and South to be obedient to this law; which is in their favor, as much as they have been obedient to laws that have been against them, and their Constitutional rights." Discuss.

Discussion Questions
1. How might such civil rights activists as Martin Luther King, Jr., and Stokely Carmichael have viewed the last sentence of the resolution?

2. Compare and contrast the sentiments expressed in this resolution with those of the Hale County citizens. How might you explain their differences and similarities?

Nos. 1 - 5

54

A JOINT RESOLUTION STATING THE POLICY OF THE STATE OF NORTH
CAROLINA WITH REFERENCE TO THE MIXING OF THE CHILDREN OF
DIFFERENT RACES IN THE PUBLIC SCHOOLS OF THE STATE, AND
CREATING AN ADVISORY COMMITTEE ON EDUCATION.

WHEREAS, Governor William B. Umstead, shortly before
his death, appointed a Special Advisory Committee on Education,
composed of outstanding citizens of our State of both races,
to study the difficult and far reaching problems presented by
the May 17, 1954, decision of the Supreme Court of the United
States on the question of segregation in the public schools,
and our present Governor, Honorable Luther H. Hodges, recom-
missioned that Committee soon after assuming the duties of
Governor of North Carolina, and said Committee filed its report with the Governor on December 30, 1954, which report
stated, among other things, the following:

> "The mixing of the races forthwith in the public
> schools throughout the state cannot be accom-
> plished and should not be attempted. The schools
> of our state are so intimately related to the
> customs and feelings of the people of each com-
> munity that their effective operation is impos-
> sible except in conformity with community atti-
> tudes. The Committee feels that the compulsory
> mixing of the races in our schools, on a state-
> wide basis and without regard to local conditions
> and assignment factors other than race, would
> alienate public support of the schools to such
> an extent that they could not be operated suc-
> cessfully." and

WHEREAS, his Excellency, the Governor of North Carolina, has transmitted the report of this Special Committee to
this General Assembly recommending it as the policy for this
State to follow, and

WHEREAS, the Attorney General of the State of North
Carolina has filed a brief with the Supreme Court of the United
States in the pending segregation cases before said court, which
brief states, among other things, the following:

2

"The people of North Carolina know the value of
the public school. They also know the value of
a social structure in which two distinct races
~~can live together as separate groups,~~ each proud
of its own contribution to that society and recognizing its dependence upon the other group.
They are determined, if possible, to educate
all of the children of the State. They are also
determined to maintain their society as it now
exists with separate and distinct racial groups
in the North Carolina community.

"The people of North Carolina firmly believe that
the record of North Carolina in the field of education demonstrates the practicability of education of separate races in separate schools. They
also believe that the achievements of the Negro
people of North Carolina demonstrate that such
an educational system has not instilled in them
any sense of inferiority which handicaps them
in their efforts to make lasting and substantial
contributions to their state."

NOW, THEREFORE,

Be it resolved by the House of Representatives, the Senate

concurring:

Section 1. That the report of the Governor's Special

Advisory Committee on Education and the brief of the Attorney

General of North Carolina, filed in the Supreme Court of the

United States in the pending segregation cases, are hereby ap-

proved as a declaration of the policy of the State of North

Carolina with respect to the serious problems in public edu-

cation created by the opinion of the Supreme Court of the

United States handed down on May 17, 1954.

Sec. 2. That the mixing of the races in the public

schools within the State cannot be accomplished and if attempted

would alienate public support of the schools to such an extent

that they could not be operated successfully.

Sec. 3. (a) In order to provide for a continuing study of the problems which may arise as a result of the decision of the United States Supreme Court on May 17, 1954, and to provide counsel and advice to the Governor, the General Assembly, the State Board of Education and the county and local school boards throughout the State, there is hereby created a committee to be known as The Advisory Committee on Education.

(b) The Committee shall consist of seven members to be appointed by the Governor for terms of two years, or until their successors are appointed. Two members of the Committee shall be appointed from the membership of the Senate, two from the membership of the House of Representatives, and three from the public at large. The Governor shall designate one member of the Committee to be its Chairman.

(c) The Committee shall be authorized to employ an executive secretary and such other assistants as it may from time to time, with the approval of the Governor, find necessary. The salaries of the executive secretary and of all other assistants employed by the Committee shall be fixed by the Committee, with the approval of the Governor, and shall be paid, together with all other necessary and proper expenses of the Committee, from the Contingency and Emergency Fund.

(d) The Committee shall make a continuing study of the problems which exist and may arise in this State directly or indirectly from the decision of the Supreme Court of the United States on May 17, 1954, in the matter of separate schools for the races. The Committee shall from time to time report to the Governor its findings and recommendations, and shall, so far as it may find practicable, provide counsel, information and advice to the General Assembly, the State Board of Education and the county and local school boards when requested by them to do so.

(e) The Committee is authorized to call upon the Attorney General for such legal advice as it shall deem necessary.

Sec. 4. This resolution shall be in full force and effect from and after its adoption.

Questions for Students

1. When was the resolution written? What U.S. Supreme Court decision is it in response to?

2. Based on this resolution, what would be the policy of North Carolina toward desegregation?

Discussion Questions

1. What do these reasons reveal about the climate of opinion in North Carolina at the time? What do they tell us about the relation between social customs and the law? How valid do these reasons seem today?

2. Suppose that you are the superintendent of schools for a North Carolina school district. You believe in school integration. How does this resolution affect you as a school administrator? As a citizen of North Carolina?

WEST KENTUCKY VOCATIONAL SCHOOL
1400 Thompson Avenue
Paducah, Kentucky

I & C   1261

APR 26 '61   757478

Apr 20 15 09 PM 1961

INTERSTATE COMMERCE   April 13, 1961
COMMISSION
RECEIVED

APR 2 4 1961

BUREAU OF INQUIRY AND
COMPLIANCE
OFFICE OF THE DIRECTOR

Chairman
Interstate Commerce Commission
Washington 25, D. C.

Dear Sir:

On traveling through the states of Louisiana, Mississippi, Tennessee, one
observes signs on the waiting rooms as follows:

    Colored Waiting Rooms Intrastate Passengers

    White Waiting Rooms Intrastate Passengers

According to the signs, there is no waiting room (either White or Negro) for
Interstate Passengers.

These signs are more ridiculous and more confusing than the original "White and
Colored Room" signs. The intention of such foolish signs is quite obvious.
They are intended to do just what they are doing, confuse the issue and evade the
law. The whole thing boils down to segregated waiting rooms, which is contrary
to your ruling. It seems to me if the Interstate Commerce Commission or other
agencies of the Federal Government concerned with the problem really wanted to
do the right thing, it (or they) would force all ethnic signs removed, partitions
torn away and only the sign "Waiting Room."

Too, I do not see how morally or legally your department can continue to permit
segregated lunch counters at bus and railway terminals under the guise that they
are operated by private companies. How can anything so public as a lunch counter
in a bus station be a private concern?

It has now been approximately seven years since the 1954 Supreme Court Decision,
and I honestly think that there has been ample time for the discountinuance of
all indecent undemocratic practices such as I have memtioned in this letter. I
see no reason why the proper agency of the Federal Government would not now be
justified in enforcing its own law just as the appropriate Federal Agency does the
Income Tax Law. If the payment of Income Tax were left to the conscience and discretion of individuals, I am sure the Government would soon become bankrupt. It

is the same way with other areas. As long as the Federal Government remains spineless and continues to leave racial matters to the conscience and discretion of individuals and localities, injustices will continue to prevail and the United States will continue to be ridiculed as a big hypocrite among nations.

I hope the Interstate Commerce Commission and all other agencies combined will start and effect a real revolution not merely to do something in name or for the purpose of saving face or impressing the Russians or some one else, but to bring about real Democracy. I think tearing down White and Negro signs, tearing out partitions in bus and train stations will be an effective beginning.

I trust this letter will be considered seriously, because far too long have we played the hypocrite. Far too long has the Federal Government been too lax in these matters, acting like the spineless, infamous Pilate. I hope Attorney General Kennedy will probed into discriminatory practices as deeply and as vigorously as he has probed into the very bottom of price fixing by the big corporations.

Sin and mal-practices should be fought in all areas. If we are to ever be the Democracy we profess to be, we must practice true Democratic Principles.

Respectfully yours,

(Miss) Osceola A. Dawson

OAD/jaw
CC
    Mr. Clarence Mitchel
    President Kennedy
    Attorney General Kennedy
    Courier Journal
    Louisville Defender
    Sun Democrat
    Senator John Cooper
    Attorney Dearing
    Mr. Roy Wilkins
    Civil Rights Commission

Vocabulary: intrastate, interstate, Interstate Commerce Commission, Pilate, 1954 U.S. Supreme Court decision.

Questions for Students

1. Explain the difference between interstate and intrastate.

2. Why do you think the waiting room signs distinguish between white and colored waiting rooms for intrastate passengers?

3. What action does Dawson want taken? By whom?

4. List the reasons Dawson gives for her demands. What do you think of her reasons?

5. Why do you think Dawson refers to the 1954 U.S. Supreme Court decision?

Discussion Questions

1. Why did civil rights groups focus on inequities in bus and train station facilities?

2. Consider the date of this letter and the reasons why, seven years after the Brown case, segregated facilities remained.

3. "Americans seem to want laws expressing high ideals but they seem also to want the convenience of ignoring or violating many of them with impunity." Monroe Berger, *Equality by Statute* (New York, 1968), p. 1. Discuss.

BAKKE SYLLABUS

NOTE: Where it is feasible, a syllabus (headnote) will be released, as is being done in connection with this case, at the time the opinion is issued. The syllabus constitutes no part of the opinion of the Court but has been prepared by the Reporter of Decisions for the convenience of the reader. See *United States* v. *Detroit Lumber Co.*, 200 U.S. 321, 337.

SUPREME COURT OF THE UNITED STATES

Syllabus

REGENTS OF THE UNIVERSITY OF CALIFORNIA *v.* BAKKE

CERTIORARI TO THE SUPREME COURT OF CALIFORNIA

No. 76-811. Argued October 12, 1977—Decided June 28, 1978

The Medical School of the University of California at Davis (hereinafter Davis) had two admissions programs for the entering class of 100 students—the regular admissions program and the special admissions program. Under the regular procedure, candidates whose overall undergraduate grade point averages fell below 2.5 on a scale of 4.0 were summarily rejected. About one out of six applicants was then given an interview, following which he was rated on a scale of 1 to 100 by each of the committee members (five in 1973 and six in 1974), his rating being based on the interviewers' summaries, his overall grade point average, his science courses grade point average, and his Medical College Admissions Test (MCAT) scores, letters of recommendation, extracurricular activities, and other biographical data, all of which resulted in a total "benchmark score." The full admissions committee then made offers of admission on the basis of their review of the applicant's file and his score, considering and acting upon applications as they were received. The committee chairman was responsible for placing names on the waiting list and had discretion to include persons with "special skills." A separate committee, a majority of whom were members of minority groups, operated the special admissions program. The 1973 and 1974 application forms, respectively, asked candidates whether they wished to be considered as "economically and/or educationally disadvantaged" applicants and members of a "minority group" (blacks, Chicanos, Asians, American Indians). If an applicant of a minority group was found to be "disadvantaged," he would be rated in a manner similar to the one employed by the general admissions committee. Special candidates, however, did not have to meet the 2.5 grade point cut-off and were not ranked against candidates in the general admissions process. About one-fifth of the special applicants were invited for interviews in 1973 and 1974, following which they were given benchmark scores, and the top choices were then given to the general admissions committee, which could reject special candidates for failure to meet course requirements or other specific deficiencies. The special committee continued to recommend candidates until 16 special admission selections had been made. During a four-year period 63 minority students were admitted to Davis under the special program and 44 under the general program. No disadvantaged whites were admitted under the special program, though many applied. Respondent, a white male, applied to Davis in 1973 and 1974, in both years being considered only under the general admissions program. Though he had a 468 out of 500 score in 1973, he was rejected since no general applicants with scores less than 470 were being accepted after respondent's application, which was filed late in the year, had been processed and completed. At that time four special admission slots were still unfilled. In 1974 respondent applied early, and though he had a total score of 549 out of 600, he was again rejected. In neither year was his name placed on the discretionary waiting list. In both years special applicants were admitted with significantly lower scores than respondent's. After his second rejection, respondent filed this action in state court for mandatory injunctive and declaratory relief to compel his admission to Davis, alleging that the special admissions program operated to exclude him on the basis of his race in violation of the Equal Protection Clause of the Fourteenth Amendment, a provision of the California Constitution, and

§ 601 of Title VI of the Civil Rights Act of 1964, which provides, *inter alia*, that no person shall on the ground of race or color be excluded from participating in any program receiving federal financial assistance. Petitioner cross-claimed for a declaration that its special admissions program was lawful. The trial court found that the special program operated as a racial quota, because minority applicants in that program were rated only against one another, and 16 places in the class of 100 were reserved for them. Declaring that petitioner could not take race into account in making admissions decisions, the program was held to violate the Federal and State Constitutions and Title VI. Respondent's admission was not ordered, however, for lack of proof that he would have been admitted but for the special program. The California Supreme Court, applying a strict-scrutiny standard, concluded that the special admissions program was not the least intrusive means of achieving the goals of the admittedly compelling state interests of integrating the medical profession and increasing the number of doctors willing to serve minority patients. Without passing on the state constitutional or federal statutory grounds the court held that petitioner's special admissions program violated the Equal Protection Clause. Since petitioner could not satisfy its burden of demonstrating that respondent, absent the special program, would not have been admitted, the court ordered his admission to Davis.

Held: The judgment below is affirmed insofar as it orders respondent's admission to Davis and invalidates petitioner's special admissions program, but is reversed insofar as it prohibits petitioner from taking race into account as a factor in its future admissions decisions.

18 Cal. 3d 34, 553 P. 2d 1152, affirmed in part and reversed in part.

MR. JUSTICE POWELL concluded:

1. Title VI proscribes only those racial classifications that would violate the Equal Protection Clause if employed by a State or its agencies. Pp. 12-18.

2. Racial and ethnic classifications of any sort are inherently suspect and call for the most exacting judicial scrutiny. While the goal of achieving a diverse student body is sufficiently compelling to justify consideration of race in admissions decisions under some circumstances, petitioner's special admissions program, which forecloses consideration to persons like respondent, is unnecessary to the achievement of this compelling goal and therefore invalid under the Equal Protection Clause. Pp. 18-49.

3. Since petitioner could not satisfy its burden of proving that respondent would not have been admitted even if there had been no special admissions program, he must be admitted. P. 49.

MR. JUSTICE BRENNAN, MR. JUSTICE WHITE, MR. JUSTICE MARSHALL, and MR. JUSTICE BLACKMUN concluded:

1. Title VI proscribes only those racial classifications that would violate the Equal Protection Clause if employed by a State or its agencies. Pp. 4-31.

2. Racial classifications call for strict judicial scrutiny. Nonetheless, the purpose of overcoming substantial, chronic minority underrepresentation in the medical profession is sufficiently important to justify petitioner's remedial use of race. Thus, the judgment below must be reversed in that it prohibits race from being used as a factor in university admissions. Pp. 31-55.

MR. JUSTICE STEVENS, joined by THE CHIEF JUSTICE, MR. JUSTICE STEWART, and MR. JUSTICE REHNQUIST, being of the view that whether race can ever be a factor in an admissions policy is not an issue here; that Title VI applies; and that respondent was excluded from Davis in violation of Title VI, concurs in the Court's judgment insofar as it affirms the judgment of the court below ordering respondent admitted to Davis. Pp. 1-14.

POWELL, J., announced the Court's judgment and filed an opinion expressing his views of the case, in Parts I, III-A, and V-C of which WHITE, J., joined; and in Parts I and V-C of which BRENNAN, MARSHALL, and BLACKMUN, JJ., joined. BRENNAN, WHITE, MARSHALL, and BLACKMUN, JJ., filed an opinion concurring in the judgment in part and dissenting in part. WHITE, MARSHALL, and BLACKMUN, JJ., filed separate opinions. STEVENS, J., filed an opinion concurring in the judgment in part and dissenting in part, in which BURGER, C. J., and STEWART and REHNQUIST, JJ., joined.

Vocabulary: syllabus, regents, *certiorari,* grade point average, extracurricular, respondent, discretionary, mandatory injunction, declaratory relief, allege, *inter alia,* petitioner, strict-scrutiny standard, affirm, proscribe, violate, inherently, foreclose, chronic, remedial, concur, dissent. *(You may wish to consult a legal dictionary for definitions of some of these terms.)*

Questions for Students

1. Based on the syllabus, develop a chronological outline of the process by which Allan Bakke sought admission to the Medical School of the University of California at Davis.

2. Restate in your own words the final decision of the U.S. Supreme Court in the Bakke case.

Discussion Questions

1. What issues have arisen around the Bakke decision? Why does it appear to have historical importance?

2. What can be inferred from the number of separate opinions filed by the Justices?

3. "Technically, the Court's decision in a case applies only to the particular facts of that case and to the parties to it. But the reasoning outlined by the Court gives lower court judges a basis for deciding similar cases." James E. Clayton, *The Making of Justice* (New York, 1962), p. 85. Discuss.

4. What might be the reactions of the following individuals to the Bakke decision? What justifications might they offer for their opinions?

   a. White male, first-generation American. Your parents immigrated to America from Latvia. You earned your undergraduate degree by attending evening classes.

   b. Black female. You are the first member of your family to pursue an advanced degree.

   c. White female from middle-class professional family.

5. What comments do you have on the Bakke decision?

General Discussion

1. Compare and contrast the situations outlined in the following documents with the guarantees of the 14th Amendment. What can you conclude about the relationship between interpretation of the Constitution and prevailing social attitudes at the time?

2. Discuss the roles of the U.S. Supreme Court and the Federal Government in the regulation of our lives and social customs. Consider such areas of involvement as education, rights of the accused, abortion, death with dignity, voting practices, and privacy.

3. Discuss the nature of the relationship between State and Federal Governments as revealed in the documents. Consider how citizenship has come to be defined.

4. Discuss the role of precedents and landmark cases in lawmaking.

5. Compare and contrast the impact of a constitutional amendment and that of a U.S. Supreme Court decision. Why are women seeking a constitutional amendment to protect their rights?

6. What are the rights of minorities in a nation of immigrants, such as the United States? What have these rights been in the past and how might they evolve in the future? To what extent should minority rights be protected? How do the rights of minorities impinge upon rights of the majority?

7. Discrimination is often built into our institutional practices: for example, Jim Crow laws, voting restrictions, and housing patterns. What is the role of legislation with respect to institutional discrimination? What is the relationship between institutional discrimination and the practices of individuals toward members of minority groups?

8. Is there such a thing as a bad law? How might you define "bad" in the context of these documents? How do opinions vary among your students on the nature of a bad law? Is civil disobedience justified?

9. What constraints and limitations exist in carrying out constitutional guarantees?

10. What is affirmative action?

11. List several Federal policies directed at minority groups or women that you would classify as affirmative action programs. Consider each program in view of the following:
   a. At what group(s) was the policy directed?
   b. Why was the policy initiated?
   c. What were the goals or objectives of the program?
   d. To what extent were those goals achieved?

12. To obtain a basis for understanding the need for affirmative action programs directly related to education, students might research the history of minority education in the United States and might consider groups such as blacks, American Indians, and Mexican Americans.

13. Review the time line. What does it indicate about the status of blacks from 1865 to the present? Does it seem adequate as an overview of the status of blacks, other minorities, or women? Why, or why not? Does there appear to be repetition in the laws or policies included?

corpus. In early May, shortly before Milligan's scheduled execution, his lawyers filed a petition for a writ of habeas corpus at the U.S. circuit court in Indianapolis. The lawyers argued that a military court has no right try a citizen if a civil court is in operation. Supreme Court Justice Davis, sitting as a member of the circuit court, felt the lawyers' request to be an issue requiring a decision by the Supreme Court. But Milligan and his fellow conspirators were sentenced to hang before any of this could come to pass. Justice Davis wrote a moving letter to President Andrew Johnson asking him to stay the execution until the Supreme Court could hear the case.

President Johnson complied, reluctantly, to Justice Davis's request, first by staying the execution until June and later by commuting the sentence to life in prison. The order to commute the sentence was delivered to Edwin Stanton with instructions not to tell the prisoners until just before their scheduled execution that they were to live. Believing that even the Constitution could not save him, Milligan spent what he thought were his last days arranging his own funeral and writing an address, which he expected to deliver before he was hanged.

In due course the Supreme Court considered the case and ruled in favor of Milligan's contention that a citizen's right to a trial in a civil court could not be revoked even if war produced situations in which the privilege of the writ of habeas corpus might be revoked. Justice Davis, writing for the majority, argued that the case went to the very heart of what it meant to be a free people. He wrote into his decision a reminder that one of the grievances against King George III in the Declaration of Independence was that he had "'rendered the military power independent of and superior to the civil power.'" He went on to say, "No graver question was ever considered by this court, nor one which more clearly concerns the rights of the whole people; for it is the birthright of every American citizen when charged with a crime, to be tried and punished according to the law." On April 12, 1866, Milligan and his fellow prisoners were

released from custody by order of the U.S. Supreme Court.

The Civil War was a crisis that stretched the Constitution, but this Supreme Court decision defined just how far it could be stretched by drawing a clear line between the government's need for security and the rights of individual citizens. As Professor Allan Nevins observed, "The heart of this decision is the heart of the difference between the United States of America and Nazi Germany or Communist Russia."

This document is taken from the Records of the Office of the Judge Advocate General (Army), Record Group 153; Court Martial Records; NN3409, Box 1165.

Teaching Suggestions

Distinguishing Fact from Opinion

1. With students in groups of five, distribute a copy of the document to each student and have them read it carefully. A recorder for the group should make a list of questions that the group members raise after reading the document.

2. Instruct the group members to decide if the questions on their list can be answered with a fact (+) or by a supporting opinion (*). Have them place an appropriate mark next to each question.

3. Instruct the groups to choose their two best fact questions and their two best supporting opinion questions.

4. As the groups report, record their questions on the board in a chart like the one below.

Fact (+)	Supporting Opinion (*)

Indianapolis 28 Dec. 1864

Hon. B. M. Stanton Sec. War.

Dear Sir I have
been Condemned to die with-
-out evidence. Please examine
the facts and advise the
President do this much for
an old acquaintance and
friend —

Yours very truly

L. P. Milligan

Exploring the Constitution: Civil Liberties Search

Using the copy of the Constitution in their text, students should complete the puzzle below.

1. __ __ __ __   __ __ __ __ __ Ⓞ __

2. __ Ⓞ   __ __ __ __   __ __ __ __

3. __ Ⓞ __ __ __ __

4. __ __ __ Ⓞ

5. __ Ⓞ __ __

6. __ __ __ Ⓞ __   __ __ __ __ __

7. __ __ __ Ⓞ

Clues

1. Amendments I-X.
2. Article I, sec. 9, cl. 3, prohibits laws that are _____, i.e., retroactive criminal laws that work to the disadvantage of an individual.
3. Amendment IV says a criminal has a right to a trial that is public and _____ .
4. Protection from unreasonable search and seizure is in this amendment.
5. Amendment VIII states that this cannot be excessive.
6. Article I, sec. 9, cl. 2, promises the privilege of this writ.
7. Amendment XXVI gives this right to 18-year-olds.

Hidden clue: The circled letters when rearranged spell a Latin phrase which means "on behalf of one side only."

Moral Dilemma

Although we know little about the extent of the friendship between Milligan and Stanton, the dilemma of a public official's response to a former friend is an interesting one.

1. Have students read the story below and discuss it with their groups.

The country is involved in a civil war. You are the Secretary of Defense, and the President has had to arrest many people who disagree with him in order to protect the country. There is some question as to whether the President has acted within the Constitution, but you agree that these steps are necessary to protect the government. Much to your surprise, a letter comes across your desk one day from your old friend _____, who has been sentenced to die by a military court. What do you do? Why do you do it?

2. After they have listed and discussed their decision and the reasons for their decision, have them draft a letter to their friend explaining their decision.

For Further Research

1. Possible topics for further research could focus on

a. Treason trials in Cincinnati and Indianapolis

b. Secret societies such as The Sons of Liberty, The Knights of the Golden Circle, and The Union League

c. Supreme Court cases related to *Ex parte Milligan* such as *Ex parte Merryman*, *Ex parte McCardle*, *Ex parte Quirin*, and *Duncan* v. *Kahanamoku*.

Puzzle Answers:

1. B I L L O F R I G H (T) S
2. E (X) P O S T F A C T O
3. S (P) E E D Y
4. F O U (R)
5. B (A) L L
6. H A B (E) A S C O R P U S
7. V O T (E)

Unscrambled Word — *Ex Parte*

A Resolution on "The Indian Question"

The Vision of Wovoka

By the year 1889, Sioux Indians living in North and South Dakota had reason for discontent. The size of their reservations at Pine Ridge and Rosebud had been reduced. They had been forced by the U.S. Government to adapt from a nomadic to an agricultural lifestyle, and in 1889 their crops had failed. The Government had been slow in supplying needed money and rations. Above all, the U.S. Army had intruded further on their lands. Given all these pressures, it is no wonder that members of the tribe who had been exposed to the Ghost Dance religion were eager to bring its message of inspiration and promise to their downtrodden people.

That same year, Wovoka, a Paiute sheepherder and prophet well known to the Indians of the region, had a vision in which he went to heaven and returned to earth as the Messiah. According to Wovoka, the earth would rise and push white men from it, restoring the prairies and buffalo herds the Indians had once known. All Indians would be reunited, and the life the Indians had known before the white man arrived would be restored. To achieve this earthly paradise, God required Indians to abandon war, a difficult requirement for some warlike tribes, and to live lives of industry and honesty. The price for a reunited Indian nation was peacefulness and virtue.

The celebration of the Ghost Dance was the central ritual of Wovoka's religion. Lasting for many hours, the dance promised its participants a temporary "death" that brought them to heaven to be reunited with other Indians and their lost tribal practices. Other tribes that adopted the new religion absorbed the Ghost Dance into their own mythologies.

The Sioux and the Ghost Dance

The Sioux, led by Sitting Bull, used the Ghost Dance to vent their hatred against the white man. Although they accepted Wovoka's vision of paradise, they rejected his passive means of finding it. They believed that the dancers would be immune to bullets and that the forces of the white man could not prevail against them. Wovoka's peaceful religion, as interpreted by Sitting Bull and his followers, became militant.

The death of Sitting Bull and the incident at Wounded Knee on the Sioux Reservations in December 1890 were consequences of the inevitable clash between the Ghost Dance followers and the U.S. Army. Excerpts from the *Sixtieth Annual Report of the Commissioner of Indian Affairs to the Secretary of Interior, 1891*, reflect the position of the Government at the time. From the Standing Rock Agent: "[Sioux] cling tenaciously to the old Indian ways and are slow to accept the better order of things." From a listing in the report of the causes of the Sioux troubles: "A feeling of unrest and apprehension in the mind of the Indians has naturally grown out of the rapid advance of civilization."

PRESIDENT'S OFFICE: 219 CHESTNUT ST.,

Philadelphia, Pa., 12 mo. 17th 1890

To the Hon. John W. Noble, Secretary of the Interior:

At the 24th Anniversary of the Pennsylvania Peace Society, the following Conviction was unanimously adopted and a copy thereof ordered to be sent to the Hon. Secretary of State, viz;

9th. That the Indian question can be settled by bearing in mind that the Indian is part of the human family, was the original owner of this soil, and if half the money and time given to his subjection by warlike means, was bestowed upon schools and the teaching of a true civilization, there would be no breaking of the peace; and at this time, if we would carry out the injunction, "if thine enemy hunger, feed him," we would speedily end the troubles in the Pine Ridge and Rosebud agencies.

By order of the Society
John Collins, Cor. Sec'y

67

The letter reproduced here is found in File 39135, Box 2, Special Case 188, "Ghost Dance," in Records of the Bureau of Indian Affairs, Record Group 75.

Suggestions for Teaching
Student Activity
1. Carefully read the letter. Record the information in the document, such as the date, author, addressee, and any other elements you think important.

2. Examine the letterhead closely. What clues does it give you about the nature of The Universal Peace Union?

3. Why do you think the letter was addressed to the Secretary of the Interior?

4. What problem does the letter consider?

5. What solution to this problem is proposed?

6. What irony exists in the proposed solution? Consider the use of phrases such as "Indian question," "true civilization," and "if thine enemy hunger, feed him."

7. Why do you think this letter was written?

8. Compare and contrast the letter with the excerpts from the *Commissioner's Report.* What conflicts of values existed among whites toward the Indians?

Note: The Universal Peace Union separated from the American Peace Party in 1866. The Peace Union claimed a membership of 10,000. Its chief concerns included international disarmament, an end to imperialism, arbitration of labor disputes, and the "unity of the races." It was an active Washington lobbying group.

For Further Research
1. Investigate other incidents related to the clash of white and Indian cultures. What basic values were in conflict?

2. Investigate the status of several other American ethnic groups in the 1880s and 1890s. Rewrite The Universal Peace Union letter to reflect the status of one of those groups.

Plessy v. Ferguson Mandate

During the era of Reconstruction, black Americans' political rights were affirmed by three constitutional amendments and numerous laws passed by Congress. Racial discrimination was attacked on a particularly broad front by the Civil Rights Act of 1875. This legislation made it a crime for an individual to deny "the full and equal enjoyment of any of the accommodations, advantages, facilities, and privileges of inns, public conveyances on land or water, theaters and other places of public amusement; subject only to the conditions and limitations established by law, and applicable alike to citizens of every race and color."

In 1883, the Supreme Court struck down the 1875 act, ruling that the Fourteenth Amendment did not give Congress authority to prevent discrimination by private individuals. Victims of racial discrimination were told to seek relief not from the Federal Government, but from the States. Unfortunately, State governments were passing legislation that codified inequality between the races. Laws requiring the establishment of separate schools for children of each race were most common; however, segregation was soon extended to encompass most public and semipublic facilities.

Beginning with passage of an 1887 Florida law, states began to require that railroads furnish separate accommodations for each race. These measures were unpopular with the railway companies that bore the expense of adding Jim Crow cars. Segregation of the railroads was even more objectionable to black citizens, who saw it as a further step toward the total repudiation of three constitutional amendments. When such a bill was proposed before the Louisiana legislature in 1890, the articulate black community of New Orleans protested vigorously. Nonetheless, despite the presence of 16 black legislators in the state assembly, the law was passed. It required either separate passenger coaches or partitioned coaches to provide segregated accommodations for each race. Passengers were required to sit in the appropriate areas or face a $25 fine or a 20-day jail sentence. Black nurses attending white children were permitted to ride in white compartments, however.

In 1891, a group of concerned young black men of New Orleans formed the "Citizens' Committee to Test the Constitutionality of the Separate Car Law." They raised money and engaged Albion W. Tourgée, a prominent Radical Republican author and politician, as their lawyer. On May 15, 1892, the Louisiana State Supreme Court decided in favor of the Pullman Company's claim that the law was unconstitutional as it applied to interstate travel. Encouraged, the committee decided to press a test case on intrastate travel. With the cooperation of the East Louisiana Railroad, on June 7, 1892, Homer Plessy, a mulatto (7/8 white), seated himself in a white compartment, was challenged by the conductor, and was arrested and charged with violating the state law. In the Criminal District Court for the Parish of Orleans, Tourgée argued that the law requiring "separate but equal accommodations" was unconstitutional. When Judge John H. Ferguson ruled against him, Plessy applied to the State Supreme Court for a writ of prohibition and certiorari. Although the court upheld the state law, it granted Plessy's petition for a writ of error that would enable him to appeal the case to the Supreme Court.

In 1896, the Supreme Court issued its decision in *Plessy* v. *Ferguson.* Justice Henry Brown of Michigan delivered the majority opinion, which sustained the constitutionality of Louisiana's Jim Crow law. In part, he said:

We consider the underlying fallacy of the plaintiff's argument to consist in the assumption that the enforced separation of the two races stamps the colored race with a badge of inferiority. If this be so, it is not by reason of anything found in the act, but solely because the colored race chooses to put that construction upon it. . . . The argument also assumes that social prejudices may be overcome by legislation, and that equal rights cannot be secured except by an enforced commingling of the two races. . . . If the civil and political rights of both races be equal, one cannot be inferior to the other civilly or politically. If one race be inferior to the other socially, the Constitution of the United States cannot put them upon the same plane.

In a powerful dissent, conservative Kentuckian John Marshall Harlan wrote:

I am of the opinion that the statute of Louisiana is inconsistent with the personal liberty of citizens, white and black, in that State, and hostile to both the spirit and the letter of the Constitution of the United States. If laws of like character should be enacted in the several States of the Union, the effect would be in the highest degree mischievous. Slavery as an institution tolerated by law would, it is true, have disappeared from our country, but there would remain a power in the States, by sinister legislation, to interfere with the blessings of freedom; to regulate civil rights common to all citizens, upon the basis of race; and to place in a condition of legal inferiority a large body of American citizens, now constituting a part of the political community, called the people of the United States, for whom and by whom, through repre-

sentatives, our government is administered. Such a system is inconsistent with the guarantee given by the Constitution to each State of a republican form of government, and may be stricken down by congressional action, or by the courts in the discharge of their solemn duty to maintain the supreme law of the land, anything in the Constitution or laws of any State to the contrary notwithstanding.

Indeed, it was through the Supreme Court's decision in *Brown* v. *Board of Education of Topeka, Kansas* and congressional civil rights acts of the 1950s and 1960s that systematic segregation under state law was ended. In the wake of those Federal actions, many states amended or rewrote their state constitutions to conform with the spirit of the 14th amendment. But for Homer Plessy the remedies came too late. The document shown is the mandate (order) of the Supreme Court to the Louisiana Supreme Court to deny Plessy's request to overturn the law and to order him to bear the cost of the suit. It is part of the Records of the Supreme Court, RG 267, *Plessy* v. *Ferguson,* 163, #15248.

Teaching Suggestions

Interpreting the Document

1. Students should review what their textbooks have to say about *Plessy* v. *Ferguson.* Supplement the text with information from the preceding article.

2. Review the definitions of the following words before reading the document:

- *petitioner (n)* — person making a written request or plea in which a specific court action is asked for
- *respondent (n)* — a defendant
- *writ (n)* — formal legal document ordering or prohibiting some action
- *relator (n)* — person at whose prompting or complaint a case is begun
- *mandate (n)* — an order from a higher court or official to a lower court
- *writ of prohibition (n)* — an order forbidding something to be done
- *writ of certiorari (n)* — an order from a

70

United States of America, ss:

The President of the United States of America,

⟨ Seal ⟩

GREETING:

To the Honorable the Judges of the Supreme Court of the State of Louisiana

Whereas, lately in the Supreme Court of the State of Louisiana, before you, or some of you, in a cause between Homer A. Plessy, petitioner, and J. H. Ferguson, Judge of Section "A", Criminal District Court for the Parish of Orleans, respondent, c. to. 11,134, wherein the judgment of the said Supreme Court, entered in said cause on the 19th day of December, A. D. 1892, is in the following words, viz:

"It is ordered that the provisional writ of prohibition herein issued be now dissolved and set aside, and that the relief sought be denied at the relator's costs."

And whereas, in the present term of October, in the year of our Lord one thousand eight hundred and ninety=five, the said cause came on to be heard before the Supreme Court of the United States on the said transcript of record, and was argued by counsel:

On consideration whereof, It is now here ordered and adjudged by this Court that the judgment of the said Supreme Court in this cause be, and the same is hereby, affirmed with costs; and that the said respondent recover against the said petitioner, Homer Adolph Plessy, for his costs herein expended and have execution therefor.

May 18, 1896.

71

higher court to a lower court requesting the record of a case for review

3. Words from the vocabulary list above have been scrambled. As the students unscramble each word, one letter will fall into a circled space. Students should take the letters in the circled spaces and unscramble the word they form to find the answer to the problem.

The dissenting opinion in *Plessy* v. *Ferguson* was written by Mr. Justice _____.

a. Tralore a. _ _ O _ _ _ _
b. Fricawrtoortieri b. _ _ _ _ _ _
_ _ _ _ _ _ _ O _ _ (3 words)
Potinretie c. _ _ _ _ _ _ _ _ _ O
d. Dronspeten d. _ _ _ _ _ _ _ O _
e. Natamed e. _ _ _ _ O _ _
f. Thifribitooniworp f. _ _ _ _ _ _
_ _ _ O _ _ _ _ _ _ (3 words)

KEY: a. relator b. writ of certiorari c. petitioner d. respondent e. mandate f. writ of prohibition
L A R N A H = Harlan

4. Present the document to students and ask them to read it and answer the following questions:

a. Who sent the mandate? Who received it?

b. Who were the two parties in the case?

c. In whose favor had the Louisiana Supreme Court decided in December 1892?

d. What did the U.S. Supreme Court decide about the Louisiana Supreme Court's judgment? When?

e. Which party won the case? Which party had to pay the costs of the case?

Related Topics and Questions for Research and Reports

1. Instruct students to prepare a time line of significant legislation and events during Reconstruction from the end of the Civil War to the 1883 decision.

2. Justice Henry Brown, who wrote the majority opinion in *Plessy* v. *Ferguson*, warned that legislation would fail to end social prejudice. Ask students to research civil rights legislation adopted in the 1950s and 1960s

and develop a position paper in which they either affirm or dispute Justice Brown's assertion.

3. Ask students to conduct independent research and make reports on the following topics.

a. The opinions and lives of Justice Brown and Justice Harlan offer an interesting study in contrasts. Provide a thumbnail biographical sketch about each man, then ask students to read the passages given in the note from the judges' *Plessy* v. *Ferguson* opinions and to infer which justice wrote each opinion. Have students account for why their inferences were correct or incorrect. Ask students to read the entire decision, then to summarize the main points of Brown's opinion and Harlan's dissent.

b. *Plessy* v. *Ferguson* upheld segregation only in the use of railroad coaches. Subsequent Supreme Court decisions upheld segregation in other areas as well: *Berea College* v. *Kentucky*, 211 U.S. 45 (1908); *Cumming* v. *County Board of Education*, 175 U.S. 528 (1899); *Gong Lum* v. *Rice*, 275 U.S. 78 (1927); *McCabe* v. *Atchison, T. & S. F. Ry. Co.*, 235 U.S. 151 (1914); *Missouri ex rel., Gaines* v. *Canada*, 305 U.S. 337 (1948); *Sipuel* v. *University of Oklahoma*, 332 U.S. 631 (1948); *McLaurin* v. *Oklahoma State Regents*, 339 U.S. 637 (1950); *Henderson* v. *United States*, 339 U.S. 816 (1950); *Allston* v. *School Board of the City of Norfolk*, 112 Fed. 2d 992 (1940); *Sweatt* v. *Painter*, 339 U.S. 629 (1950). However, beginning with the 1914 McCabe case, the Supreme Court began to apply more rigid standards of equality under segregation. Ask students to investigate the circumstances that led to these cases, the arguments presented by each side, and the main points of the Supreme Court's opinion and dissent, where applicable.

c. *Brown* v. *Board of Education of Topeka* overturned *Plessy* v. *Ferguson*. Ask students to investigate the circumstances that led to this landmark case, the arguments presented by each side in the case, and the main points brought out in Chief Justice Warren's opinion, the single opinion of a unanimous court.

Photograph of a Land Auction

Since the 18th century, the Federal Government has encouraged and promoted the orderly distribution and development of publicly owned land in the United States. This has been done, in part, by the passage of legislation providing for its sale to private citizens at public auction.

The earliest ordinance dealing with land sales was that of 1785, and it was designed by the Continental Congress to establish a system for the distribution of land west of the original Thirteen Colonies. This ordinance ordered a land survey and provided for the establishment of townships 36 miles square. The smallest parcel of land, comprising 640 acres, was called a "section" and could be purchased for a minimum price of $1.00 an acre. There was no limit to the amount of land that a purchaser could buy, and speculation was both legal and common. District land offices were created by the Treasury Department to supervise the auctions at which much of this land was sold. Two years later, in 1787, the Northwest Ordinance established procedures by which the newly settled lands would become States.

Sale of public land has continued through the 19th and into the 20th centuries. The Homestead Act of 1862 encouraged farmers to settle by offering them 160 acres of land at no cost to heads of families who agreed to live on the land for at least five years. Land was also offered as a recompense for military service during the 19th century, and today it is still possible to buy remotely situated parcels of land in such areas as Alaska and the Far West.

Reproduced here is a photograph of a land auction — whether public or private is not known — in Imperial, California, in 1904. Until the 20th century, the southernmost area of California was an unpopulated, arid wasteland known as the Colorado Desert. By 1905, land developers had built a canal to connect the area with the Colorado River, which would provide necessary water. Towns were established and lots were sold. Despite occasional flooding from the Colorado River, the area prospered. Construction of the Boulder (later Hoover) Dam in Nevada in 1936 controlled the flooding in the valley and secured the future of the area. Today the Colorado Desert is called the Imperial Valley and is one of the richest agricultural areas of California.

Photographs are valuable sources for studying history. However, like written documents, they reflect the point of view or bias of the photographer and must be used with care. It is useful, for example, to know who took a photograph and for what purpose. The original of this photograph, with many others of the valley, was sent to E. A. Hitchcock, Secretary of the Interior, by A. H. Heber, president of the California Development Company. Heber was one of the developers of the Imperial Valley.

This is photograph 48-RST-7-25 in Records of the Office of the Secretary of the Interior, Record Group 48.

Suggestions for Teaching

1. You can reproduce this photograph for your students on a photocopying machine. Use it as the basis for a discussion on using photographs as historical evidence. We suggest you consider these questions in your discussion:
   a. What is happening in the

74

photograph?

b. What details in the photograph provide clues about what is happening?

c. What details in the photograph reveal the date of the event?

d. Is there evidence in the photograph to place it in a particular location?

e. If you knew that this photograph recorded a public auction, what conclusions could you draw from it?

f. Would these conclusions change if the photograph recorded an auction held by the land developer?

2. Use this photograph with others from your textbook or from other sources to discuss with students how to use photographs as evidence. Ask students to review each photograph for details. For example, they should notice such elements as means of transportation, geography, lighting fixtures, furnishings, architectural styles, and clothing. Students should also consider the possible point of view of the photographer and how his or her purpose could affect the photograph.

3. Use a map of your town as the basis for a mock land sale. Before your sale, discuss with students:

a. How would you conduct a sale fairly? Establish the rules for a public auction.

b. Would you allow real estate developers to compete with individual buyers?

c. What is a zoning ordinance? How would you determine residential and commercial zones? Where would you build parks and schools?

d. Would buyers be extended credit or be required to pay cash?

e. How would you, as a city official, use the money from the land sale?

f. Who would pay for public services, such as street lights and garbage collection?

4. Invite someone from the city development office to come and talk with your class about city policies toward land sales.

5. Develop a time line of events and legislation concerning the settlement of the West.

a. When was the last land rush?

b. When was the reservation system established for American Indians?

c. When were the national parks established?

d. When did the California gold rush begin?

e. Ask students to find photographs to illustrate some of these events.

6. Use this photograph as the basis for a small-group project. Direct students to investigate the survey system of the Ordinance of 1785. Ask them to report to the class on the township-range survey system established by the ordinance. Aerial photographs provide modern evidence of the widespread influence of this survey system.

Three Photographs of Children at Work, Circa 1908

The growth of industry after the Civil War increased the demand for workers and pulled more and more children into the labor force. In the twenty years between the census reports of 1890 and 1910, the number of working children between the ages of 10 and 15 rose from 1.5 million to 2 million. By 1910, children made up 18.4 percent of the total labor force.

In the National Child Labor Committee, a public interest group that started in New York City in 1904, opposition to child labor found a strong voice. The NCLC began its investigations with child labor conditions
in coal mines, capitalizing on the public concern raised during the nationwide coal miners' strike of 1902. Later NCLC investigations centered upon the glassmaking industry, textile mills — especially in the South — and the canning industry.

Eyewitness accounts of the kind of working conditions of child laborers that the NCLC was investigating and publicizing at the beginning of the 20th century appear in *Children and Youth in America*, Volume II, Robert H. Bremner, editor (Harvard University Press, 1971). One such account, taken from John Spargo's *The Bitter Cry of the Children* (New York, 1906), describes conditions in a glass factory:

I shall never forget my first visit to a glass factory at night ... the boys employed, about forty in number, at least ten of whom were less than twelve years of age. It was a cheap bottle factory, and the proportion of boys to men was larger than is usual in the higher grades of manufacture. The hours of labor for the "night shift" were from 5:30 pm to 3:30 am. ... Then began the work of the "carrying-in boys," sometimes called "carrier pigeons," [who] took the red-hot bottles from the benches, three or four at a time, upon big asbestos shovels to the annealing oven. ... The work of these "carrying-in boys," several of whom were less than twelve years old, was by far the hardest of all. They were kept on a slow run all the time from the benches to the annealing oven ... was one hundred feet, and the boys made seventy-two trips per hour, making the distance traveled in eight hours nearly twenty-two miles. Over half of this distance the boys were carrying their hot loads to the oven. The pay of these boys varies from sixty cents to a dollar for eight hours' work.

Another account, taken from Al Priddy's *Through the Mill* (Norwood, Massachusetts, 1911), describes conditions in a cotton mill:

The mule-room atmosphere was kept at from eighty-five to ninety degrees of heat. The hardwood floor burned my bare feet. I had to gasp quick, short gasps to get air into my lungs at all. My face seemed swathed in continual fire. ... Oil and hot grease dripped down behind the mules, sometimes falling on my scalp or making yellow splotches on my overalls or feet. Under the excessive heat my body was like a soft

sponge in the fingers of a giant; perspiration oozed from me until it seemed inevitable that I should melt away at last. To open a window was a great crime, as the cotton fiber was so sensitive to wind that it would spoil. . . . When the mill was working, the air in the mule-room was filled with a swirling, almost invisible cloud of lint, which settled on floor, machinery, and employees, as snow falls in winter. I breathed it down my nostrils ten and a half hours a day; it worked into my hair, and was gulped down my throat. This lint was laden with dust, dust of every conceivable sort, and not friendly at all to lungs.

In 1908 the NCLC hired Lewis W. Hine to investigate and to photograph the conditions of working children. The three photos that appear here are typical of the scenes that Hine captured with his camera. These photographs, numbered 102-LH-90, 102-LH-120, and 102-LH-348, are now in Records of the Children's Bureau, Record Group 102. (See pp. 106, 108, 109.)

The results of the NCLC investigations did not build immediate or widespread public support. The most vocal opponents included southern mill owners, supporters of States rights, *laissez-faire* economists, and, most significant politically and morally, President Woodrow Wilson. Nevertheless, the diligent work of the members of the NCLC resulted in the establishment of the Children's Bureau (1912), a federal information clearinghouse, and, in 1916, in the passage of the Keating-Owen Bill. The resulting law established child labor standards: a minimum age of 14 for workers in manufacturing and 16 for workers in mining, a maximum workday of 8 hours, prohibition of night work for workers less than 16, and documentary proof of age.

Today the Fair Labor Standards Act, passed in 1938, establishes minimum wages, overtime pay, and child labor standards for workers in the United States. The child labor provisions ensure children's ed-

ucational opportunities and protect their health. With the establishment of strictly enforced compulsory state education laws, full-time work for children became a thing of the past. Part-time hours vary according to hazards in the workplace. The minimum age for children employed in agriculture is 12 years, and in industry it is 14 years.

Teaching Activities

Display the photographs on the bulletin board before making assignments, and direct students to examine them closely. Remind students that Hine's photographs were used by the NCLC to arouse public interest in and concern for the plight of working children. As when they work with all documents, students should consider the point of view of the photographer as they draw conclusions from the photographs. Student assignments should directly reflect the evidence found in these photographs.

1. Direct students to select one child portrayed in the photographs. Read to them the two eyewitness accounts of working conditions at the beginning of the 20th century. Ask students to complete one of the following writing assignments from the perspective of the child laborer in the selected photograph:

a. A diary entry that describes in detail why you are working.

b. A letter to a friend that describes in detail your daily routine at your job.

c. A diary entry that describes why you like or dislike your job.

d. Your comments to the NCLC staff that is investigating conditions in your place of work.

2. Conduct a class discussion of the following question: What role should the government assume in protecting workers — especially children — from the hazards of the workplace?

3. Make a survey of students who are employed, in order to collect such information about their jobs as wage rates, hours, and safety precautions. Ask working students

the following questions:

    a. Did your employer advise you about hours or safety laws that protect you as a minor?

    b. What procedures are required of you by the Federal and State governments before you can work?

    c. Do you think that government regulations for employed minors provide you with adequate protection? or too much? or too little? Why?

Chinese Exclusion Forms

In 1886, at the entry to New York Harbor, President Grover Cleveland dedicated a statue — "Liberty Enlightening the World." Seventeen years later, the statue's pedestal was inscribed with Emma Lazarus' sonnet "The New Colossus" with its salute, "I lift my lamp beside the Golden door!" Yet no Statue of Liberty ever welcomed Chinese immigrants coming to the west coast seeking California's fabled Mountain of Gold. Instead, the Chinese faced barrier after barrier in an exception to a general historical pattern of unregulated immigration to the United States.

For a century, the U.S. Congress felt little need to use its constitutionally sanctioned powers (implied rather than stated) to regulate immigration. Efforts to do so lay mainly with the states until lobbying pressures forced Federal action in the late 19th century. By then, racial, economic, and cultural fears had produced strong anti-immigration lobbying. California provided the catalyst, for she faced the first large-scale Asian immigration. Chinese "coolies," intending only a temporary stay, came because mining and railroad industries in post-gold-rush California combined to encourage them to immigrate in large numbers as contract labor. Until 1864, from 2,000 to 3,000 Chinese arrived annually: after 1868, some 12,000 to 20,000 arrived annually, peaking in 1873 at 23,000. By then, 150,000 Chinese resided in California.

Like much of the rest of the nation, the Bear Flag state's population held inconsistent attitudes toward immigration. Some Californians favored unlimited immigration for those intending to stay, but opposed immigration of contract workers. These laborers, they believed, selfishly exploited U.S. bounty. Others welcomed Asians as laborers but not as permanent residents. A third group admired the melting pot ideal of an Anglo-Saxon United States, criticizing immigrants who maintained, as did the Chinese, their ethnic heritage. Still others opposed Americanization: they had welcomed the Chinese because of their Oriental culture, which with Americanization would be lost.

Unlike most of the nation, California's employers looked west for immigrant labor and east for Federal aid to encourage immigration. At first, Congress encouraged Chinese immigration as a way to provide cheap labor. In 1868 the terms of the Burlingame Treaty promised most-favored-nation status between the United States and China, by which citizens of the two nations would enjoy reciprocal immigration privileges. The United States would gain cheap labor. Chinese immigrants would have the right to travel in, reside in, and be educated in the United States. The treaty thus opened the door to Chinese immigration.

Union Pacific Railroad

Completion of the Union Pacific Railroad in 1869 and the 1873 depression soon threatened those treaty promises. The national financial crisis provided radical agitator Denis Kearney (himself an Irish immigrant) an opportunity to rail against both the rich and the "coolies." He struck the Chinese immigrants the hardest, however. This provoked an already uneasy San Francisco population into the so-called Sand Lot Riots of 1877, one of which resulted in the deaths of 21 Chinese. Kearney's Workingmen's Party, crying for relief from Chinese competition for wages and jobs, found great support for its slogan: "The

Form 430   APPLICATION OF ALLEGED AMERICAN-BORN CHINESE FOR PREINVESTIGATION OF STATUS   **TRIPLICATE**

No.1979-C.
No. 403-C   **Department of Commerce and Labor**
                                    IMMIGRATION SERVICE

                                                    Office of ____Commissioner____
                                                    Port of ____Philadelphia, Pa.____
                                                    April 3, _____, 123

To Commissioner of Immigration,
~~Chinese and Immigrant Inspector,~~
~~Philadelphia Immigration Station,~~
~~Gloucester City, N.J.~~
            SIR: It being my intention to leave the United States on a temporary visit abroad, departing and returning through the Chinese

port of entry of **Seattle, Washington**_____, I hereby apply, under the provisions of Rule 39 of the Chinese Regulations (Bureau Circular No. 25), for preinvestigation of my claimed status as an American citizen by birth, submitting herewith such documentary proofs (if any) as I possess, and agreeing to appear in your office personally, and to produce therein witnesses, for oral examination regarding the claim made by me.
            This application is submitted in triplicate with my photograph attached to each copy, as required by said rule.
                            Respectfully,

Signature in Chinese 簽 唐·字 名 陳明
Signature in English 簽 番 字 名 *Chin Ming*_____ (Pa.
            Address 具票人之住址 436 - 3rd Ave. Pittsburg,

相 簽 詢 委 亦 憑 國 九 而 來 人 遊 欲 委 管
三 名 問 員 親 據 出 欵 回 亦 出 外 暫 員 理
幅 稟 口 之 與 呈 世 之 茲 埠 入 邦 離 知 外
  上 供 公 證 上 所 例 依 而 之 今 美 之 人
  並 照 辦 人 查 有 在 三 由 去 港 由 國 我 入
  附 例 房 到 驗 之 美 十 埠 將   華 出 現 口

30,565   Port of _____

                                _____, 19____

Respectfully returned to
_____

        Chinese and Immigrant Inspector,
            Gloucester City, N.J.

With the information that I am ✓ prepared, on the basis of the evidence submitted with the original of this application, to approve said application.

        11—2847

                                    Officer in Charge.

Chinese must go."

By 1879, having adopted a state constitution with anti-Chinese provisions, Californians pressed for congressional action. Legislators in other states, concerned with Mexican or European immigrants, agreed that Federal action should be taken. Union leaders shared Kearney's concern about Chinese pay scales undercutting conventional rates. Some groups, preferring the melting pot, despaired of even trying to Americanize the highly ethnic-bound Chinese; therefore, these groups wanted to keep out the Chinese. Big landowners, once in favor of cheap labor and therefore opposed to Federal restrictions on labor, now feared that white supremacy might be undermined and joined anti-immigration factions. The violence in California only cemented the congressional perception that the situation might explode.

What could Congress do? Given the Burlingame Treaty's guarantees of the right to immigrate freely, could Congress restrict immigration? First, Congress moved to modify the Burlingame Treaty's guarantees by ratifying the treaty of November 17, 1880. Here the United States narrowed its focus from Chinese immigration in general to Chinese laborers. The 1880 treaty claimed for the United States the right to "regulate, limit or suspend" Chinese labor immigration. Congress could not, however, absolutely prohibit Chinese immigration.

The changes thus gave the U.S. government the right to limit future immigration of laborers whenever it "affects or threatens to affect" U.S. interests or "good order." Teachers, students, merchants, and Chinese travelers "proceeding from curiosity," as well as their servants, would be welcome. For nonlaborers, Burlingame's most-favored-nation status still held.

For Chinese, laborers or not, already in the United States, the 1880 modifications retained Burlingame's promise of the "rights, privileges, immunities and exemptions" due most-favored-nation populations. The Federal Government promised

to punish any violation of those protections. Thus the Congress distinguished between promising protection for the Chinese already in the United States and protecting the United States against further labor immigration.

Fortified by the new treaty with China, Congress soon bowed to lobbyist pressures. In the 1880s, Congress passed legislation establishing immigration barriers. In doing so, it resorted to regulation by law, which effectively circumvented the spirit of the immigration provision of the Burlingame Treaty and actually reduced immigration posed by the 1880 treaty. In the spring of 1882, Congress passed and President Chester A. Arthur signed the Chinese Exclusion Act, which provided an absolute 10-year moratorium on Chinese labor immigration. For the first time, Federal law proscribed entry of an ethnic working group on the premise that it endangered the good order of certain localities.

Chinese Exclusion Act

The Chinese Exclusion Act required the few nonlaborers who sought entry to obtain certification from the Chinese government that they were qualified to immigrate. But this group found it increasingly difficult to prove that they were not laborers, because the 1882 act defined excludables as "skilled and unskilled laborers and Chinese employed in mining." Thus, while the treaty did not totally prohibit Chinese immigration, in reality very few could enter the country under the 1882 law.

The 1882 exclusion act also placed new requirements on Chinese who had already entered. If they left the United States, they had to obtain certificates to re-enter. Congress, moreover, refused State and Federal courts the right to grant citizenship to Chinese resident aliens, although these courts could still deport them.

When the exclusion act expired in 1892, Congress extended it for 10 years in the form of the Geary Act. This extension, made permanent in 1902, added restrictions by requiring each Chinese resident to register and obtain a certificate of residence. Without a certificate, she or he faced deportation. With the congressional law providing such restrictions, the Burlingame Treaty guarantees and the 1880 modifications made little difference.

The Geary Act regulated Chinese immigration until the 1920s. With increased postwar immigration, Congress adopted new means for regulation: quotas and requirements pertaining to national origin. By this time, anti-Chinese agitation had quieted. In 1943 Congress repealed all the exclusion acts, leaving a yearly limit of 105 Chinese, and gave foreign-born Chinese the right to seek naturalization. The so-called national origin system, with various modifications, lasted until Congress passed the Immigration Act of 1965. Effective July 1, 1968, a limit of 170,000 immigrants from outside the Western Hemisphere could enter the United States, with a maximum of 20,000 from any one country. Skill and the need for political asylum determined admission.

The document of the month, "An Application of Alleged American Born Chinese for Preinvestigation of Status," is found in the Chinese Case Files of Records of the Immigration and Naturalization Service (Record Group 85), National Archives — Philadelphia Branch. It also is included in National Archives Microfilm Publication M1144, roll 30.

Teaching Suggestions

1. After students examine the form carefully, ask the following questions: What does it require of the Chinese? What do those requirements illustrate? What is the place of residence?

2. Ask students to read sections on Chinese immigration and European immigration in their textbooks. Discuss with the students the similarities and differences in the textbook coverage of the two groups.

3. Locate sketches of the Colossus of Rhodes and the Statue of Liberty and a copy of Emma Lazarus' "The New Colossus." Discuss the vocabulary before analyzing the poem. How are the Colossus and the Statue of Liberty different? Ask students to write an essay contrasting the promise of immigration with its reality for a recent immigrant group such as the Boat People.

4. Have students begin a genealogical study of their families or of a family from another ethnic group. List ethnic groups on the blackboard. Assign an oral history project of interviewing family members or neighbors about their ethnic background and how they have adapted to the United States. Find out what laws prevailed for their ethnic groups when they immigrated and what laws exist now.

Censoring the Mails: What Is Your Opinion?

During the early years of the 20th century, postal regulations authorized postmasters to confiscate mail under certain conditions. By authority of section 480 of the 1916 postal laws and regulations, the Post Office Department could deny mailing privileges to publishers of:

Every obscene, lewd, or lascivious, and every filthy book, pamphlet, picture, paper, letter, writing, print, or other publication of an indecent character, and every article or thing designed, adapted, or intended for preventing conception or producing abortion. . . . And the term "indecent" within the intendment of this section shall include matter of a character tending to incite arson, murder, or assassination.

The Blast, an anarchist publication edited and published by Alexander Berkman, was one of several publications confiscated by postal authorities. Published biweekly in San Francisco from January 1916 to June 1917, *The Blast* included articles to rally public opposition to capitalism and to all government authority. *The Blast* also promoted the causes of activists such as Margaret Sanger, who advocated women's rights to information pertaining to birth control.

Not long after *The Blast* appeared for sale, San Francisco Postmaster Charles W. Fay confiscated three issues and then recommended that the Post Office Department deny Berkman second-class mailing privileges. In a letter of March 25, 1916, to the Third Assistant Postmaster General, Fay described *The Blast:*

Since the first issue, the character of the paper has become more and more violent until with the publication of the last issue it would seem to come within several of the regulations that would bar it from the mails. It is obscene, incendiary, defamatory, and in every way undesirable.

Despite the resistance of Postmaster Fay, Berkman succeeded in getting his message through the mails to subscribers for a year and a half. On the one-year anniversary of *The Blast,* Berkman wrote to his subscribers:

[He had overcome] chicken-hearted printers, fearful of what their respectable customers would say; sly underhand wire-pulling by grafters, high and low; bitter opposition of Mother Grundies in silk shirts and overalls; stupid censorship and arbitrary deprivation of second class rights.

With the entry of the United States into war in the spring of 1917, Berkman's criticism of the government became even more vitriolic. On June 15, 1917, Federal marshals arrested Berkman and his longtime friend Emma Goldman for conspiring to discourage draft registration. They were tried, convicted, and sentenced within a month of their arrest. Imprisonment of Berkman succeeded in stopping the pub-

45217

Bishop, Cal.

April, 21st, 1916.

Postmaster General

Washington, D.C.

Sir:-

About three months ago I sent one
dollar to a publication known as the Blast, published
in San Francisco, and as I have not received the last
two issues, I wrote the publisher to ascertain the
cause of this. I have his reply before me stating that
my paper has been held up by the postal authorities
on the grounds that it carries "forbidden" articles.
Now I resent greatly your interference in this matter,
as I can not see by what right you exercise the power
of censoring my mail. I think that I am in much better
position than yourself to judge what for me would be
forbidden literature. But perhaps since you have set
yourself up as my literary censor, you will reimburse
me my one dollar. You have no more right to hold up my
paper, which I have paid for in actual money, than the
highwayman to hold up and rob me.

I DEMAND THAT YOU REMOVE YOUR
EMBARGO OR REFUND MY MONEY.

Yours,

F. E. vanCleave.

Introductory Exercise:
Written Document Analysis Worksheet

1. TYPE OF DOCUMENT (check one):
   - ☐ Newspaper
   - ☐ Letter
   - ☐ Patent
   - ☐ Memorandum
   - ☐ Map
   - ☐ Telegram
   - ☐ Press release
   - ☐ Report
   - ☐ Advertisement
   - ☐ Congressional record
   - ☐ Census report
   - ☐ Other

2. UNIQUE PHYSICAL QUALITIES OF THE DOCUMENT:
   - _____ Interesting letterhead
   - _____ Handwritten
   - _____ Typed
   - _____ Seals
   - _____ Notations
   - _____ "RECEIVED" stamp
   - _____ Other

3. DATE(S) OF DOCUMENT: _____

4. AUTHOR (OR CREATOR) OF THE DOCUMENT: _____

   POSITION (TITLE): _____

5. FOR WHAT AUDIENCE WAS THE DOCUMENT WRITTEN? _____

   _____

6. DOCUMENT INFORMATION: (There are many possible ways to answer A-E.)
   A. List three things the author said that you think are important.
      1. _____
      2. _____
      3. _____
   B. Why do you think this document was written?

      _____
      _____

   C. What evidence in the document helps you to know why it was written? Quote from the document.

      _____
      _____

   D. List two things the document tells you about life in the United States at the time it was written.
      1. _____
      2. _____
   E. Write a question to the author that is left unanswered by the document.

      _____
      _____

Opinion Survey: Censorship of the Mails

Directions: Read each statement to decide which of the five opinions you support. In the spaces to the left, write the abbreviation of that opinion.

Strongly Agree	Agree	Neutral	Disagree	Strongly Disagree
SA	A	N	D	SD

_____ 1. The government has an obligation to censor obscene material that might corrupt American youth.

_____ 2. The reader, not the government, should decide what literature is obscene.

_____ 3. Censorship of the mail is a violation of a citizen's First Amendment rights.

_____ 4. The government should reimburse a subscriber of confiscated literatare.

_____ 5. Under no circumstances should the government remove literature from the mails.

Below, indicate the statement that you found most difficult to answer and explain why.

Do you think your responses reflect the opinions of most Americans? Which groups might take a different position?

lication of *The Blast,* even though denial of mailing privileges had failed to do so.

The independent United States Postal Service replaced the Federal Post Office Department as the carrier of the mails in 1970. In the reorganization of the mail system, the Postal Service retains authority to confiscate "pornographic" and "incendiary" material. Today, however, postal inspectors are most concerned with identifying instances of mail fraud, rather than pornographic or incendiary materials.

The letter reproduced here is from file #45217, series 40, Records Relating to the Espionage Act, 1917-21, Records of the Post Office Department, Record Group 28.

Suggestions for Teaching

1. Opinion Survey: Censorship of the Mails:

a. Provide each student with a copy of the opinion survey below. Collect the completed survey and ask student volunteers to tally the responses.

b. As an alternative to suggestion a, make a transparency of the survey to display on an overhead projector.

c. Discuss the survey results with the class. Ask students to consider: What issues might be considered "forbidden" by the government in the early 20th century? Today? Are there any circumstances that you think would justify government censorship of the mails?

d. Provide each student with a copy of the document. Discuss with students the following questions: Does the government have an obligation to reimburse Mr. vanCleave for his financial loss? How do you think the government responded to Mr. vanCleave's letter? What further action might Mr. vanCleave have taken if he did not receive *The Blast* or his money?

2. Written Document Analysis:
The Written Document Analysis Worksheet below helps students to analyze systematically this letter or any written document. It focuses students' attention on documents and their importance to the historian and serves as a valuable beginning exercise for students who are unfamiliar with documents.

German Propaganda Leaflets in World War I

Today, propaganda, like the gun, is a common weapon of war. It was not until World War I, however, that the U.S. Government developed its first massive propaganda campaign. Largely responsible for this effort was the Committee on Public Information created by President Woodrow Wilson. Headed by George Creel, the Committee mobilized citizen support for the war through patriotic speeches, poster campaigns, newspaper stories, films, and pamphlets. Abroad, the Committee operated a worldwide information service, distributed films, and with the U.S. Army directed propaganda materials at the enemy.

Germany also had a well-organized propaganda machine. At the start of the war, the Germans focused on keeping the U.S. out of the European conflict. In this country, German diplomats and businessmen and some German-American citizen groups waged a propaganda campaign that consisted primarily of the distribution of anti-British publications. On the battlefront, German military intelligence directed propaganda at Allied soldiers.

Generally, propaganda leaflets intended for use along the front were designed to demoralize the soldier so that he would lay down his arms and surrender. Materials prepared by the Allies emphasized the humanistic war aims of President Wilson and called on German troops to overthrow the Kaiser. The two leaflets presented here are examples of German efforts to encourage black and German Americans to give up the fight. Leaflets such as these were sent behind the lines in a variety of ways. Most often they were carried in hot-air balloons; other times they were dropped from airplanes or packed in shells and literally fired across enemy lines.

These documents are photographs 165-WW-164A-1 and 165-WW-164A-7 in Records of War Department General and Special Staff, Record Group 165.

Suggestions for Teaching

Before completing this activity, have the class discuss the meaning and use of propaganda.

The following questions are designed to help your students develop a written analysis of these documents. They may also be used as the basis for class discussion.

1. To whom are these documents addressed?

2. Who do you think wrote them?

3. What points are being made by the authors?

4. What arguments are used to make these points?

5. Do you find these arguments convincing? Why or why not?

6. Describe the tone of the documents.

7. Compare and contrast the two documents. How are they alike or different?

To the American soldiers of German descent.

You say in your loose leaf that you serve in an honorable way in the U. S. Army. Do you think it honorable to fight the country that has given birth to your fathers or forefathers? Do you think it honorable to fall·upon any country after it has heroically defended itself for four years against a coalition of peoples tenfold its superior in numbers? Look at the map and compare that tiny little spot representing Germany with the vast territories assigned to Russia, England and the United States, to mention only the biggest of Germany's adversaries, and you cannot remain in doubt that the heroism is entirely on Germany's side. We are fighting for every thing dear to us, for our homes, our very existence. What are you fighting for, why did you come over here, fourthousand miles away from your own home? Did Germany do you any harm, did it ever threaten you? Your leaders are Misleaders, they have lied to you that we were slaves of a tyrant, and you are guilty of gross ignorance if you believe one word of it. Everybody knowing anything about human nature and the history of European nations will tell you that slaves can never stand up against the whole world of fierce enemies, only free man fighting for their hapiness in life will endure so many years of fighting against the most colossal odds that ever a nation encountered. An everlasting shame that twenty millions of German-Americans could not prevent that man Wilson, who never was a genuine American but rather an English subject in disguise, to raise his hand against their mother country! Read Washington's Farewell Adress and imagine what he. would have to say of the total collapse of real Americanism in our days. His golden words to his fellow citizens to only mind their own business have been thrown to the winds by the present administration. Go and repent ere it is too late, we shall welcome every lost sheep that finds its way back to its herd. There is more freedom in Germany indeed than in the land of Dictator Wilson. We do not try to deceive you, we do not promise you a farm, but we assure you that every honest man willing to work has infinitely better chances in Germany where we do not suffer corrupt politicians, deceiving land speculators, nor cheating contractors. Lay down your gun, your innermost soul is not in this fight. Come over to us, you will not regret it.

To the colored soldiers of the U. S. Army.

Hallo boys, what are you doing over here? Fighting the Germans? Why? Have they ever done you any harm? Of course, some white folks and the lying English-American papers told you that the Germans ought to be wiped out for the sake of humanity and democracy. What is Democracy? Personal Freedom, all citizens enjoying the same rights socially and before the law! Do you enjoy the same rights as the white people do in America. the land of Freedom and Democracy? Or aren't you rather treated over there as second class citizens? Can you go into a rest urant where white people dine, can you get a seat in a theater where white people sit, can you get a Pullman seat or berth in a rail roadcar or can you even ride, in the South, in the same street car with white people? And how about the law? Is lynching and the most horrible cruelties connected therewith a lawful proceeding in a democratic country?

Now, all this is entirely different in Germany, where they do like colored people, where they treat them as Gentlemen and not as second class citizens. They enjoy exactly the same social privileges as every white man, and quite a number of colored people have migthy fine positions in business in Berlin and other big German cities.

Why then fight the Germans only for the benefit of the Wallstreet robbers to protect the millions they have lent to the English, French and Italians? You have been made the tool of the egotistic and rapacious rich in England and in America, and there is nothing in the whole game for you but broken bones, horrible wounds, spoiled health or — death. No satisfaction whatever will you get out of this unjust war. You have never seen Germany, so you are fools if you allow ■■■■ to teach you to hate it. Come over to see for yourself. ■■■■ do the fighting who make profit out of this war; don ■■■■ em to use you as cannon food. To carry the gun in th ■■■ ce is not an honor but a shame. Throw it away and come over to the German lines You will find friends who help you along.

8. What assumptions have the authors made about the people addressed?

9. How is the information in the documents organized? How does this affect the message?

10. Is there information in the documents that links them to a particular event in U.S. history?

11. Why do you think these documents were written?

12. Do you consider these documents to be examples of propaganda? Why or why not?

13. List examples of propaganda techniques used in the period in which these documents were created. How are they similar to or different from present-day techniques?

The Zimmermann Telegram

Historical Background

Between 1914 and the spring of 1917, the European nations engaged in a conflict that became known as World War I. While armies moved across the face of Europe, the United States remained neutral. In 1916, Woodrow Wilson was elected President for a second term, largely because of the slogan "He kept us out of war." Events in early 1917 would change that hope. In frustration over the effective British naval blockade, Germany in February broke its pledge to limit submarine warfare. In response to the breaking of the *Sussex* pledge, the United States severed diplomatic relations with Germany.

In January of 1917, British cryptographers deciphered a telegram from German Foreign Minister Arthur Zimmermann to the German Minister to Mexico, von Eckhardt, offering United States territory to Mexico in return for joining the German cause. This message helped draw the United States into the war and thus changed the course of history. The telegram had such an impact on American opinion that, according to David Kahn, author of *The Codebreakers,* "No other single cryptanalysis has had such enormous consequences." It is his opinion that "never before or since has so much turned upon the solution of a secret message." In an effort to protect their intelligence from detection and to capitalize on growing anti-German sentiment in the United States, the British waited until February 24 to present the telegram to Woodrow Wilson. The American press published news of the telegram on March 1. On April 6, 1917, the United States Congress formally declared war on Germany and her allies.

Reproduced here is a copy of the telegram from Zimmermann to von Eckhardt and a copy of the decoded message. The coded telegram is signed "Bernstorff" because it was transmitted through the United States and Bernstorff was the German ambassador in Washington.

The story of British intelligence efforts to decipher the German code is fascinating and complicated. *The Zimmermann Telegram* by Barbara Tuchman recounts that story in all of its exciting detail. It is an excellent historical account for high school students.

The telegram reproduced here is from Decimal File 862.20212/82A (1910-1929), and the decoded telegram is from Decimal File 862.20212/69 (1910-1929), General Records of the Department of State, Record Group 59.

Teaching Suggestions

1. Decoding a message: In this exercise, students decode a fictitious message using a simple substitution code. In substitution codes, the letters of the plaintext (message to be put into secret form) are replaced by other letters, numbers, or symbols. In this code system, each letter in the alphabet and each of the numbers from 1 to 9 appears in the matrix of the grid. Each letter in the grid is replaced by two letters in the coded message. The first letter in the message is from the vertical axis of the grid, and the second letter is from its horizontal axis. For example, if "DG" were the first two letters to decipher in a cryptogram, you would find the letter "D" on the vertical axis and the letter "G" on the horizon-

GERMAN LEGATION

MEXICO CITY

130	13042	13401	8501	115	3528	416	17214	6491	11310
18147	18222	21560	10247	11518	23677	13605	3494	14936	
98092	5905	11311	10392	10371	0302	21290	5161	39695	
23571	17504	11269	18276	18101	0317	0228	17694	4473	
22284	22200	19452	21589	67893	5569	13918	8958	12137	
1333	4725	4458	5905	17166	13851	4458	17149	14471	6706
13850	12224	6929	14991	7382	15857	67893	14218	36477	
5870	17553	67893	5870	5454	16102	15217	22801	17138	
21001	17388	7446	23638	18222	6719	14331	15021	23845	
3156	23552	22096	21604	4797	9497	22464	20855	4377	
23610	18140	22260	5905	13347	20420	39689	13732	20667	
6929	5275	18507	52262	1340	22049	13339	11265	22295	
10439	14814	4178	6992	8784	7632	7357	6926	52262	11267
21100	21272	9346	9559	22464	15874	18502	18500	15857	
2188	5376	7381	98092	16127	13486	9350	9220	76036	14219
5144	2831	17920	11347	17142	11264	7667	7762	15099	9110
10482	97556	3569	3670						

BERNSTOPFF.

Charge German Embassy.

CANCELED
Letter 1-8-58
V. ....erson, State Dept.

By *Mark G Eckhoff Archivist*

Date *Oct 27,1958*

FROM 2nd from London # 5747.

"We intend to begin on the first of February unrestricted submarine warfare. We shall endeavor in spite of this to keep the United States of America neutral. In the event of this not succeeding, we make Mexico a proposal of alliance on the following basis: make war together, make peace together, generous financial support and an understanding on our part that Mexico is to reconquer the lost territory in Texas, New Mexico, and Arizona. The settlement in detail is left to you. You will inform the President of the above most secretly as soon as the outbreak of war with the United States of America is certain and add the suggestion that he should, on his own initiative, invite ~~the~~ Japan to immediate adherence and at the same time mediate between Japan and ourselves. Please call the President's attention to the fact that the ruthless employment of our submarines now offers the prospect of compelling England in a few months to make peace." Signed, ZIMMERMANN.

Cryptogram

Directions: Decipher the cryptogram message using the grid.

```
                      FGAFA   AAVXA   DGAVX   VADAD   DVDDD   VGA
VXVDX   DVDDF   AFDXG   XGDDG   AVFDV   X
        VAAFX   GDADX   VDDXD   AVXXV
        AAAVD   AVXDA   VVGDD   XAVDG   DXGXV   XVDVF   VVAFD   XAVAF
VXDXV   DFDAF   XAVVV   FAVAF   VVVVV   ADGXV   AXAFD   GGXFX   AFAVV
ADGDF   VFAXV   DVXXF   DAVXG   DVAAF   XGDAD   XVDVF   AVAFV   FDGAV
AFVXV   DAXAF   DGXDA   FAFVA   AADGV   VVVXV   VDDFV   VGDVD   AVVXD
FVDVX   DADXA   F
        AAAFA   VDFVV   VXVDA   VFGFG   XFDGV   VGDDA   DFFXV
XVDDF   FDDX
```

Grid

	A	D	F	G	V	X
A	B	2	E	5	R	L
D	I	9	N	A	1	C
F	3	D	4	F	6	G
G	7	H	8	J	0	K
V	M	O	P	Q	S	T
X	U	V	W	X	Y	Z

tal axis. Trace them across the grid to their intersection at the letter "A" in the plaintext.

To decode the fictitious message, students should begin by grouping each set of two letters starting with the first two letters (FG) and continuing through the message. The code letters are arbitrarily arranged in groups of five letters. Some letter pairs will carry over from one line to the next. As students locate each letter in the grid, they should write that letter above the pair of code letters to which it corresponds. There are no punctuation marks in the telegram, so students may need some direction in clarifying the message.

As homework, students can be asked to write a message using the code, and then exchange the messages for decoding.

Decoded Message:

February 22, 1917

To: von Eckhardt
  Mexico City
  British crack top secret code. U.S. press may leak German plot with Mexico. Prepare to leave embassy on short notice.
Bernstorff
Washington, D.C.

2. The Zimmermann telegram provides an opportunity to review geography with your students. Ask them to locate England, Germany, Mexico, and Japan on a world map or globe. Direct students to indicate on the map or globe the territory offered by the Germans to the Mexicans in the telegram. Ask them to calculate how much the territory offered to Mexico would increase the size of that country. What geographical advantages would the Germans gain by Mexican entry into the war? What was the role of Japan?

3. Discussion questions:
  a. What other documents have changed the course of American history? For example, consider the effects of the Emancipation Proclamation, the Monroe Doctrine, and the DeLôme Letter.
  b. What events in 1916 and 1917 contributed to the impact the Zimmermann telegram would have on the American public?
  c. Would the United States have remained neutral if the Zimmermann telegram had not been revealed?

The Black Soldier in World War I

The contribution of American black soldiers during World Wars I and II is touched on lightly in United States history texts, and the subject is sometimes ignored in the social studies curriculum, even during black history celebrations. Usually Crispus Attucks, the Tenth Cavalry, and the Tuskegee Airmen are all that is popularly known about blacks in the United States military during wars. This document focuses on the black soldier of World War I and the period of intolerance that followed the Armistice.

Poor race relations in the United States resulted in inequitable draft practices and conflicting attitudes among white commanders toward black troops. In World War I blacks were drafted out of proportion to their numbers in the population. Under the Selective Service Act of 1917, 36 percent of eligible black males were drafted as compared with 24 percent of eligible white males.

Military commanders dealt with the race issue in various ways. Gen. Thomas H. Brady, Camp Grant (Illinois), chose to ignore the issue of color in his directive about the use of recreational areas, announcing that "The only color recognized in Camp Grant is to be O.D. — the olive drab of the Army uniforms." Gen. C. C. Ballou issued Bulletin 35 to the black 92nd Division at Camp Funston (Kansas) ordering them to "avoid every situation that can give rise to racial illwill. Attend quietly and faithfully to your duties, *and don't go where your presence is not desired*." Capt. Eugene C. Bowan was court-martialed for refusing to obey an order to assemble a troop formation that included black and white forces.

Records show that a number of white officers were separated from service for discrimination against "colored" soldiers and for unwarranted acts of cruelty in dealing with them. Yet both black and white soldiers faced the same hazards at the front. Just like his white counterpart, the black male enlisted or was drafted and received basic training. He sailed across the Atlantic on a troopship to fight in the trenches of France. He killed, was killed or maimed, was decorated or buried. He returned home to a victory parade. But the black soldier's return to United States soil was often followed by a period of confusion and disillusionment. Although he had changed as a result of the experience of war, his status at home had not. The potential for conflict for the black veteran, both internal and external, was heightened by this realization.

During the early postwar years, violence against blacks increased in the United States. Old stereotypes of the black persisted, including fear of his supposed unbridled lust and fear that he would intermarry with whites. The black soldier was suddenly seen as capable of doing well in a number of trades and therefore became an economic as well as a social threat to the white worker. White contempt of blacks gave way to hostility and mindless killing. In 1918, 68 people were lynched, of whom 58 were black. By 1919 a new element of terror was added as blacks were burned alive. Of the 83 people killed by mobs in 1919, 77 were black and 11 of those were burned to death.

This bigotry produced a group of black protest writers and journalists. W.E.B. DuBois and Marcus Garvey were particularly active publicists, developing an audience among disenchanted black veterans. Some writers recommended direct action for redress of their grievances. Others sought unity among blacks to provide both protection and action against the violence that confronted them.

At the peak of the violence, DuBois, writing in *Crisis,* called for a war for equal rights:

> Behold the day, O Fellow Black Men! They cheat us and mock us: they divide our misery. When we plead for the naked protection of the law, there, where a million of our fellows dwell, they tell us to "Go to Hell!" To Your Tents, O Israel! And Fight, Fight, Fight for Freedom!

But the white workingman also sought unity and security through organized labor, but the activity of labor organizers, particularly those who were associated with the International Workers of the World (IWW), was perceived by many other elements of American society as part of a Bolshevist plot to undermine the American way of life. It was an easy exercise to relate the writings of DuBois and the active black press to Karl Marx's rallying cry, "Workers of the world unite. You have nothing to lose but your chains." The so-called Red Scare of the 1920s wound up fanning racial hatred, as well as fear of communism, for years to come.

This document is found in the National Archives Record Group 28, Records of the Office of the Solicitor, under Records Related to the Espionage Act of World War I, File B-584. Under section 12 of the June 1917 Espionage Act, the Postmaster General was authorized to deny mailing privileges to newspapers, periodicals, and other materials that advocated treason, insurrection, or forcible resistance to any law of the United States. The Solicitor was appointed to take charge of legal matters arising from the enforcement of this act. Correspondence of the Solicitor in the file of *The Favorite Magazine* included a letter from the postmistress of Melbourne, Florida, samples of two issues of the magazine, and this poster. In a letter dated August 5, 1919, she asked the Postmaster General, "Are the inclosed [sic] periodicals and newspapers in accordance with postal rules and regulations?" The memo from the Solicitor's Office provided no clear decision regarding the suitability of this document for mailing.

Teaching Activities

Before the foregoing background of the document is presented to the students, use an inquiry approach to the document to introduce the subject.

1. Pass the document around the class or project it with an opaque projector. Ask the students to examine it carefully.

2. Discuss the major content of the document, using the following questions: What is the family doing? What war is depicted in this poster? What does the blue star flag in the window indicate? Why is the portrait of Lincoln higher than the father's portrait? What features appear to be out of place? Are sex-roles obvious in this print? Why is the poster titled "True Blue"? [Note: The blue star flag in the window indicates that a person in that home is serving in the military.]

3. Discuss the use of propaganda. Ask the students to write a paragraph answering the question: Is the poster an example of wartime propaganda? If NO, why not? If YES, who is the audience, what is the desired effect of the work, and what might be some undesirable effects of it?

4. Students could do additional research for oral or written reports on the contributions of the black soldier during all the wars of the United States. They could attempt to determine how many served, where they served and in what capacities, and who the heroes and villains were. They could also attempt to report on the racial composition of the current Armed Forces.

True Blue

5. Students should consider launching oral history projects, using their families as primary sources. Students can be encouraged to talk to family members about their experiences of race relations in the military. This special project could compare the experiences of the several generations to determine if conditions have changed since Harry Truman's Executive Order in July 1948 to desegregate the military forces.

 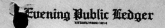

PUBLIC LEDGER COMPANY

INDEPENDENCE SQUARE
PHILADELPHIA

June 14th

Dear Brother Palmer:

I am enclosing an editorial from yesterday's
PUBLIC LEDGER and am sorry I did not have the full report of your overwhelming testimony before me when I
wrote it since I might have been more emphatic in certain particulars. It is unfortunate that the newspapers
carried such poor accounts of your testimony. I believe
that your report ought to be sent personally to every
responsible editor in the country, especially in those
centers in which the aliens predominate and where so
many so-called intellectuals sympathize with the type of
people represented by Wallerstein and Kane who in turn
play into the hands of the half-baked crowd that are for
Bolshevism though they do not know why. But it is unfortunate
that it will not get into the hands of all those who should
have it in newspaper offices and if there is any way in
which you could send out an abstract, I think it would be
a good idea. You have certainly shown them up, and even
before I had your report I had suspected that the innocent
school meetings and study meetings which they describe so
pathetically were really anarchist or Bolshevist meetings. I
notice that you speak about the radical publications and say
you will send a list to the Senate. May I get a copy of this
list? I should also like to have any material which will
further offset the outrageous charges of Post and his lawyer
and the so-called National Government League. I really wish you
could get what you have done before the public more fully but I realize how

difficult this is.

Yours sincerely,
Harvey M. Watts

I hope you win out at
San Francisco, but I
suppose McAdoo is to
be the Philippe "Egalité"
candidate on a
radical platform.
I like Harding and
Coolidge; they're
real folks and
my kind.

a democracy?

e. What effect has media coverage had on national events? Cite examples of significant instances in which media coverage of an event in progress may have altered its outcome.

4. Ask students to examine other periods in U.S. history when people were obsessed with malign influences. The students should compare and contrast the atmosphere and methods of the Red Scare with those of McCarthyism, the Know-Nothing movement, and the Salem witch trials. Ask students to share their findings through oral or written reports.

5. The Red Scare has been compared by many to the hysteria of the Salem witch trials. In her book *The Devil in Massachusetts: A Modern Inquiry into Salem Witch Trials,* Marion Starkey develops the hypothesis that such periods of persecution follow a pattern. A genuine problem generates such fear that authorities curtail liberties of people who are poor, lacking in status, or unpopular. The persecution spreads to people who consider themselves middle-class, "respectable" folk, then rages on to threaten the powerful and wealthy before it wanes. Ask students to identify how this document fits into this general pattern.

Note: Kane and Wallerstein were defense attorneys for accused "Reds." William G. McAdoo was President Wilson's son-in-law, Secretary of the Treasury, and a rival to Palmer for the 1920 Democratic presidential nomination with backing of the party's liberals. French nobleman Louis Philippe Joseph d'Orléans renounced his title and assumed the name Philippe-Égalité; he was a liberal reformer who worked to overthrow Louis XVI.

Schools for Americanization

Historical Background

At the close of World War I, public pressure mounted to assimilate immigrants more rapidly into American culture. The postwar influx of Southern Europeans into America — immigrants who differed in religion and culture from many of those who had come before — fueled that pressure.

In the 1920s, local and state governments actively encouraged a policy of Americanization, to which English-language instruction was basic. Previously, churches and social clubs founded by immigrants had offered such language instruction without support from public funds. With the Americanization program, the Federal Government prepared appropriate textbooks that local communities could use to teach English and citizenship to immigrants, both young and old. Localities opened classroom space in public schools to the newest Americans and recruited volunteer teachers from service clubs, immigrant social organizations, and even labor unions. The remarks of a young Armenian high school graduate in Watertown, Massachusetts, capture the spirit of the Americanization movement:

> I was only seventeen years old when I first came to America, the land of heroes and great men. My dream was always to come into this great and free country, to live as a free man, without fear that my life was in danger. . . . I was not able to speak English at all, but today, with the aid of the night school, I can speak and read and write very well the English language. I love and admire America because she helped me many times and because she is the only unselfish nation in the world.

During the period 1919-20, according to the Department of Commerce and Labor fiscal year 1920 report, more than half a million immigrants took their seats in classrooms to learn English; of these, 26,000 were adults. The concentration of new Americans within each state determined the number and type of programs offered. By the end of World War I, twenty towns in Illinois, for example, offered English instruction; and the ranks of students numbered over 4,000. Granite City, Illinois, a steel-producing town north of East Saint Louis, where the program announced in this document was located, offered English instruction through the Americanization program to its immigrant population of mostly Hungarians. The poster reproduced here appeals to immigrants in Granite City to attend classes at one of four Americanization schools.

Today, an Americanization school concept persists, retaining the character of its early years. The Immigration and Naturalization Service continues to provide adult immigrants who are not regularly enrolled in public schools with textbooks and home study materials. However, the initiative for Americanization, while affected by waves of political refugees like the South Vietnamese and Haitian boat people, remains a local and state responsibility. Across the country today, communities provide space for classes in public schools and recreation centers, and voluntary organizations recruit instructors for citizenship and English classes.

The poster reproduced here is from file 27671/44, Americanization files, Records of the Immigration and Naturalization Service, Record Group 85.

GRANITE CITY
AMERICANIZATION SCHOOLS

Beginning
Monday,
September
the 27th,
1920

Underwood & Underwood

These two men are brothers, one is an American Citizen and the other has just come to this country with their old mother. See the difference in the way they dress and look. America is a great country. In America everybody has a chance. Everybody who comes to America from the old country ought to learn the American language and become an American citizen. If the people that come to America do not become Americans, this country will soon be like the old country.

Monday
and
Thursday
Evenings
7:30 p. m.

SCHOOLS:

HIGH SCHOOL, 20TH AND D STREETS
LINCOLN PLACE, 917 PACIFIC AVENUE

LIBERTY SCHOOL, 20TH AND O STREETS
MADISON SCHOOL, 1322 MADISON AVENUE

Keep America Great.   Become an American Citizen   **Learn The Language.**

Press-Record Publishing Co. 1834 D St., Granite City, Ill

Teaching Activities

Provide each student with a copy of the document or post it on the bulletin board for easy reference.

1. Assign students to develop a list of all the reasons, stated and implied by the poster, for attending the Granite City Americanization School. Discuss the meaning of the statement: "If the people that come to America do not become Americans, this country will soon be like the old country." According to the evidence in the poster, what is "the American Dream"?

2. Ask students for their definitions of the American Dream. Classify these definitions by types of dreams: e.g., economic, political, social, educational, and so forth. Assign students to solicit a parent's definition of the American Dream. In class, compare and contrast the types of dreams described by each generation and consider: Do members of the same family seem to have the same dreams? Does the age of the parent seem to affect the dream? How have the dreams changed over time?

3. Direct the students to redesign the center square of the poster to illustrate their visions of the American Dream and to appeal to new Americans today.

4. America has been described both as a "melting pot" (a blend of the elements of many cultures into a new culture) and as a "nation of nations" (a mixture of many cultures, each retaining its unique elements). Discuss with students each of these descriptions and consider which is more accurate and which creates the fewest problems in national life.

5. At various times in our history, different political groups have acted to ensure access to the American Dream for *all* Americans. Direct students to identify the following terms and to indicate that aspect of the American Dream that each seeks to protect: affirmative action, equal employment opportunity, Head Start, unemployment compensation, social security, mainstreaming, and bilingual education. Direct students also to investigate government actions that ensure access to the American Dream: e.g., amendments to the Constitution, Supreme Court decisions, and Congressional acts.

A Letter from a Mother

In May 1929, in an effort to stem the increase of criminal activity in the United States, President Herbert Hoover created the National Commission on Law Observance and Enforcement. Called the Wickersham Commission after its chairman, George Wickersham, the 12-member group gathered information on particular aspects of criminal law enforcement, including penal institutions and juvenile delinquency. The major part of the Commission's investigation, however, focused on the problem of enforcing prohibition under the provisions of the 18th Amendment. That amendment prohibited the manufacture, sale, and transportation of alcoholic beverages. (For a more detailed discussion of the Wickersham Commission, see "A Political Cartoon" on page 116.

Found in the records of the Commision at the National Archives are thousands of letters from citizens expressing their concerns about the causes of crime and the increase in criminal activity. Letters reporting crimes associated with prohibition violations were common. Citizens presented arguments both for and against the 18th Amendment. The following excerpts from letters sent to the Commission suggest the range of American opinion on the causes of crime:

From Tulsa, Oklahoma (May 25, 1929):

This great wave of crime is due to the use of cigarettes and nothing else. The indiscriminate use of hooch, poison liquor, wine, Jamaica ginger and any other product that has a kick, is due to the use of cigarettes and nothing else.

From Seattle, Washington (May 23, 1929):

From Seattle, Washington (May 23, 1929):
The first thing to be observed, perhaps, is that the increase of crime is not from the increase of netural [sic] criminals, but the great increase of criminal opportunity afforded by the invention of the auto. The easy means by which the auto can be used for robbery . . . as well as the disposing of liquor, have caused vast increase in those forms of crime.

From Baltimore, Maryland (June 10, 1929):

Second, the newspapers seem to be making law enforcement more difficult by giving crime great value as "news" and assigning headlines accordingly.

From Spokane, Washington (June 13, 1929):

The present prohibition law has offered to the bootlegger a lucrative occupation and this fraternity harbors criminals of all kinds from the gentleman bootlegger who caters to so-called respectable trade to the burglar and highwayman who finds the business almost as profitable and not nearly as dangerous as the one previously followed.

The letter reproduced here in full is an expression of a mother's concern over increased crime as it affects her family. It is from the Correspondence Files; Anonymous Letters Expressing Complaints, Grievances (April 1929-August 1931); Records of the National Commission on Law Observance and Enforcement, Record Group 10.

Teaching Activities

The following activities vary according to ability level and skill focus. We recommend that you review the activities and select the one most consistent with your class objectives.

Activity 1: The Letter as Evidence of Life in the 1920s
(Locating information, drawing conclusions, and discussing)
1. Provide students with copies of the letter and allow time for them to read it carefully.

2. Write the following items on the board in a column, directing students to reread the letter to find factual information about the 1920s in each category.
    a. the cost of living
    b. the level of technology
    c. the enforcement of prohibition laws
    d. citizen faith in government
    e. public attitude toward immigrants
    f. the generation gap
    g. peer pressure

3. As a concluding activity, discuss with the class the problem of using this document to draw generalizations about life in the United States during the 1920s.

Activity 2: The Letter as a Reflection of the Individual and Society
(Locating information and making generalizations)
    Most written documents can be used effectively with this activity.

Ask students to read the document silently, or select one student to read it orally while other students follow the letter on an overhead projection or a copy.

2. Write on the board the two column headings that follow:

Individual	Society
1.	1.
2.	2.
3.	3.

3. Direct students to locate evidence in the letter that gives information about the individual who wrote it. Students may work as a class or independently. Then direct the class to repeat the process, focusing on

information about the society in which the individual lived. Record the information on the board. (Be sure to include the significance of the "received" stamp, the notation, and the absence of an identifiable signature.)

Activity 3: The Letter as a Skill Exercise
(Writing, punctuating, and spelling)
1. Provide each student with a copy of the letter. Direct students to use a red pen or pencil to correct punctuation errors. Students should underline spelling and typographical errors.

2. As an alternative, ask students to rewrite one or two paragraphs of the letter with corrections.

Activity 4: Mr. Wickersham's Reply
(Synthesizing, evaluating, and writing)
As background for this exercise, discuss with students the function of the National Commission on Law Observance and Enforcement and the role of Mr. Wickersham as its chairman.

2. Before proceeding with the exercise described below, direct students to read the document carefully and, in a class discussion, to consider the letter's content and purpose.

3. Direct students to compose a letter from Mr. Wickersham in reply to the mother's letter. Be sure that students address the mother's concerns and offer a solution to her dilemma. Students should consider how the government might solve such a problem.

Activity 5: Using the Letter for Role Playing
(Problem solving and valuing)
1. After students have read and discussed the letter, ask for volunteers to play the parts of the mother, the son, and the son's companions. Direct students to recreate the following incidents, drawing on information they know about human nature, prohibition, and life in the 1920s.
    a. The decision to get a drink after

Phila: Pa.
7/22/29

Mr Wickersham;
Dear Sir,

Please hear the plea of a heartbroken
mother and send some reliable person to investigate the
 condition of an Italian joint,where children are sold rum
for ten cents a drink. My boy with several companions Went
swimming and after the swim they suggested he go with them
to get something to warm them up consquently my thirteen
year old boy was brought home to me in a drunken stupor.
        Willingly would I send you his name but I dread the
publicity his father is dead I am alone trying to rear him
an honorable American but how canI when this foreigner I
doubt if he has ever been naturlized is allowed to ruin my
boy.
        The City wont close him up he has been arrested
several times,he keeps right on doing business,he has been
in this vicinity for the last six years and in this present
location the last three.
        This Italian is known by the name of Nick he had a
shack at 63 and Lindberg Boulevard a man bought the ground
put up a Sun Gasoline Station and knowing that he sold rum
built him a resturant right in the station that is where
my boy bought his, then they moved the old shack across
the road and that is where it is hid in and around the
old shack.
        Send one of your men to 63 &Lindberg Boulevard on
the Back Road stay around that Sun Station watch the Res_
turant an the shack across the road, noon hour is a good
time that is when I went down to remonstrate with him
never in my life did I meet with such insults he was
surrounded with bums and ordered me out under threat that
he would have one of them throw me out, I dont know why I
didnt kill him. I am desperate no one can touch him so I
come to you last with my plea please help save these boys
from that poisoned rum.
        My boy is a good boy a pupil of the Tilden Junior
High and carried off the highest honors in his class
last term.

                        Truly Yours.

RECEIVED   A Mother

JUL   1929

NATIONAL COMMISSION ON LAW
OBSERVANCE AND ENFORCEMENT

swimming.
(son, son's friends)

    b. The confrontation between the mother and the drunken son and one or two of his companions.
(mother, son, and companions)

2. Follow up this role-playing activity with a discussion of specific issues of conflict between parents and teenagers today. How do students and their parents resolve conflicts?

Activity 6: Topics for Discussion
(Comprehending, synthesizing, and evaluating)

    This document provides a versatile range of topics for discussing life in the 1920s. Many of the issues raised then parallel issues of current concern and make interesting comparisons. For example, prohibition of alcohol in the 1920s and prohibition of marijuana today; intolerance of eastern European immigrants in the 1920s and intolerance of Asian and Hispanic immigrants today; conflicts between the older and younger generations then and now; attitudes toward government in the 1920s and the post-Watergate attitude of the 1970s.

The Unfinished Lincoln Memorial

Today a majestic marble likeness of Abraham Lincoln stares across the reflecting pool at the Washington Monument on the capital's grassy mall. This memorial to Lincoln has been the backdrop for many important public protests and events since its completion in 1922. It was on the memorial's steps that singer Marian Anderson gave her Easter Sunday concert in 1939 after being turned away from Constitution Hall by the Daughters of the American Revolution and where Dr. Martin Luther King, Jr., delivered his "I Have a Dream" speech in August 1963. Antiwar protesters came to the memorial steps in the late 1960s and early 1970s to raise their voices against the U.S. role in Vietnam.

Construction began on the memorial to Lincoln in 1915, fifty years after his assassination. American sculptor Daniel Chester French designed the statue to honor the 16th President. French had gained a national reputation with his earlier portrayal of "The Minute Man," a statue to honor those colonials who died at Lexington and Concord in 1775. In describing his tribute to Lincoln, French said: "The memorial tells you just what manner of man you are come to pay homage to; his simplicity, his grandeur, and his power." President Warren G. Harding dedicated the building and the sculpture on May 30, 1922.

The photograph shown here captures workers assembling French's statue of Lincoln in 1920. It is a haunting reminder of the unfulfilled promises implicit in Lincoln's Emancipation Proclamation, for the 1920s commenced an era of strained race relations in this country. The causes for the increased tensions included fierce competition for jobs among demobilized soldiers, both black and white; the migration of rural blacks to urban centers in the North and the South; and the infusion into the melting pot of immigrants who differed in cultural background from those who had come earlier. One consequence of these tensions was the rise of nativism, or giving first place to "native" Americans; another was the rebirth of the Ku Klux Klan in all its virulence. The headless image of Lincoln is prophetic of the somber aspects of the decade that is most remembered for its flappers, flivvers, and frivolity.

This photograph is from Records of the Office of Public Buildings and Public Parks of the National Capital, Record Group 42, item No. 42-M-J-1. The photographer is unknown, as is the identity of the central figure in the photograph.

Teaching Suggestions

1. Photographs, like all evidence, should be examined with care. Students should be aware that, like written documents, photographs reflect a point of view, may even be staged, and should be used with other sources of evidence. Before discussing this photograph with students, post it on the bulletin board for several days and direct students to look at it closely. It is useful to divide a photograph into quadrants and to look at each in turn, noting striking details.

2. Photographs freeze events in time and evoke in the viewer a memory of the event. In this way many photographs become symbols of an event or series of events — the student kneeling by her slain classmate at Kent State, Lyndon Johnson's swearing-in as President aboard Air Force

One, and the Marines raising the American flag on Iwo Jima. Discuss the photograph of Lincoln's statue as a symbol of the 1920s. Develop a list of photographic images that are symbolic for students. Consider with students how to judge the validity of a photograph as a symbol.

3. Develop a list of students' images of President Abraham Lincoln: for example, self-taught youth, great debater, advocate of abolition of slavery, assassinated hero. Direct students to investigate these images of Lincoln to see if they stand up under scrutiny.

4. Abraham Lincoln has been honored in many ways (Lincoln Tunnel in New York City, the Lincoln penny, Lincoln University, etc.). Assign students to survey all the ways that Lincoln has been honored. Has your town honored Lincoln with a park, school, or street named for him? Create a bulletin board that illustrates the many ways that we honor past Presidents.

5. Washington, DC, is the site of memorials to most former Presidents and other prominent Americans. There are also memorials to those who served and died in American wars. The memorial to those who served and died in Vietnam was dedicated on Veterans Day in November 1982. The final design for the memorial created some controversy among veterans' groups. Assign students to investigate the areas of controversy and the compromise solution.

6. Citizens' groups successfully lobbied Congress to honor slain civil rights leader Dr. Martin Luther King, Jr., by declaring his birthdate a national holiday. Direct students to discover how national holidays are created.

7. If you come to Washington, DC, be sure to visit the Lincoln Memorial. It is especially moving to see it at night. Or, if you find yourself in Stockbridge, MA, visit Chesterwood, the home and studio of sculptor Daniel Chester French.

A Political Cartoon

We have selected a cartoon as the document because many texts include cartoons. As you use your textbook, keep in mind that the illustrations can be used to create interesting classroom lessons. We offer here an approach to analyzing political cartoons, as well as a sample cartoon from the holdings of the National Archives.

The chart included here is designed to enable students to analyze any political cartoon. The questions on the chart begin at the basic level of comprehension and build to a higher level that requires the use of interpretive skills. You may wish to assign the first questions on the chart to individual students and to discuss the higher level questions with the class as a group. Keep in mind that cartoons are also excellent vehicles for vocabulary development.

In preparation for using the cartoon chart, you may wish to discuss the nature of symbols with your students. As an exercise, you can ask your students to develop their own visual or written symbols for people (teachers, principals, parents); institutions (school, home, local "hangout"); or ideas (energy conservation, political philosophies, fads). Students might also be asked to develop a list of common American symbols frequently used by cartoonists (Uncle Sam, John Q. Public, the Democratic donkey, the Republican elephant, etc.).

We recommend that you use political cartoons as a summarizing activity at the end of a unit of study. Because cartoons are symbolic, subtle, and ironic, the more background information that students bring to the cartoon, the better able they will be to grasp the cartoonist's meaning.

The Cartoon in Historical Context

Prohibition

By 1917, 19 States had already adopted their own laws concerning the prohibition of alcohol. On December 18, 1917, the Congress adopted and submitted to the States an amendment to the United States Constitution prohibiting the manufacture, sale, and transportation of alcoholic beverages. The 18th Amendment was ratified by three-fourths of the States on January 16, 1919, beginning a 14-year period of national prohibition of alcohol.

For many Americans, such as members of the popular Women's Christian Temperance Union and the Anti-Saloon League, the ratification of the 18th Amendment culminated an extensive campaign against the moral and social evils of alcohol. Many more Americans, however, supported prohibition as a patriotic act to help conserve grain and fruit needed to support the United States war effort during World War I. Ironically, by the time the amendment was ratified the pressures of war had passed.

From the outset, the 18th Amendment provoked controversy. Opponents of prohibition attacked the government's efforts to enforce the law. They pointed to the widespread illicit liquor traffic, racketeers and gangsters, and corruption in government as proof of the amendment's failure. Supporters acknowledged the shortcomings in enforcement of the law but gave credit to the amendment for the general prosperity that existed in the country between 1923 and 1929.

The Wickersham Commission

Despite arguments to the contrary, it was evident by 1929 that enforcement of the 18th Amendment was ineffective. President Herbert Hoover, in response both to public demand and his own personal convictions, appointed a commission to study the problems of law enforcement, with particular emphasis on prohibition. Hoover designated former Attorney General George Wickersham as the head of

Cartoon Analysis

	Visuals	Words
Level Three	1. List the objects or people you see in the cartoon.	1. Identify the cartoon caption and/or title. 2. Locate three words or phrases used by the cartoonist to identify objects or people within the cartoon. (Not all cartoons include words.) 3. Record any important dates or numbers that appear in the cartoon.
Level Two	2. Which of the objects on your list are symbols? 3. What do you think each of the symbols means?	4. Which words or phrases in the cartoon appear to be the most significant? Why do you think so? (Not all cartoons include words.) 5. List adjectives that describe the emotions portrayed in the cartoon.
Level One	A. Describe the action taking place in the cartoon. B. In your own words, explain how the words in the cartoon explain or clarify the symbols. C. In your own words, explain the message of the cartoon. D. What special interest groups would agree/disagree with the cartoon's message? Why?	

the National Commission on Law Observance and Enforcement, popularly known as the Wickersham Commission. The 11 other Commissioners included such distinguished public figures as Secretary of War Newton Baker, U.S. Circuit Judge William Kenyon, and Dr. Ada Comstock, president of Radcliffe College. Each of the Commissioners headed a subcommittee that investigated and reported on the effectiveness of one aspect of criminal law enforcement (the police, juvenile delinquency, penal institutions, etc.). The Commission's report on enforcement of prohibition, however, was the part of this $100,000 study that attracted the most public attention.

The Wickersham Commission presented its report to the President on January 20, 1931. The Commission members disagreed among themselves on the question of prohibition enforcement, but the majority opinion was to support the continued existence and enforcement of the 18th Amendment. Two members voted for its repeal, six for its modification (but not to the extent of allowing the manufacture of light wine and beer), and four for further efforts at its stringent enforcement.

Political cartoonists satirized the Commission's report as a waste of taxpayers' money, because the Commissioners arrived at no new solutions to the prohibition problem. So disgusted was the public by the government's failure to enforce the law consistently that by 1932 the Democratic National Convention included the repeal of the 18th Amendment in its platform. The strong Democratic victory in November of that year pushed the Congress to approve an amendment for repeal. The 21st Amendment was ratified in less than a year by the necessary three-fourths of the States, and by 1933 national prohibition was over.

The cartoon reproduced here, "The Big Specialist Reports His Findings," appeared in the *Dispatch* (Columbus, Ohio) on January 21, 1931, and is found as part of the Subject Files of Editorial Cartoons, 1930-1931, Records of the National Commission on Law Observance and Enforcement, Record Group 10.

Suggestions for Followup Student Activities

1. Based on the information in the cartoon, write a paragraph describing the Wickersham Commission findings.

2. Collect several political cartoons and use the chart presented here to analyze the elements of each cartoon.

3. Design a cartoon that illustrates your opinion on a specific issue of interest to you.

4. Compare and contrast a political cartoon with one of your favorite comic strips. What are the differences in the symbols, characters, and messages of each?

A Questionnaire on Moral Problems and Discipline, c. 1924

The Children's Bureau was established in 1912 to investigate and report on matters pertaining to childhood in America. Among these concerns were maternity care and infant mortality, the conditions of working mothers, juvenile delinquency, desertion of children, child health, and state and local administration of child welfare laws. Now a part of the Department of Health, Education and Welfare, the Bureau was, at the time these records were created, part of the Department of Labor.

During the 1920s the Bureau began to take an interest in social movements in the United States concerned with morality and social behavior. In 1924, its publication *Child Welfare Summary News* carried an article on crime and the punishment of criminals. In response to the article, numerous religious and sectarian organizations with a similar concern submitted proposals and plans for improving the morals and behavior of American youth. One such organization was the Pathfinders of America, which was founded in Detroit, Michigan, in 1914. Its members described themselves as follows:

The Pathfinders of America is an organization sponsored by Detroit business and professional men, with the approval and cooperation of the judges, prison officials and school authorities. Early in the history of this organization it was discovered that the prison work to which they had confined their efforts hitherto was not the most effective way of stemming the tide of crime; in fact it was found that this was very similar to trying to purify a stream at its mouth instead of its source. Consequently the work was introduced into the schools, giving moral instruction to the children without the use of the Bible and permitting no religious discussion whatsoever. The efficacy of their work is best proven by the fact that it is growing by leaps and bounds and is spreading rapidly in the schools and prisons of the country.

The document is from general file 9-6-0, box 213, in Records of the Children's Bureau, Record Group 102.

Suggestions for Teaching

Before having students complete the exercise below, discuss with them the nature of public opinion surveys.

1. What type of document is this?

2. Who wrote it?

3. What kind of information does it contain?

4. This document was distributed in 1924. How might you describe that year in American history? Using any clues found in the document and information you have about the 1920s, explain why you think the questionnaire excerpt was developed.

5. What student attitudes and/or behaviors are emphasized in the excerpt?

Pathfinders' of America

Scientific Character Builders

—: HUMAN ENGINEERING :—

For Every Nationality, Color, Tongue and Creed

Motto—"To Know the Law and Live a Life of Service to Mankind."

J. F. WRIGHT, Executive Secretary and Leader, 311 Lincoln Bldg.

DETROIT, MICH.

June 13th, 1924.

U. S. Department of Labor,
Children's Bureau,
Washington, D. C.

Gentlemen:-

In the last issue of the "Child Welfare News Summary" we note an article on the Marshall Stillman Movement for Crime Prevention quoted from "The World's Work".

The purposes of the Pathfinders of America are very similar to that of the Marshall Stillman movement and for your information we are attaching a brief survey of our work which you may wish to use in your publication, and also a little pamphlet that may interest you.

Yours in service,

J. F. Wright

Encs.

123

Excerpts from a Questionaire relative to Moral Problems in the High Schools as judged by the students, North Central Association of Colleges and Schools, covering 19 States. Edited by Prof. C.O. Davis, University of Michigan, Ann Arbor, Michigan.

The chief moral qualities exhibited by pupils:
Honesty 30%
Fellowship 12%
Clean habits 19%
Courtesy lowest with only 9%

The most regretable practices of boys in school:
Smoking 38%
Swearing 19%
Drinking 8%
Telling vulgar stories 5%

The most regretable practices of girls in school:
Cosmetics 17%
Flirting & petting 14%
Profane language 12%

Factors tending to develope high moral qualities among pupils:
Teacher 31%
School Organization 18%
Athletics 17%

Invidious factors tending to undermine right conduct:
Certain low minded people 63%
Poor discipline 11%
Immoral parties 11%

How could school help to develope morality among pupils?
Course in morals 32%
Stricter Rules 21%
Talks 19%

Is a course in moral education desirable?
61% of replies said "Yes",
39% of replies said "No".

Some forces which are the most helpful:
Mother 20%
Father 17%
Teacher 11%

Influences which made pupils do what they should not have done:
Evil companions 55%
Personal weakness 10%
Immoral movies 9%
Wish to be popular & desire for a good time 6%.

Highest school ambitions:
To be all around capable person 62%
Excellent student 31%

Things pupils are proud of:
The High School spirit 22%
Athletic Activities 20%
Moral strength 12%

What change in class procedure advocated?
More class discussions 23%
More recitations by pupils 20%
More explanations 23%

Things making a boy popular:
Athletics 21%
Scholarship 14%
Good looks 10%
Dependability has 1%
Capability only 2%
Character only 2% & takes 12th place of 18 questions asked.

Things that make a girl popular:
Appearance 17%
Scholarship 13%
Personality 9%
Morality 4%
Character only 3% & takes 15th place of 18 questions asked:

What would you expect to learn fr. a course in marriage, home & parenthood?
How to make married life a success 36%
Sex instruction (what it is all about) 21%
Parenthood 19%

Characteristics of an ideal boy:
Education 10%
Good morals 10%
Athletics 10%

Characteristics of an ideal girl:
Honesty 10%
Education 10%
Good looks 9%
Morality 5%
Capability 3%

Present causes of worry:
Choice of vocation 27%
Money matters 21%
Studies 16%
Religious matters 2% (lowest of ten questions).

Future life problems:
Marriage 19%
Money 19%
Vocation 17%
Service 4%

Admission from pupils of using vulgar or profane language:
Yes 31%, No. 69%.

Flying into fits of violent temper:
Yes 27%, No. 73%
Telling or willingly listening to vulgar stories: Yes 34%, No. 66%.

Note: That a goodly number of pupils regret the fact that the full meaning of life is not made clear to them by the school.

Pathfinders of America, Human Engineers, 311 Lincoln Bldg., Detroit, Mich.

6. Is there information in the document that supports the note at the bottom of it?

7. Does the excerpt indicate that the questionnaire was sexist? Why or why not?

8. Does the excerpt indicate whether or not the questionnaire was "scientifically" developed? Why or why not?

9. What does the word "edit" mean? Does it appear that Professor Davis was more concerned with editing for content than for style? Why or why not?

10. Why do you suppose the Pathfinders submitted the document to the Children's Bureau?

Final Exercise

Have students work in groups to develop questionnaires that seek to make recommendations for resolving issues related to discipline, using whatever meaning of the word they choose. Have the class criticize the questionnaires before they are distributed to the student body.

A Telegram from Persia

The transcript of the decoded telegram reproduced here describes the events surrounding the death in 1924 of Robert Imbrie, a United States Vice Consul to Tehran, Persia. The mob attack that killed Imbrie took place while he, a relatively new member of the consular staff, and Melvin Seymour, a United States citizen in the custody of the consulate, were touring the sights of the capital city.

As a result of this incident, the United States demanded from the Persian government: (1) an official apology; (2) indemnities for Imbrie's widow and for Seymour, who survived the attack; (3) appropriate Persian military honors for Imbrie's remains; (4) compensation for the costs of sending the USS *Trenton* to retrieve the body; and (5) punishment of the participants in the attack. The Persian government quickly met the first four demands and eventually executed by firing squad three members of the mob. By early 1925 all United States demands in response to the incident had been met.

For Persia, this "international incident" had important repercussions. Only three years earlier, in 1921, the ambitious Reza Khan, leader of the Persian Cossack forces, took part in a *coup d'état* that purged the Persian government of outside influence and expelled Russian officers from the armed forces. After the *coup*, Reza Khan was named commander of the Persian Army, and in 1923 he became Prime Minister.

Now, as a result of Imbrie's death, Prime Minister Reza Khan established martial law in Tehran, thereby buttressing his growing political influence with military strength. Within 18 months he was able to lead the National Assembly in deposing Ahmad Mirza Shah, the last of the long-ruling Kajar dynasty, and to be named Shah himself. He ruled Persia, which he renamed Iran in 1935, until 1941. By then, his associations with Nazi Germany had so unsettled Allied nations that British and Russian troops occupied Iran. He was forced to abdicate in favor of his son, Mohammad Reza Shah Pahlavi, and died in exile in 1944. His son, only the second Shah of Iran in the Pahlavi dynasty, was himself exiled in 1979. For a more detailed account of the Imbrie incident, see Bruce Hardcastle's article, "A Death in Tehran," *The New Republic* (December 19, 1979): 10-12.

Details of the Decoded Telegram

• "Green" at the top, righthand side of the document signifies that this telegram was transmitted in a particular code, called Green. Other diplomatic codes in common use at that time were Red, Gray, and Blue.

• "Vice Consul" is the lowest of the three main "consular" posts within the United States Foreign Service. Consular officers perform the specific function of protecting the commercial and private interests of United States citizens on foreign soil.

• "Bahais" were a 19th-century offshoot of the Shia Muslims' (Shiites) religious majority in Persia. Their ideals of unity among all religions, universal education, world peace, and the equality of men and women made them subject to harsh discrimination by the Shiites.

• "Seymour" is Melvin Seymour, a United States citizen who was being held in the custody of the United States consul-

TELEGRAM RECEIVED

FROM

GREEN

TEHERAN

Dated July 18, 1924.

Rec'd 7:22 p.m.

Secretary of State

Washington.

Very Urgent, 52, July 18, 6 p.m.

Vice Consul Imbrie died at three p.m. today of shock following murderous assault by Persian mob which practically cut and beat him to death. For past ten days there had been many religious demonstrations in which Bahais have been denounced. At eleven a.m. today Imbrie and Seymour prisoner of consulate, stopped in front of one of these demonstrations. It is alleged that Imbrie had taken pictures. Mob became furious crying that he was a Bahais and rushed on him. Servant of Dr Packard shouted that he was the American Consul. Taking no heed of this statement mob dragged them from their carriage and attacked them savagely. Though Teheran streets are always crowded with police and military only two policemen were slightly scratched in delivery victims.

I have viewed body of Imbrie. Took deposition from carriage driver. Seymour's condition grave and he could make no statement. Department's instruction urgently requested.

KORNFELD.

HPD

ate because of his involvement in an assault against another United States citizen in Tehran in 1923; thus, he is referred to as "prisoner."

• "Kornfeld" is Joseph Kornfeld, the head of the United States mission in Tehran who sent the telegram.

The telegram reproduced here is from Decimal File 123 Im 1/78 (1910-1929), General Records of the Department of State, Record Group 59.

Suggestions for Teaching

The teaching strategies suggested below begin with students examining the specific details of the document and conclude with students discussing questions about the implications of an international incident such as Imbrie's death.

1. Document Details. Help students examine the document for details by asking them to answer the following questions:

a. When was the document written?

b. How long did it take to reach the Department of State? (Remind students that the time difference between Tehran and Washington is 8½ hours.)

c. When was a reply made to Tehran? In what form was the reply?

d. When was the document filed? What is its file number?

e. Look carefully at the received stamps and markings made by the Department of State. What do they tell you about the organization of that department?

2. Locating the Facts. Direct students to read the telegram and answer the following content questions:

a. Who wrote the telegram? Where was he located?

b. To what religious group did the Persian mob think Imbrie belonged?

c. Describe the sequence of events leading to the death of the Vice Consul.

d. What were Kornfeld's sources of information about the attack on Imbrie?

e. What request did Kornfeld make to the State Department?

3. The Diplomatic Dilemma: A Role Play.

On July 19, 1924, Kornfeld sent a second urgent telegram to the Department of State that implicated the Persian military in the death of Imbrie. This second telegram ended with these words: "Very drastic action on the part of the government is fully justified."

a. Ask students to assume the role of State Department officials who have received both of these telegrams. Tell them it will be their task to determine the best diplomatic response to this incident to recommend to President Calvin Coolidge.

b. Ask the class to discuss the possible government responses and list them on the board. Their list might include: demanding an official apology from the Persian government, boycotting imports from Persia, recalling all United States diplomats in Persia, expelling Persian diplomats in the United States, refusing visas to Persian visitors to the United States, dispatching troops to guard United States diplomats in Persia, refusing to export goods to Persia, demanding punishment of mob attackers, and compensating the victims.

c. Discuss with students what the consequences of each of these actions might be for the United States. Consider the economic, political, military, and diplomatic advantages and disadvantages that might result from each action. Ask the class to decide which response would be most appropriate.

d. To conclude the activity, share with students the actual actions taken by the United States government (see Historical Background). Compare the students' ideas with the official actions of the government.

4. Discussion Questions

a. Why did Kornfeld send this message to the Department of State by telegram?

b. How would you rate the reliability of Kornfeld's sources of information about the death of Imbrie?

c. How much responsibility should the government of a country assume in protecting the safety of foreign diplomats?

d. How do you think United States military and law enforcement officers would have responded under similar circumstances?

e. What do you think is the best way to obtain justice in a criminal case involving two countries?

f. Should diplomats serving in foreign countries be immune to the laws of the host country? Why? Why not?

A Letter on Employment of Married Women

With the passage of the National Recovery Act in June 1933, there was considerable public optimism that this New Deal program would help to alleviate the nation's unemployment. Through the National Recovery Administration (NRA), each industry established its own guidelines (codes) to promote cooperation among businesses, to reduce unfair competition, and to improve working standards. Individual businesses voluntarily signed the codes and displayed the "blue eagle" to symbolize their support for the government's efforts.

Many citizens wrote to President Roosevelt or to General Hugh Johnson, NRA chief, describing their financial struggles and offering suggestions for implementing the NRA codes. Domestic workers, labor leaders, business persons and others wrote to lesser government officials to suggest industrial standards, encourage collective bargaining, and point to NRA code violators. Several citizens even composed music to rally public sentiment for this New Deal program.

Miss Kubicki's letter typifies several hundred letters sent to the NRA that complain about the employment of married women whose husbands are also employed. Writers, like Miss Kubicki, used adjectives such as "greedy" to describe married women who "cheat" their single sisters and drain the lean job market.

Miss Kubicki is typical of working women of her time because single women (divorced and widowed) were 71 percent of the female labor force, although women were only 21 percent of the total labor force in 1930. At 37, she is also in the most employed age group of women in 1930; 64 percent of working women were between the ages of 20 and 44 years. While some statistics on working women have changed, one pattern is unchanged: 61 percent of working women today are still between the ages of 20 and 44 years. However, women are now 42 percent of the total labor force. Of this group, there are more married working women (55 percent) than single working women (44 percent).

Although Miss Kubicki wrote to President Roosevelt, her letter was referred to the correspondence branch of the NRA for reply. That reply was sympathetic, but not altogether reassuring. It urged her to write members of Congress and suggested that increased public criticism on the subject of working/married women might result in "some action" in the current session of Congress; yet it informed her firmly that ". . . the authority vested in this administration by the National Industrial Recovery Act does not permit us to intervene in matters of this type and the government cannot say just whom a certain firm shall or shall not employ."

The reply also addressed the issue of technological unemployment, which Miss Kubicki had brought to the attention of the NRA. It indicated that the government proposed to ". . . offset this problem by shortening the number of working hours

Kansas City, Missouri.
December 20th, 1933.

President Franklin D. Roosevelt,
Washington, D. C.
United States of America.

Dear Mister President;

Having long been an admirer of your integrity and wisdom,
I am taking the liberty of writing to you of a problem which is
getting more serious each day.

I am thirty seven years old, and for fourteen years held
the position of assistant bookkeeper in a large department store
in Kansas City. Recently, this company changed hands, the new
president bringing in an efficiency engineer. This man put in a
new system in the office, which required bookkeeping machines
and calculators. So far, there has been eight of us to lose our
jobs.
No consideration was given as to who needed jobs, in fact
it seemed that those who needed them most, were fired. Not one
married woman in that office was fired, and each and every one
of them has a husband employed. This deplorable condition seems
to be prevalent in this city and other cities of this country.
Every-where I go to look for a job I find these women, some of
them my friends, working- and I have found that nine cases out
of ten their husbands have good jobs. I do believe there are
about ten percent of these cases where husbands are out of work.

I understand that some employers say that the married woman
is more efficient. Naturally, the half-starved, worried, single
woman hasn't a chance with a well-kept married woman who has two
incomes to meet her greedy demands. I have come in contact with
quite a few single women since I have been out of work, and many
of them are eating only one or two meals a day. My heart aches
for these women, Mr. President, and I know you would feel the
same way, if you knew this condition as it really exists.

The greedy type of married woman does not only cheat her
single sisters, but she makes conditions worse for the single
and married men who are out of work. They are also a stumbling-
block to the boy and girl out of school. The people of Kansas
City are greatly incensed over this, but of course it is up to
the employers to act- and only a few of them have done so. So
far, the N. R. A. has done nothing about it. It seems to me,
Mr. President, that it could be handled through this source.

Wishing you and yours a Glorious Christmas and a Merry
New Year, I am

Sincerely,

Miss Frances M. Kubicki,
3012 Montgall, Kansas City, Mo.

131

". . ." and suggested that ". . . a satisfactory solution [to unemployment] is forthcoming as the result of the working of the NRA." Such optimism is predictable from an administration committed to innovative programs to solve the nation's widening depression.

While we are uncertain about Miss Kubicki's employment future, we do know that, as a federal policy, the government never ruled against hiring married women, although some state regulations and popular sentiment were generally opposed to married women working at that time.

The letter reproduced here is in file 622, drawer 3017, Classified General Files, 1933-35, Records of the National Recovery Administration, Record Group 9.

Teaching Suggestions

Skills Activities:

1. *Identifying the main ideas.* Number each paragraph in the letter from 1 to 6. Direct students to number their papers from 1-6. Ask them to write next to each number a sentence that describes the main idea of each of the six paragraphs. For example, paragraph 1 — Miss Kubicki expresses her admiration for the President. When students have identified the main ideas, compare their answers. Consider: Do you think Miss Kubicki has written a persuasive letter to the President? Why or why not?

2. *Reading for understanding.* After students have read the letter, ask them if Miss Kubicki would *agree* or *disagree* with the following statements. You may wish to reproduce this as a worksheet.

Agree Disagree

_____ _____ 1. Whenever possible, machines should be used to promote efficiency.

_____ _____ 2. Married women are more efficient workers than single women.

_____ _____ 3. The NRA should require employers to fire married women with working husbands.

_____ _____ 4. Roosevelt is powerful enough to solve the problems of single women seeking jobs.

_____ _____ 5. Married women take jobs that should go to unemployed men and single women.

As a culminating assignment, ask students to write a paragraph explaining why they agree or disagree with Miss Kubicki's idea about giving unemployed men and single women job priority.

Discussion Ideas:

1. Discuss the following generalization with students: In times of economic depression, married women should give their jobs to unemployed men or single women. Ask students if they agree or disagree with Miss Kubicki's arguments.

2. Miss Kubicki complains that machines are contributing to unemployment. Ask students to consider: Do you think the government should protect workers from being replaced by machines? Why or why not? Note the government's response to Miss Kubicki on this issue in the background essay.

3. Ask students to imagine themselves as a "typical" woman living in 1930 and answer the following questions. Direct them to answer also the questions as they would be answered today.

1930 Today

_____ _____ a. If you are employed, what would your status most likely be?
(1) Married (2) Single

_____ _____ b. What percentage of the labor force would you as a woman (whether married or single) represent?
(1) 20 percent (2) 40 percent (3) 60 percent

_____ _____ c. As a working woman, in what age group would you most likely be?
(1) 16-19 years
(2) 20-44 years
(3) More than 45 years

After students have answered the questions, provide them with the statistical information on working women in the background essay to check their answers against. Discuss the changes with students.

4. Consider with students: How should the government have replied to Miss Kubicki's requests? Do you think that the government should have power to regulate private industries? Share with students relevant information from the NRA's response to Miss Kubicki, which is included in the background essay.

Writing a Letter of Appeal

During the Depression years, thousands of Americans wrote directly to President Franklin Roosevelt and Eleanor Roosevelt describing in great detail their personal situations, as well as proposing solutions to the nation's economic crisis. These letters frequently were referred to the appropriate Government agency for reply.

Louis Kroll's letter is typical of this correspondence; and it was referred to the Subsistence Homesteads Division, then in the Department of the Interior. Under the National Recovery Act (1933), the Division had been set up to assist destitute workers by relocating them from cities where employment opportunities were limited to small communities where they could find work and supplement their income through farming.

Suggestions for Teaching

Activities 1-3 seek to emphasize writing skills in social studies, while activities 4-6 focus primarily on historical observation and research skills. Select from these ideas those activities that best serve your objectives.

1. Ask each student to read carefully Louis Kroll's letter and write a short paragraph paraphrasing it. When the paragraphs are complete, discuss the following points with the students:
   a. Are the writer's points clearly stated? Why or why not?
   b. What is the style of the letter? What determines the style?
   c. How do you identify tone? (Consider vocabulary, sentence structure, and the like.)
In light of the students' paragraphs and your subsequent discussion, what is the impact of Kroll's style, tone, vocabulary, and sentence structure on the facts presented in the letter?

2. Using one of the following profiles, direct students to write a similar letter to President Roosevelt or Eleanor Roosevelt.
   a. You are a veteran of World War I, partially disabled, with a large family. You live in Oneida, Pennsylvania, and before the war you were a coal miner.
   b. You are an eighth-grade student writing on behalf of your family. Your father is unemployed and your mother is ill. Your six-year-old brother has quit school to work at odd jobs to help support the family.
   c. You are a woman writing from Iowa, where farmers are unhappy about the Government's apparent indifference. You want to see more done for small family farms.

Students might exchange their letters and compare them in terms of style, tone, and content.

3. Ask students to read carefully the Kroll letter and discuss it as a source of historical information. Direct them to write a paragraph (based on answers to the following questions) that describes the letter as a historical source:
   a. What information in the letter places it in a particular time period?
   b. Does the letter provide details about the writer's personal situation?
   c. What is the purpose of the letter?
   d. What factual information is in the letter?
   e. What inferences, generalizations, and conclusions might be drawn from the letter?

If students have completed the second

LOUIS KROLL
~~Xxxxxxxxxxxxxx~~
COUNSELLOR AT LAW

MURRAY HILL 2-5540
CABLE: MATAVIC

535 FIFTH AVENUE
NEW YORK

August 9th, 1933.

Hon. Franklin D. Roosevelt
Hyde Park, New York.

Dear Mr. President:

Sincere apologies for taking up
your valuable time, but the exigency of the matter
fully warrants the interuption.

My dad has been out of employment
for more than two years. His many endeavors to obtain assistance, not charity, through the proper agencies have met with one disappointment after another.

About a year ago, while you were
our Governor, a movement was started to have as many
people as possible ~~migrate from city to~~ farm. Dad, on
reading thereof, believed that Golden opportunity was
knocking at the door and hastily wrote a letter to the
person in charge. Particular stress was laid upon the
facts that Mother was, and by the way is more so now
because of our financial condition, tuburcular and that
dad and three sons and daughter would be willing to
work their fingers to the bone to help mother. He
however received as an answer the statement that at
present nothing was being done but that as soon as the
movement got under way he would be remembered. At the
writing of this plea we have heard naught. Conditions now
are such that dad has given up all hope and in fact has
threatened drastic things so that mother might benefit
by the insurance monies dad was able to save. Were I in
a position to help this letter would not be written but I
as a young attorney have all I can bear to try to make ends
meet for my wife and child.

I know that you are wholeheartedly concern-
ed with the welfare of your people; that making a plea to you
is not the same as talking or writing to these agencies. Can't
you please do something, not for me but for Dad and Mother?.

Fervently awaiting a reply, I am

Respectfully yours,

activity, they might direct these questions to their own letters.

4. Use Kroll's letter as the basis for a discussion of the sources of history and how historians use primary and secondary sources in writing history.

5. Use Kroll's letter as the basis for an opening discussion of Roosevelt's New Deal. Review the letter carefully as evidence of the nation's needs during the Depression.

6. Students might further investigate the Subsistence Homesteads Division to discover more about it and evaluate its work. They might also compare this New Deal project with current urban homesteading efforts.

The letter reproduced here is found in File Kai-Las, Drawer 37, General Correspondence, 1933-35, Subsistence Homesteads Division, Farm Security Administration, Records of the Farmers Home Administration, Record Group 96.

Related Readings

Agee, James, and Walker Evans. *Let Us Now Praise Famous Men.* New York: 1974. Paperback edition. Difficult reading for some students, but has excellent photographs.

Hunt, Irene. *No Promises in the Wind.* Chicago: 1970. Fiction.

Lange, Dorothea, and Paul Taylor. *American Exodus.* New Haven: 1969. Excellent photographs.

Steinbeck, John. *Grapes of Wrath.* New York: 1939. Fiction.

Terkel, Studs. *Hard Times.* New York: 1970. Oral histories with much local color.

Man of the Hour...
A Comparison
of Leadership

The year 1933 was one of great change in Germany and the United States. As the year opened, President von Hindenburg named Adolf Hitler chancellor of Germany and Franklin Roosevelt succeeded Herbert Hoover as President of the United States. On opposite sides of the Atlantic, two journeys to world power began almost simultaneously.

Let's compare the first 100 days of Roosevelt's leadership with Hitler's first 100 days of leadership to see how each sought to handle the severe economic and political distress in his nation. Keep in mind that Hitler came to power over a 14-year-old republic with little democratic tradition, while Roosevelt assumed the reins of a government with 150 years of democratic experience. Nevertheless, we shall proceed as if the two leaders started from the same place at approximately the same time, and that both faced the same problems in approximately the same context — an economic depression within a democratic republic.

As you can see, both leaders moved quickly and dramatically to fulfill their goals — Hitler in the political arena and Roosevelt in the economic realm. Both used extraordinary measures not seen in their countries before. You will notice that Hitler used his position to solidify his own control and subsequently to stifle all political opposition. Roosevelt, on the other hand, set out to tackle the nation's economic troubles, borrowing ideas and assistance from many quarters. Their first 100 days of governing set the tone for their subsequent years of rule, which in both cases ended with death in April 1945.

The document reproduced is a telegram from U.S. Ambassador Frederic M. Sackett to Secretary of State Cordell Hull. The telegram reports on Hitler's actions to consolidate his power on March 23, 1933. (See time line.) On the basis of the Empowering Act, referred to in the telegram, Hitler and the cabinet assumed all powers of government, rendering the actions of the Reichstag without authority. With the subsequent abolition of the political parties except the National Socialists in July, the Reichstag lost its representative function entirely and served only as a conduit for *der Fuehrer's* decrees. In August 1934, after the death of President von Hindenburg, Chancellor Hitler further consolidated his power by assuming the presidency himself.

The document is No. 862.00/2930, in the Decimal File, 1930-39, Records of the Department of State, Record Group 59.

Teaching Activities

Before you begin to discuss the telegram with students, be sure that they understand the following terms used in the document.

Reichstag — The lower house of the German legislature created by the 1919 Constitution. The Reichstag was popularly elected and possessed the power to make law.

Reichsrath — The upper house of the legislature, which was a council of state government representatives (from Prussia,

TELEGRAM RECEIVED

FROM

MET .

GRAY

Berlin

Dated March 24, 19 33

Rec'd 11:05 a. m.

Secretary of State,

Washington.

DEPARTMENT OF STATE

MAR 24 1933

DIVISION OF
WESTERN EUROPEAN AFFAIRS

44, March 24, 10 a. m.

The empowering law submitted to the Reichstag by
the parties represented in the government and passed
last night gives the Hitler Cabinet practically
unlimited powers. It transfers certain presidential
prerogatives to the Chancellor while the legislative
powers of the Reichstag and Reichsrath are to be
assumed by the Cabinet as a whole. It gives the
Cabinet the right to enact legislation modificative
of the constitution which normally requires a
two-thirds majority in the Reichstag, with the sole
limitations that the President's powers are to remain
unaffected and that the Cabinet may not enact laws
abolishing the Reichstag and the Reichsrath as such.
The prorogatives of these two bodies, however, are
quite thoroughly emasculated by the very next article
of the law.

On

On the basis of this law the Hitler Cabinet can reconstruct the entire system of government as it eliminates practically all constitutional restraints. The law remains in effect till April 1, 1937 unless the present Reich Government is sooner replaced by another in which event it becomes void.

Law was passed by 441 votes against 94 belonging entirely to the Social Democrat party. The two Catholic parties swallowed the bitter pill, the spokesman of the Center saying that his party would vote for the law in spite of many misgivings "which in normal times could scarcely have been overcome".

Upon the announcement of the result of the vote the Reichstag was adjourned sine die.

Text and translation of the law being forwarded by mail.

WMB-CSB   SACKETT

1933 — United States

March 4 Franklin Delano Roosevelt inaugurated President.

March 6 President Roosevelt declares four-day national banking holiday to prevent further bank closings.

March 9 Roosevelt convenes Congress in special session. Congress introduces and passes Emergency Banking Relief Act, granting broad discretionary powers to the President to meet the economic crisis.

March 10 Roosevelt requests passage of Economy Act to cut government salaries and veterans' pensions to ease strain on government budget. Bill passes March 20.

March 12 Roosevelt broadcasts first radio "fireside chat" to reassure populace of government's ability to solve economic crisis.

March 22 Roosevelt requests amendment to Volstead Act to legalize and tax the sale of wine and beer, thus increasing federal revenues. Passes April 1.

March 31 Congress creates Civilian Conservation Corps to put to work thousands of unemployed young men.

April 19 United States abandons gold standard.

May 12 Congress enacts Federal Emergency Relief Act to provide states with matching grants for relief for the unemployed.

May 12 Congress passes Agricultural Adjustment Act to relieve farmers through subsidies for reducing acreage in production and other financial support. (The Supreme Court would declare the AAA unconstitutional three years later.)

May 18 Congress authorizes Tennessee Valley Authority, first giant federal public utility project, to harness the power of the Tennessee River in Alabama for the production of electricity, to serve the region's energy needs, to create jobs, and to develop area's natural resources.

June 6 Congress establishes Employment Service to coordinate and streamline state employment efforts.

June 13 Congress passes Home Owners Refinancing Act, establishing the Home Owners Loan Corporation to refinance long-term home mortgages at lower interest rates.

June 16 Congress establishes Federal Bank Deposit Insurance Corporation to federally insure bank deposits to restore depositor confidence.

June 16 Congress passes Farm Credit Act to refinance long-term, low interest mortgages for farms, providing same support for farmers that the HOLC offers home owners.

June 16 Congress authorizes National Industrial Recovery Act to revive business and to decrease unemployment through increased business cooperation. Creates Public Works Administration to provide jobs through public works projects. (The Supreme Court would declare the NRA unconstitutional in 1936.)

June 16 Special session of Congress adjourns.

1933 — Germany

January 30 President von Hindenburg appoints National Socialist (Nazi) party leader Adolf Hitler chancellor of German Federal Republic. Hitler tops a cabinet of three National Socialist ministers and eight ministers from other parties.

February 1 Hitler pressures von Hindenburg to dissolve Reichstag and to call for new elections in an effort to strengthen Nazi representation in that body.

February 4 Under pressure from Hitler, von Hindenburg issues a decree limiting freedom of the press and prohibiting free assembly.

February 6 In an effort to centralize political control, Hitler pressures von Hindenburg to disband Prussia's representative legislature. Similar actions in other states across Germany would follow.

February 27 Reichstag building in Berlin is destroyed by fire. Hitler blames incident on Communist Party.

February 28 President von Hindenburg declares a state of emergency, suspending *habeas corpus* and other civil liberties. (The state of emergency would remain in effect until Hitler's death.)

March 5 In the national election of a new Reichstag, 89% of the German voters cast their votes. The National Socialists win 43.9% of the votes. The traditional coalition of four moderate parties, long the basis of majority actions in the Reichstag, can no longer outvote the Nazi members.

March 8 Concentration camps established for internment of political "undesirables."

March 13 Hitler names Joseph Goebbels to newly-created position of minister of propaganda.

March 23 Reichstag passes Empowering Act, surrendering its own constitutional authority to make law to Chancellor Hitler and the cabinet.

April 1 First government-sponsored boycott of Jewish businesses fails. German people refuse to cooperate and pressure is brought to bear on the German government by the international business community.

April 7 National Socialist Civil Service Act establishes new standard for government service, including removal of all non-Aryans and opponents of Nazi rule from the service.

Bavaria, etc.) and could, according to the Constitution, veto laws passed by the Reichstag.

Chancellor — Leader of the *cabinet* of ministers, which made policy and executed laws for the federal government. The chancellor and cabinet were appointed by the *president.*

President — The popularly elected leader of the republic with four main powers: the appointment of governmental officials (including chancellor and cabinet), the conduct of foreign affairs, the leadership of the military, and the authority to declare a state of emergency for the nation.

sine die — Latin term meaning "without fixing a day for future action or meeting."

Sackett — Frederic M. Sackett, U.S. Ambassador to Germany, appointed by Herbert Hoover; sender of the telegram to Cordell Hull.

During the 1920s and 1930s, seven major political parties held seats in the Reichstag: the National People's Party, the People's Party, the Democratic Party, the Catholic Center Party, the Social Democratic Party, the Communist Party, and the National Socialist (Nazi) Party. The rise of popularity of the Nazi Party was dramatic. It captured only 2.6 percent of the popular vote in the Reichstag elections in 1928, but by the 1932 elections, Nazi Party members had gained 33.1 percent of the vote. However, a coalition of parties still maintained a ruling majority in the Reichstag. The March 1933 elections gave the Nazis 43.9 percent of the vote, for the first time overcoming the strength of the coalition.

You may wish to reproduce or post the time lines for handy reference for your students.

1. Consider one or more of the following questions raised by the telegram with students.

a. How did the new law described in the telegram increase Adolf Hitler's power?

b. Why is it significant that the new law allowed the cabinet rather than the legislature to change the constitution?

c. What is the meaning of the sentence beginning: "The two Catholic parties swallowed the bitter pill. . . ."?

2. Consider the following ideas for class discussion and further inquiry.

a. It has been said that extraordinary circumstances sometimes demand extraordinary measures by governments. Discuss the meaning of this concept with students and develop a list of circumstances that would require a government to assume extraordinary powers: e.g., war, civil disruptions, natural disasters. Once students have developed a list, review it and discuss the limitations on government authority that might be appropriate for each situation.

b. Both Hitler and Roosevelt assumed extraordinary governing powers in their respective countries. Discuss the uses of extraordinary powers by each and how they were alike and different.

c. Develop a list of possible reactions to the German situation that the U.S. Secretary of State might have recommended to the President. As a writing assignment, direct students to draft a reply to Sackett's telegram outlining the U.S. position.

d. President von Hindenburg had the position and authority to resist Adolf Hitler's power plays and yet he did not. Direct students to investigate von Hindenburg — his background, selection as president of the Weimar Republic, and relationship to Adolf Hitler. In a short writing assignment, ask students to describe von Hindenburg's role in Hitler's rise to power.

Constitutional Issues: Separation of Powers

It is safe to say that a respect for the principle of separation of powers is deeply ingrained in every American. The nation subscribes to the original premise of the framers of the Constitution that the way to safeguard against tyranny is to separate the powers of government among three branches so that each branch checks the other two. Even when this system thwarts the public will and paralyzes the processes of government, Americans have rallied to its defense.

At no time in this century was the devotion to that principle more vigorously evoked than in 1937, when Franklin Roosevelt introduced a plan to add justices to the Supreme Court. The conflict set off by the President's plan is more understandable when viewed in the historical context of expanding judicial power as well as in the contemporary context of pro- and anti-New Deal politics.

In the early national period, the judiciary was the weakest of the three branches of government. When Chief Justice John Marshall established the principle of judicial review in *Marbury* v. *Madison* by declaring an act of Congress unconstitutional, he greatly strengthened the judiciary. Even though the high court only exercised this prerogative one other time prior to the Civil War *(Dred Scott* v. *Sanford),* the establishment of judicial review made the judiciary more of an equal player with the executive and legislative branches.

After the Civil War, the Court entered a phase of judicial activism based on a conservative political outlook that further enhanced its own power. In accepting the view that the 14th Amendment should be interpreted to protect corporations, the Court struck down laws that protected workers, such as minimum wage laws and laws prohibiting child labor. Critics of the Court's stand, including Justice Oliver Wendell Holmes, argued that these decisions were not based on the Constitution but upon the laissez-faire theory of economics. By 1937 the Court was widely regarded by the public as an enemy of working people.

This sentiment was exacerbated by the Great Depression. In 1935-36, the Court struck down eight of FDR's New Deal programs, including the National Recovery Act (NRA) and the Agricultural Adjustment Act (AAA). Public antijudicial sentiment intensified; many critics questioned the constitutionality of the concept of judicial review itself. As a result of this reaction, several constitutional amendments were introduced into Congress in 1936, including one that would require a two-thirds vote of the Court whenever an act of Congress was declared unconstitutional; another that would permit Congress to revalidate federal laws previously declared unconstitutional by repassing them with a two-thirds vote of both houses; and even one that would abolish altogether the Court's power to declare federal laws unconstitutional.

FDR remained silent, hoping that the

doesn't like

The Gannett Newspapers

Frank E. Gannett
President

A STATEMENT BY   *Ried*   Executive Offices
Rochester, N. Y.

FRANK E. GANNETT, PUBLISHER GANNETT NEWSPAPERS

President Roosevelt has cleverly camouflaged a most amazing and startling proposal for packing the Supreme Court. It is true that the lower courts are slow and overburdened, we probably do need more judges to expedite litigation but this condition should not be used as a subtle excuse for changing the complexion and undermining the independence of our highest court. Increasing the number of judges from nine to fifteen would not make this high tribunal act any more promptly than it does now, but it would give the President control of the Judiciary Department.

A year ago I predicted that this is exactly what would happen if Roosevelt was reelected. The Supreme Court having declared invalid many of the administration measures the President now resorts to a plan of creating a Supreme Court that will be entirely sympathetic with his ideas. Provision has been made for amending the Constitution. If it is necessary to change the Constitution it should be done in the regular way. The President is mistaken, if he thinks he can conceal his real purpose of packing, influencing and controlling the Supreme Court by confusing that objective with a long dissertation on the slow action of our various courts.

The Supreme Court has been the anchor that has held America safe through many storms. Its absolute independence and integrity must never be in doubt.

Our Government is composed of three departments, Legislative, Executive and Judiciary. These are the foundations of our Democracy. As a result of the election and the transfer of powers by so-called emergency measures, the Executive now dominates the Legislative Department. The President now proposes also to dominate the Judiciary. Do we want to give to this man or any one man complete control of these three departments of our Government which have from the beginning of the Republic been kept entirely separate and independent?

This proposal should give every American grave concern for it is a step towards absolutism and complete dictatorial power.

Frank E. Gannett

antijudicial public sentiment would continue to grow without his having to enter the fray. He avoided any direct references to the Court in the 1936 election campaign. After his election victory, however, he submitted to Congress early in February 1937 a plan for "judicial reform," which forever came to be known as his attempt to "pack" the Supreme Court. Given Roosevelt's record for legislative success, it is interesting to discover why this plan to reconstitute the Court with justices more favorable to the New Deal backfired.

Franklin Roosevelt and his Attorney General, Homer Cummings, had considered several options. They could have attacked the issue of judicial review head on, as the Congress' proposed amendments had sought to do, but they chose not to, perhaps anticipating the public's attachment to the idea of the judiciary as the guardian of the Constitution. Instead, they chose to change the number of justices on the Court, which had been done six times since 1789. Their plan had a different twist, however, for it proposed adding a justice for every justice over the age of 70 who refused to retire, up to a maximum of 15 total.

This proposal was all the more appealing because Justice Department lawyers had discovered that the very same idea had been proposed by Justice McReynolds, one of the most conservative justices then sitting on the Court, when he was Wilson's Attorney General in 1913. The administration could not resist the appeal of such irony, and without consulting Congress, the President and his New Deal aides blundered into one of the biggest political miscalculations of their tenure. By masking their true intentions, they created a split within their own party from which they never fully recovered.

It was expected that the Republicans would cry foul, but when the chairman of the House Judiciary Committee, Democrat Hatton Sumners of Texas, announced his opposition, the plan was as good as dead. Further resistance to the plan devel-

oped in Congress as the Court began a reversal of its previous conservative course by ruling in favor of such legislation as the National Labor Relations Act and the Social Security Act. Congressmen urged the White House to withdraw the bill, but confident of victory, FDR refused to back down. The cost was to alienate conservative Democrats and to lose the fight in Congress.

Letters poured into the White House and the Justice Department both attacking and supporting the President's plan. Many of the letters of support came from ordinary citizens who had worked in industries hurt by the Great Depression. The Worker's Alliance of Kalispell, Montana, wrote, "We consider that Recovery has been delayed materially by the dilatory action of the Supreme Court. . . . An immediate curb on the Supreme Court is of *utmost* importance, then an amendment to put it in its proper place would be well and good." But others, most notably the legal establishment and the press, thought that the Supreme Court was already "in its proper place."

One of the most outspoken members of the press was the Rochester, New York, newspaper publisher, Frank Gannett. The document shown here was sent by Gannett to the Office of the Solicitor in the Justice Department and then referred to the Attorney General. Like many others in the file, it expresses the concern that the real issue is not judicial reform but the continued expansion of executive power.

Even those who trusted Roosevelt, and who believed in what the New Deal was trying to accomplish, were wary. The following excerpt from a telegram to President Roosevelt is typical.

Please watch your step while attempting to curb the powers of the honorable Supreme Court of the United States. Such action may be in order while so able a person as your excellency may remain in the president's chair but please let us look to the future when it might be in order for the citizenship of our great country to look to the Supreme Court for guidance which we might justly require.

This month's document and the others quoted here can be found in the records of the Justice Department, Record Group 60: Correspondence of the Attorney General, case file 235868.

Teaching Suggestions

Vocabulary

1. Review the definitions of the following words before reading the document.

camouflage (verb) — to disguise in order to conceal

expedite (verb) — to hasten

litigation (noun) — lawsuit

dissertation (noun) — a formal and lengthy report

absolutism (noun) — system where ruler has unlimited powers

integrity (noun) — honesty, wholeness

tribunal (noun) — court of justice

2. After reading and working with the document, ask students to write a brief story of the court-packing controversy using five words from the list.

Reading for the Main Idea

Students should review what their textbook has to say about the court-packing controversy. Ask them to read the document and answer the following questions.

1. How many justices does FDR want to add to the Supreme Court?

2. What does Gannett feel will be the result of this increase?

3. What alternative method for changing the system does Gannett propose?

4. List three principles of government that Gannett mentions in this statement.

The Constitutional Issue

1. Ask students to define the constitutional issue. Why was this issue so controversial?

2. In paragraph 4, Gannett expresses his fear that the executive will dominate the other two branches of government. Ask students to recall other times in our history when one of the three branches became too powerful.

3. Some have argued that our system of separation of powers and checks and balances paralyzes the efficient working of government and that we should amend the Constitution to provide for a parliamentary system of government. Ask interested students to research and stage a debate for the class on the question: RESOLVED that the Constitution should be amended to provide for a parliamentary system of government.

Thinking Metaphorically

1. In the third paragraph, the author uses a metaphor when he compares the Supreme Court to an anchor. Play with this idea with your students. How is the Court like an anchor? If the Court is the anchor, what is the ship? What is the sea? What other storms might there have been in our history? Invite them to suggest other possible metaphors for the Court's role in our system.

2. Supporters of Roosevelt's plan would have seen the Supreme Court differently. Follow the steps below to help students write their own metaphorical statement.

   a. List on the board how the supporters of the President's plan might have viewed the Supreme Court.

   b. Ask students to look at the list and suggest something in nature or something mechanical that has those qualities. List their suggestions on the board.

   c. Ask students to write several possible metaphorical statements that FDR's supporters might have used to describe the Court.

Techniques of Persuasion

Ask students to reread the document and underline the parts that are particularly persuasive, and then to complete one of the following activities.

1. Rank in order of importance the three most persuasive sections and discuss why they are most persuasive.

2. Write a brief paper describing the reasons why this document is or is not persuasive.

For Further Study

The number of justices on the Supreme Court has been changed six times in our history: 1789, 1801, 1802, 1837, 1863 and 1869. Ask students to investigate the circumstances under which the number was changed.

Eleanor Roosevelt Resigns From the DAR: A Study in Conscience

In February 1939, Howard University, a black institution in Washington, DC, invited internationally famous black contralto Marian Anderson to give a concert. Because their own auditorium was too small to accommodate the expected audience, Howard officials asked Washington-headquartered Daughters of the American Revolution (DAR) to use the DAR auditorium, Constitution Hall, on April 9. The DAR refused, explaining in a press interview reported in the New York *Times* on April 19 that local conditions and custom did not favor such a move. Some years earlier, the interview revealed, the DAR had defied the local custom of segregated seating at public events when it opened Constitution Hall to another distinguished black singer, tenor Roland Hayes. Hayes had refused to sing in a segregated hall, so the DAR responded with open seating. Hayes sang, but those who attended the concert protested the mixed seating so loudly that the DAR subsequently decided to avoid any future problems by adopting a "black exclusion" rule. That rule was invoked in Anderson's case. Washington was a city still reflecting southern racial attitudes.

The District of Columbia Board of Education refused to let Anderson sing in the auditorium of its largest high school unless she agreed to segregated seating, something she would not do. But the DAR deci-

sion was even more uncompromising, even more controversial. Not only did the organization refuse to permit her to perform in a segregated facility, it denied her the use of the hall altogether.

Protest over Anderson's exclusion blazed from black artistic and religious communities, threatening to turn the incident into a national scandal. But when DAR member Eleanor Roosevelt resigned from that organization in protest to its rejection of Anderson's request, the social and political reverberations rang widely and deeply. Eleanor Roosevelt was a member of a family who had come to America in 1640 and had produced two Presidents of the United States. Her beliefs as they evolved were simple, visionary, deeply religious and, in America of the 1930s, revolutionary. In a society where poverty was thought to be the fault of the poor rather than of the economic or social system, Eleanor Roosevelt believed in a social order in which everyone had enough to live on and poverty did not exist. She was concerned for the young, for women, and for peace. Raised in gentility, she believed in political action.

Unsure of her own powers or direction for many years, Eleanor Roosevelt nevertheless became a quiet, persistent, and powerful moral force upon her husband and cousin, Franklin. After his election in 1932, she began to emerge as a political figure in her own right, becoming deeply involved in the Women's Division of the Democratic party (which her husband saw as a way into the American home), in black and white youth groups, in advocacy for the poor, and in writing for newspapers and magazines. By 1939, in her husband's second term as President, she was proud that every week she received thousands of letters from Americans asking for advice, solace, and relief from the rigors of the Depression. She had broken the traditional mold for First Ladies that had existed since Martha Washington and had been exemplified by her immediate predecessors, Mrs. Coolidge and Mrs. Hoover.

Her support of Marian Anderson was not a surprise to the black community. She had supported justice and equal opportunity for blacks for many years, though her views were not so much in advance of her time as to include integration. (Her gently forthright position was exemplified in her reply to a critic who protested that she had her picture taken eating with a black child at a Hyde Park picnic. ". . . I believe it never hurts to be kind. Eating with someone does not mean you believe in intermarriage," her biographer, Joseph Lash, quotes her as saying.) As early as 1932 she had been vilified in cartoons and in print by the southern press and some northern newspapers for attending black meetings, inviting racially mixed groups to the White House, urging her husband to appoint a black woman to head Federal black relief programs, visiting black sharecroppers in their homes, and supporting NAACP anti-lynching legislation.

Her husband trod gently in these arenas, fearing the loss of white southern votes. But Republican efforts in the election of 1936 to split southern Democratic votes by exploiting Eleanor's racial views failed miserably; the party was solid. In the North, historically Republican blacks switched for the first time to the Democratic party. At the heart of this profound shift in party loyalty was the admiration blacks felt for Eleanor Roosevelt's moral determination and her activity on their be-

half. Years later, Walter White, longtime president of the NAACP, said that in his darkest moments the thought of Eleanor Roosevelt kept him from hating all white people.

Although her support of blacks had helped President Roosevelt's reelection in 1936, members of his Cabinet mistrusted Eleanor's activity, and her resignation from the DAR in 1939 on behalf of Marian Anderson confirmed that mistrust. Henry Wallace, Secretary of Agriculture, into whose departmental restaurant no black dared come; John Nance Garner, Vice President and prospective Democratic candidate for the presidency in 1940; and James Farley, Chairman of the Democratic party, disapproved of her action. Only Harold Ickes, Secretary of the Interior and a past NAACP chapter president, proved to be a supporter.

To the nation, Eleanor's personal act of conscience in resigning from the DAR was a stunning public statement. A Gallup poll reported that 67 percent of the public approved her action. Moving on this tide, both impresario Sol Hurok, Anderson's manager, and Walter White proposed to Ickes that Anderson give an open-air concert at the Lincoln Memorial. Ickes promptly agreed, and the concert was widely publicized. On April 9, when Marian Anderson sang at the foot of the great statue of Lincoln, 75,000 people, most of them black, were there to hear her. She began with "America" and ended with "Nobody Knows the Trouble I've Seen." Ickes, who introduced her, later wrote, "I have never heard such a voice . . . the whole setting was unique, majestic and impressive." An artistic and political triumph, the concert received overwhelming press and public approval. Whatever her reason, Eleanor Roosevelt did not attend.

The event had political consequences. The most immediate was the collapse of John Nance Garner's hopes for the 1940 Democratic party presidential nomination. His refusal even to acknowledge the invitation sent to him alienated both blacks and

February 26, 1939.

My dear Mrs. Henry M. Robert, Jr.:

I am afraid that I have never been a very
useful member of the Daughters of the
American Revolution, so I know it will
make very little difference to you whether
I resign, or whether I continue to be a
member of your organization.

However, I am in complete disagreement
with the attitude taken in refusing
Constitution Hall to a great artist.
You have set an example which seems to
me unfortunate, and I feel obliged to
send in to you my resignation.   You
had an opportunity to lead in an enligh-
tened way and it seems to me that your
organization has failed.

I realize that many people will not agree
with me, but feeling as I do this seems
to me the only proper procedure to
follow.

Very sincerely yours,

whites. The longer-range consequences, though harder to measure, were great. FDR won a third term in 1940 with the overwhelming support of white liberals and northern blacks. Eleanor Roosevelt's role as a White House lobbyist on behalf of blacks was strengthened, and her support of black concerns was influential in keeping the black vote Democratic. As war approached, the issue of black rights in the military became a central one, and Eleanor was her husband's constant conscience and mover. Oddly enough, she had never viewed her resignation from the DAR as more than a personal statement, one that would neither engage public attention nor change events.

Teaching Activities

The following activities vary according to ability level. We recommend that you review the activities and select the one most consistent with your class objectives.

1. *The Inductive Detective.* These documents lend themselves to some detective work. Present both letters to the students. Ask them to determine the facts of the situation. *The unsigned letter:* What is the date of the letter? Who is Mrs. Robert? What and where is Constitution Hall? Who is the "great artist"? Who wrote the unsigned letter? Why is the letter unsigned? What is the complaint? What action is the writer taking? What is the tone of the letter? *The response from Mrs. Robert:* Why is it a handwritten note? What is Mrs. Robert's response? What is her tone?

As a summary of the activity, read the historical background to the students.

2. *Interpretations of Purpose and Intent.* After explaining the historical background of the two letters, provide the students with copies of the letters. Allow time for the students to read them carefully. Ask the students to interpret the content of the following question: Is Mrs. Roosevelt's letter a move of an activist or a personal act of conscience? Is there a difference between the two? If so, what is the difference? What factors might separate a "personal"

statement from a "political" one? What elements of Mrs. Roosevelt's letter suggest a position of strong protest? Do any phrases indicate a position of weakness or casual concern? What could explain Mrs. Roosevelt's failure to use the artist's name? What evidence in the response indicates that the DAR is concerned about Mrs. Roosevelt's resignation? Does the response of the DAR attempt to change Mrs. Roosevelt's opinion? Knowing the historical background surrounding the DAR's decision, do you consider the response to Mrs. Roosevelt firm, adequate, or weak? Would Mrs. Roosevelt consider the response adequate? Would another member of the DAR consider the response adequate?

3. *Related Topics and Questions for Research and Reports.* For further study of the issues surrounding these letters, ask the students to conduct independent research and make reports from the following suggestions.

a. What is the current position of the DAR regarding black membership, the Marian Anderson incident, and current humanitarian efforts?

b. What role did Eleanor Roosevelt play in the elections of Franklin D. Roosevelt; in the formation of FDR's views and actions on racial issues; in the campaigns of Adlai Stevenson; and in issues that were important to labor, women, children, immigrants, the aged, and the unemployed? What influences did Mrs. Roosevelt's syndicated column "My Day" have on readers?

c. Read biographical materials and report on Marian Anderson's childhood, education, career, accomplishments, and awards.

d. Read biographical material on current minority musical stars to determine the general type and quality of their education and training.

e. Conduct personal interviews with musicians or artists on the subject of travel and accommodation restrictions during the 1930s, '40s, and '50s.

f. Investigate current practices with respect to race and gender of organizations such as Rotary International, Elks Club,

MRS. HENRY M. ROBERT, JR.
PRESIDENT GENERAL
NATIONAL SOCIETY DAUGHTERS OF THE AMERICAN REVOLUTION
MEMORIAL CONTINENTAL HALL, WASHINGTON, D.C.

My dear Mrs. Roosevelt:

Your letter of resignation reaches me in Colorado upon my return from the far West. I greatly regret that you found this action necessary. Our society is engaged in the education for citizenship and the humanitarian service in which we know you to be vitally interested.

I am indeed sorry not to have been in Washington at this time. Perhaps I might have been able to remove some of the misunderstanding and to have presented to you personally the attitude of the Society.

With best wishes always. Very sincerely

Sarah Corbin Robert

Puzzle to Discover the Name of the Mystery "Great Artist"

1. H _ ◯ _ _ _ _ _ _ I A N
2. _ ◯ ◯
3. C _ _ _ _ ◯ _ _ _ _ _ _ H ◯ _ _
4. E _ _ _ ◯ _ R
5. _ _ S I G _ ◯ _ _ _ ◯
6. _ _ ◯ _ Y
7. ◯ _ _ _ G H T _ _
8. _ _ _ ◯ _ _ _ _
9. ◯ E G _ _ _ _ _ _
10. _ _ _ _ C R I M _ _ _ _ _ ◯ ◯

Using these clues, fill in the blanks in the words above:

1. one who has regard for the interests of all mankind
2. Daughters of the American Revolution (abbreviation)
3. performance auditorium in the District of Columbia
4. Mrs. Roosevelt's first name
5. the act of resigning
6. stuffed animal named after Mrs. Roosevelt's famous uncle (T.R.)
7. to give intellectual light to
8. the second month
9. to separate races in, for example, housing, schools, transportation
10. the act of treating one person or group differently from another

In the order in which they occur above, place the circled letters on the following spaces to name the mystery "great artist."

The artist is _ _ _ _ _ _ _ _ _ _ _ _ _ _ _ .

DAR, and public and private country clubs.

   g. Compare the roles of the First Ladies. What are the various models (e.g., traditional, political activist, social and moral reformers)? Contrast the involvement of recent First Ladies as political and social activists.

4. *Discussion.* Consider and discuss with the students the question: Are there ever any valid reasons for which the use of a public auditorium or stadium might be denied to an individual or group?

A Poster on Inflation

No economic problem has been as persistent and intractable in recent times as inflation. President Carter, for example, in an effort to halt today's rising price spiral, established voluntary wage-price guidelines in October 1978. Difficulties caused by rapidly rising prices have emerged periodically throughout American history. Inflation is especially acute in time of war, when unemployment is low, people have money to spend, and goods are scarce — factors that drive prices upward.

From 1914 to 1918, for example, the impact of World War I increased prices by a staggering 60 percent. After the United States entered World War II, the Government, anxious to keep the lid on inflation, established the Office of Price Administration (OPA). Congress authorized the OPA to "fix" prices on goods and rents, and the OPA set the prices prevailing in March 1942 as ceiling prices. To charge anything higher was illegal. The OPA regulated prices on products ranging from automobiles to toilet tissue in an effort to hold the line on practically all consumer goods and services.

In addition to fixing prices, the OPA set up a distribution system for goods in short supply. Wartime shortages occurred principally among goods that the military now used in greater quantity than in peacetime and also among imported goods because of transportation difficulties. Because the consumer demand for such goods as sugar, coffee, meat, tires, and gasoline exceeded the supply, the OPA limited by "rationing" the amount of these items that an individual could purchase. Every person received ration coupons, which were turned in at the time of purchase.

In order for its programs to be effective, the OPA needed wide public support. It used a variety of methods to encourage the public to buy from retailers who observed OPA regulations and to discourage people from buying on the "black market," where scarce products could be purchased illegally at prices considerably higher than levels set by the OPA. The OPA sought public cooperation by explaining its objectives and citing the dangers of inflation in brochures, speeches, school programs, radio shows, films, and posters. It also sponsored a campaign in which 15 million housewives signed the pledge, "I pay no more than ceiling prices. I accept no rationed goods without giving up ration stamps."

Was the OPA successful in holding the line against inflation? The cost of living rose 30 percent during World War II, which was a significant improvement over the rate of inflation during the First World War. Yet, the rise in prices was still troublesome. After the war, when President Truman gradually relaxed OPA regulations, the dislocations in the economy caused by wartime price controls contributed to a sharp increase in prices and a serious inflationary cycle.

The poster reproduced here is an example of the OPA's campaign to convince the American people to help control inflation. It is part of a collection of over 3,700 posters in Records of the Office of Government Reports, Record Group 44, in the Audiovisual Division of the National Archives.

Suggestions for Teaching

Allow time for the class to study the

poster. Then review the four steps in an inflationary cycle (see poster), making certain that students understand how each step follows the other. Now choose a particular industry — clothing, for example — and again go through the four stages to see how inflation affects the industry.

Questions to Discuss with the Students

1. At whom was this poster directed? How could citizens help the OPA fight inflation?

2. In what way would each person be affected by inflation? Who would be harmed the most? Who might benefit: a homeowner, a Government worker, a retired couple with a fixed income, a father with a large family, a minimum wage earner, a manufacturer?

3. Inflation occurs when the amount of money in circulation exceeds the total availability of goods and services; deflation occurs when people lack sufficient buying power to purchase the available goods and services. When in American history has deflation been a problem?

4. We are living in a highly inflationary period. What recent price jumps have you observed? How do you react to the higher prices? Discuss how the Carter administration planned to control it.

Posters as Historical Documents

1. Should this poster be saved as a historical document? Why?

2. What artistic details make this an effective poster?

3. Posters are frequently used in citizen participation campaigns. What characteristics do they have that make them popular?

An English Theme Written About the Relocation of Americans of Japanese Ancestry

Historical Background

The reasons why the United States government decided to evacuate people of Japanese origin from the West Coast and Hawaii following the attack on Pearl Harbor in 1941 are complex. However, in February 1942, a frightened U.S. Defense Command and a hostile West Coast citizenry, convinced that Japanese-Americans supported Japanese naval raids on the West Coast, combined to lead President Roosevelt to sign Executive Order 9066, authorizing the Secretary of War to establish military areas vital to the defense of the United States and to exclude therefrom "any or all persons." One month later, through Executive Order 9102, the President created the War Relocation Authority (WRA) to remove, relocate, maintain, and supervise the excluded persons. Although neither order specifically said so, both were implicitly directed at Japanese-Americans, citizens and aliens alike.

World War II brought a change in everyone's life, but for Japanese-Americans, the change was fundamental. On March 2, 1942, the western coast of the United States, including Washington, Oregon, California, and a strip of Arizona along the Mexican border, was declared military zone #1, from which Japanese-Americans were to be excluded. Later that month, the government ordered all Nisei (persons born in the United States of immigrant Japanese parents and therefore United States citizens), Issei (Japanese immigrants), and Kibei (native United States citizens of Japanese immigrant parents but educated largely in Japan) from their homes and jobs and transported them to assembly centers and then to isolated relocation centers behind barbed wire.

Eating in mess halls, using communal washroom facilities, living in hastily constructed barracks with tar-paper exteriors and knotholes in the flooring were enormous hardships for family-oriented Japanese-Americans. The WRA did what it could to make life bearable: each camp became a colony with hospitals, theaters, parades, newspapers, and even flower arrangement competitions. There were schools, usually fully staffed, for children of all ages and adults. Despite these signs of ordinary activity, these transplanted Americans lived with the undeniable fact that their freedom was gone. Except for an ironic exercise in absentee voting, the United States government deprived these citizens, who included World War I veterans, of both the privileges and responsibilities of citizenship.

The government established ten relocation centers for Japanese-American citizens and aliens. The Tule Lake Relocation Center was one of them. The document reproduced here (minus certain information deleted to maintain privacy) is an exact copy of an English theme written by a ninth-grade student at the Tule Lake Center's Tri-State High School. This theme, with other compositions and samples of student art work, added uniqueness and luster to an otherwise drab statistical report of the superintendent of schools at Tule Lake to the WRA project director for the center. From the document, one can sense the feelings and frustrations created by Executive Order 9066.

Tule Lake Relocation Center, opened in May 1942, was situated in northern California near the Oregon border. From the spring of 1942 to March 1946, internees residing at the Tule Lake Relocation Center totaled 29,498, a figure that took into account 1,490 births and 331 deaths. Tule Lake was little different from the nine other centers until June 1943, when it was designated a segregation center. After that date, it housed Japanese-Americans who either proclaimed their loyalty to Japan or had been designated by the Department of Justice as disloyal to the United States.

Because of its status as a segregation center, Tule Lake was often the scene of turbulence. Schools closed for a time, the Army interceded briefly, and the colony suffered strikes, demonstrations, and near riots. Through all of this turmoil the WRA offered, as nearly as possible, uninterrupted social services for the Tule Lake inhabitants. Tule Lake Project Director Raymond Best, in his final 1946 report, expressed the regrets of many government officials when he wrote, "It was finis of a section of a chapter of history which, pray God, America neither may be called upon

nor see fit to repeat."

The theme presented is from Field Basic Documentation Records, File Box 90, Folder: Education Reports, Records of the War Relocation Authority, Record Group 210.

Suggestions for Teaching
Before Reading the Document:
Imagine that you and your family were ordered to leave your home within a week's time. You could take only what you could carry and had to dispose of all the rest of your property, including real property (land and buildings). Think through and then write down the problems your family would face. Or you may write a letter to a special friend telling of your feelings about the eviction experience. When your work is completed, compare it with the first part of Chieko's paper.

After Reading the Document:
Learning Centers
The following five exercises are designed as individual activities that students complete independently as parts of a learning center, or station, in the classroom or library.

A list of suggested reference readings is included with each exercise. They are not essential to complete the activity, but provide information to enrich the document and the information given here on this subject. Each reference provides the author's last name and the specific chapter or page number of the reading. A complete citation of the publication is located at the end of the suggested activities.

If teachers do not choose to organize their class time to accommodate individual work, they may adapt any one exercise for use by the entire class.

1. According to the document, Chieko's family was not forced to leave its home until May 13, 1942. Write five diary entries for one member of Chieko's family, describing what might have gone through his or her mind between the attack on Pearl Harbor

in December 1941 and actual evacuation the following May.
Suggested references: Bosworth, chapter 4; Hosokawa, chapter 16; Houston, chapters 1 and 2.

2. What do you suppose Chieko's family did with property that could not be taken with them? How could this be accomplished in a week's time? Assume the role of a Japanese-American family member, and write a paragraph describing this ordeal to your non-Japanese friends.
Suggested references: Hosokawa, chapter 19; Houston, chapter 2; Miyakawa, chapters 6-9.

3. Pretend you are a radio news reporter and you are reporting on the military contributions of Nisei servicemen during World War II. You may editorialize. Write your script and record it on tape.
Suggested references: Bosworth, chapter 1; Myer, chapter 11; Shirley, total book.

4. Take the position of either a United States government official or a representative of the American Civil Liberties Union. Write a list of either the pros or the cons of confinement of Japanese-American citizens living in the United States following Pearl Harbor.
Suggested references: Hosokawa, chapters 17 and 18; Myer, chapter 20; TenBroek, chapters V-VII.

5. Look at the detailed map of the United States provided by your teacher, and by using information from your readings, at a list of the relocation and assembly centers where Japanese-Americans were located during World War II. Identify geographical features common to the sites of these centers.
Suggested references: Myer, chapter 1; Hosokawa, chapter 19; Thomas, chapter II.

Extended Learning Activities
1. For a feature magazine article, describe what life was like living in D-section and in block 58.
Suggested references: Houston, chapters 2-4, 9, 12; Miyakawa, chapters 10-13; Sone,

chapters IX and X; Conrat, total book.

2. Life for most persons in a relocation center was often boring. Even for those who worked, there had to be recreation and aesthetic relief. You are the recreation director at Tule Lake Center. What artistic and recreational projects or events would you organize? Consider the cultural traditions of Japan in planning these projects.
Suggested references: Eaton, total book; Okubo, total book, especially page 134; Spicer, pages 218-229.

3. Write a research paper on the history of anti-Asian legislation, both at the federal and state levels. Include the adjustments and contributions made by Asian immigrants despite their less than warm welcome.
Suggested references: Hosokawa, chapters 1-13; Myer, chapter 2; TenBroek, chapter I.

4. Write and produce a one-act play showing the life of a family forced to leave home, jobs, and friends for an unknown future in a confinement camp.
Suggested references: Houston, chapters 1-2; Miyakawa, chapters 1-8; Thomas, chapter I.

5. Invite speakers from a local civil rights commission in your community to speak to your class about current civil rights violations and the commission's programs for correcting these abuses.

Bibliography

Bosworth, Allan R. *America's Concentration Camps.* New York: W. W. Norton and Company, Inc., 1967.

Conrat, Maisie and Richard. *Executive Order 9066.* California Historical Society, 1972.

Eaton, Allen H. *Beauty Behind Barbed Wire.* New York: Harper and Brothers, 1952.

Hosokawa, Bill. *Nisei.* New York: William Morrow and Company, Inc., 1969.

Houston, Jeanne Wakatsuki. *Farewell to Manzanar.* Boston: Houghton Mifflin Company, 1973.

Chieko Hirata
Period II, English I

My Last Day At Home

The month of May when I was attending school, all the
residents of Hood River county, as well as the people of the
whole western coast was surprised to receive such an unexpected
order of evacuation.

Promptly after hearing about the order I with my folks
went to register and then for a brief physical examination.
Then I helped my folks pack and prepared to leave my dear home
on May 13, 1942.

On May 8, 1942 I withdrew from Parkdale Grade School,
where all my friends and teachers bid me farewell with sorrow-
ful face and tears. Our packing never seem to cease, we kept
on packing then finally we were finished. Then came May 13th,
my most dreaded day which I shall never forget the rest of
my life. On the afternoon of the 13th, I board the train headed
for Pinedale, California.

On the night of the 15th we arrived. The weather was
pretty hot. In Pinedale I lived in the D-section which had
forty barracks, which had vie apartments to a barrack.

I stayed at the Pinedale Assembly Center about two
months. Then around July 15, 1942 we received our order to
evacuate for Tule Lake. Then on July 18th we evacuated for
Tule Lake and spent a night on the train. I arrived in Tule
Lake. At present I am living in Block 58. The residents of
this block is most Tacoma folks which I am not very much ac-
quainted with as yet. Being that my cousin lives in Block 57
I am always visiting them.

I am always hoping that this war will end, so that I
will be able to go back to Parkdale, my home town and see all
my old friends, and live to my dying days in my old home in
Parkdale, Oregon.

                              Herbert Yoshikawa

Miyakawa, Edward. *Tule Lake*. Walport, Ore.: House by the Sea Publishing Company, 1979.

Myer, Dillon S. *Uprooted Americans*. Tucson: The University of Arizona Press, 1971.

Okubo, Mine. *Citizen 13660*. New York: Columbia University Press, 1946.

Shirley, Orville C. *Americans — The Story of the 442nd Combat Team*. Washington, D.C.: Infantry Journal, Inc., 1946.

Sone, Monica. *Nisei Daughter*. Boston: Little, Brown and Company, 1953.

Spicer, Edward H. *Impounded People*. Tucson: The University of Arizona Press, 1969.

TenBroek, Jacobus. *Prejudice, War, and the Constitution*. Berkeley: University of California Press, 1954.

Thomas, Dorothy Swaine. *The Spoilage*. Berkeley: University of California Press, 1946.

Victory Gardens in World War II

"Food will win the war and write the peace," announced Agriculture Secretary Claude Wickard in a statement to the press in early 1943. "We need more food than ever before in history. If a suitable space is not available at home, all who can do so are asked to obtain plots on community or allotment gardens that can be reached by bus or street car."

Even before the United States entered the war in 1941, U.S. farmers were producing at record levels to supply the food needs of the Allies. After the Japanese bombing of Pearl Harbor, getting food and equipment to our troops strained production and distribution systems to their limits. Farm labor was in short supply as men left for military service. The Office of Civil Defense was given primary responsibility for convincing nonfarm families to produce and preserve some of their food at home.

It was not difficult to generate willingness to participate. Although by the 1940s most people in the United States lived in towns and cities, many felt some romantic nostalgia for the farm life their parents and grandparents had left. Food rationing, begun in 1942 by limiting purchases of coffee and sugar and later expanded to other products, added practical necessity to nostalgia. Patriotic fervor was contagious. Victory Gardens sprang up everywhere, in sunny backyards, vacant lots, and community spaces. Local governments supported the food production effort by reducing water rates, changing zoning laws to allow chickens and rabbits to be kept in town, and passing stronger laws to punish vandalism and theft.

From 1941 until the end of the war, the Office of War Information and the Office of Civil Defense worked with private industry to mount an intensive publicity campaign to promote Victory Gardens. Posters, cartoons, and press releases found in the records of the Office of Civil Defense urged citizens to "Help Uncle plant his garden" in order to "beet" the enemy. Companies like Philco and Standard Oil incorporated Victory Garden encouragement and advice in their newspaper and magazine advertising. The publishers of *Better Homes and Gardens* financed the production of a short film, "The Gardens of Victory," that was widely shown. Entertainers added Victory Garden comments and jokes to radio scripts, and newspapers were filled with gardening and recipe tips.

Antidote to Mental Depression

Food production was the primary goal of the Victory Garden campaign, but other benefits were cited as incentives. Gardening was promoted as healthy exercise, which would build strength and stamina for whatever lay ahead. Garden work could be a way to fight mental depression. "There's no quicker way to get your mind off the sordid, horrible side of war than to roll up your sleeves and dig in on a new Victory Garden — no better way to forget about taxes than to plant radishes," said the Pasadena, California, *Star-News* on August 19, 1943. The article continued: "A Victory Garden . . . is an admirable defense against the bad effects of too much worry, too much thinking, too much of everything we have all gotten too much of lately."

Another goal is not stated explicitly in the Victory Garden advertising campaign materials in the National Archives, but it

163

does appear in the Office of Civil Defense records. These records contain a letter to officials of the Idaho Defense Council from Frank Gaines, Assistant Director for Organization and War Services. Gaines' letter suggests that youth group garden projects could be an antidote for juvenile delinquency. Young people, he wrote, would find in gardening a good way to channel pent-up aggressive energy into co-operative and productive labor.

Although officials estimated that in many areas one family in three had a food garden, the program was not an unqual-ified success. Some hastily assembled in-struction pamphlets gave advice unsuited to local conditions. The expertise of ex-tension agents at state colleges, an impor-tant resource, was not fully recognized or used by backyard farmers. Shortages of equipment and fertilizer combined with adverse weather conditions discouraged many, and the demands of tending a gar-den through long, hot summer days made gardening less romantic and joyful than at spring planting time. The product some-times seemed not worth the effort. "Many men particularly, as well as youngsters, think green leafy vegetables are a curse. There is a reason. So often they are served in such a way that they look and taste like steamed hay," complained H.W. Hochbaum in a speech to the Seattle Vic-tory Garden Advisory Council in the sum-mer of 1943. He reported that his survey of gardens in the Chicago area left him en-couraged but concerned. "Vacant spaces in these so precious garden plots are slacker spaces and must not be tolerated," he announced.

Despite difficulties, many people worked in the sunshine and managed to grow and preserve a significant part of the family food supply through the war years. But Victory Gardens were a constant re-minder of a difficult and painful struggle, a war not yet won. Peace brought higher family incomes, more consumer goods, the end of rationing, and the end of the patri-otic fad of victory gardening. Families eagerly embraced the peacetime luxury of processed, packaged, quick-to-fix foods newly available in well-advertised abun-dance. Not until the back-to-nature move-ment of the 1960s and the energy crisis of the 1970s would home food gardening again become a popular hobby for millions of Americans.

The poster shown here, "Plant a Victory Garden," is item number 208-PMP-34, Records of the Office of War Information (RG 208), National Archives, Washington, DC. All quotations are found in Civilian War Services Branch, Records of the Of-fice of Civil Defense (RG 171), National Archives, Washington, DC.

Teaching Activities

1. Make a transparency of the poster if this is to be a group activity, or reproduce the poster for individual study and written or oral reporting. Have students list and de-scribe the symbols they see in the poster, both pictorial and written. They should identify and describe the propaganda de-vices used. What devices promote the idea that garden work is war work? Can you think of ways to change this poster to strengthen the message?

2. Discuss with students the concept of ad-dressing messages to a particular audience. To what segments of the home front pub-lic would this poster be most likely to ap-peal? Who is being encouraged to garden, and why? Who or what group would be likely to plan an ad campaign to convince people to garden today? What are some of government's concerns today regarding land use? Define a different target audi-ence and design an appropriate pro-garden poster.

3. Not only was food in short supply but so were other resources. Sugar rationing made it difficult for families to preserve the fruit they grew, although extra supplies of sugar were available for canning. Not only was sugar used as food, but it was also made into industrial alcohol needed in the production of synthetic rubber. Why was natural rubber not available? What other essential resources were unavailable or in

short supply? Use maps of World War II to answer these questions.

4. Rationing added to the popularity and utility of Victory Gardens. Have students find out about the rationing program during the war. What goods were rationed? Why? How did the system work?

5. Many people in this country have vivid memories of World War II on the home front. Students should have no difficulty finding family members or family friends who were involved with the Victory Garden program in some way. Have the group plan interview questions in advance; they need to ask specific questions for best results. Consider inviting or visiting people from a nearby garden club or senior center. Consider videotaping or audiotaping the interview, or ask individual students to transcribe their interviews and share them with the class.

6. The government promoted many citizen involvement programs on the home front: collecting and recycling scrap metal and fats, fitting windows with darkening shades for air-raid blackouts, buying war bonds and stamps, and so on. It has been suggested that the government's real goal was to promote patriotism and war awareness in citizens otherwise relatively untouched by a distant war not yet made present by television, and that civilian defense activities in themselves had little effect on increasing usable resources for the war effort. How can students prove or disprove this contention? What kind of data might suggest answers, and where could they get it?

7. Look closely at advertising aimed at shaping civilian participation on the home front in World War II. Locate and bring copies of old newspapers to class for this activity. Ask the students to scan the newspapers and find answers to the questions that follow. Did the government have an interest in maintaining or in changing traditional social patterns and practices in this period? For instance, was it specific government policy to get women to take jobs outside the home during the war and then to go home again when the war ended? Did private custom lead to government policy, or vice versa?

Campaign Slogans and Fliers

"I like Ike." "All the Way with LBJ." "Re-elect the President." Presidential election campaign slogans often linger in our memories like the jingles of television commercials, even though the candidates, especially the vice presidential aspirants, are long forgotten.

The 1944 election flier seen here documents a most unusual presidential campaign. This campaign was unique because Franklin Roosevelt was running for an unprecedented fourth term as president and because the electorate was engaged in supporting and fighting a second World War. Despite these unusual conditions, the party nominating conventions, campaign speech-making, and subsequent election proceeded as usual. In the summer of 1944, Roosevelt and his running mate, Missouri Senator Harry S Truman, squared off against Republicans Thomas E. Dewey, Governor of New York, and John W. Bricker, former Governor of Ohio.

The rancorous Democratic nomination of Roosevelt for President in 1940 had broken the tradition of a two-term presidency. Roosevelt's renomination in 1944 caused no such rancor; the nation was coping with the international crisis. Roosevelt accepted his renomination, declaring that if elected he would serve as "Commander in Chief to us all." In November, Roosevelt defeated Dewey by a margin of 333 electoral votes. His election and that of a Democratic Congress reflected the nation's confidence in Roosevelt's wartime leadership. Roosevelt's death in April 1945, less than three months after his fourth inauguration, cut short the longest presidential tenure in U.S. history.

Roosevelt's 12 years as President, coupled with the pressures of war, swung the balance of power toward the executive branch. With Roosevelt's death, Congress sought to reassert its authority. One aspect of this effort was the introduction of a constitutional amendment to limit the presidency to two terms. Despite much congressional debate, including accusations that the amendment only represented Republican anti-Roosevelt sentiment, the amendment passed Congress and was subsequently ratified by three-fourths of the states by February, 1951.

The flier is found in the Campaign Literature Collection, Franklin D. Roosevelt Presidential Library.

Teaching Activities

1. Discuss with students the meaning of the following elements of the campaign flier: "The man who fights for human rights," "Win the war/Win the peace," "Just another American," and "Roosevelt saved America in 1933." Ask students to consider why these elements would be included in such a flier.

2. In class, develop a list of presidential campaign slogans that have been used over the years (e.g., "Tippecanoe and Tyler, too"; "Keep Cool with Coolidge"; and "Fritz and Grits in '76"). Compare and contrast these slogans with the images of Roosevelt represented in the flier.

3. The flier attaches many apparently desirable character traits to the candidate. Direct students to review the flier and develop a list of these characteristics. Which are desirable in a candidate? Which are necessary to a good president? Discuss the

★ **THE MAN WHO FIGHTS FOR HUMAN RIGHTS** ★

AMERICA MARCHES ON TO GREATER GLORY IN 1944

WIN THE WAR **WITH PRESIDENT ROSEVELT** WIN THE PEACE

Justice

Security

LIBERTY

PROSPERITY

JUST ANOTHER AMERICAN

"In the dim distant past," says President Roosevelt, "his ancestors may have been Jews or Catholics or Protestants— what I am more interested in is whether they were good citizens and believers in God—I hope they were both."

★ Columbus Discovered America in 1492 ★

Roosevelt Saved America in 1933 ★

Fearless
•
Democratic
•
Reliable
Outspoken
Outstanding
Sincere
Experienced
Valiant
Efficient
Loyal
Truthful!

AND NOW! WITH THE GREAT LEADERSHIP OF PRESIDENT ROOSEVELT
AMERICA HAS SAVED THE WORLD!

The Greatest President of the Greatest Nation
SELECTED TO BE RE-ELECTED
For the Freedom and Security of America and its People

statement: "The qualities that make a good candidate may make a poor or inadequate president." How has campaigning by television accentuated the differences between a good candidate and a good president?

4. Campaign literature often includes photographs of the candidate. Direct students to compare the photograph of Roosevelt on the flier with others in their textbook. Suggest that students look at other photographs of Roosevelt taken at the time of the campaign. How do they compare? What accounts for the differences? (N.B.: In 1921, FDR was stricken with infantile paralysis. Upon his election as President, the press refrained from publishing photographs that revealed the extent of the President's disability. As a result of this practice, some citizens were unaware that FDR could not walk unaided.)

5. The 1940 and 1944 presidential campaigns were unique in U.S. history. Direct students to research the candidates and issues for each campaign and to write a summary of each election.

6. Discuss with students the advantages and disadvantages of a two-term presidency. Ask them to consider carefully how being at war might affect their opinions.

7. Ask students to imagine that they are presidential candidates and to design campaign fliers like the Roosevelt flier, using their own names as the centerpiece.

A Letter of Appeal on Behalf of Raoul Wallenberg

On January 17, 1985, bells at the Church of Saint John the Divine in New York City tolled 40 times for Raoul Wallenberg, a man whose disappearance has diminished all of humankind.

Back in the spring of 1944, President Franklin D. Roosevelt had broadcast a radio appeal to Hungarian Christians and antifascists to help the Jews of Hungary survive the Nazi occupation. The U.S. War Refugee Board was authorized to raise funds for rescue efforts in Hungary through a group called the Joint Distribution Committee. Because Hungary and the United States were at war with each other, it was necessary to find a neutral nation to distribute these American funds. Sweden agreed to cooperate with the United States in this humanitarian action.

The Swedish national who took charge of the mission in Hungary was Raoul Gustav Wallenberg. Born in Sweden on August 4, 1912, Wallenberg was a 1935 graduate of the Architectural School of the University of Michigan. He accepted the post of special attaché and second secretary to the Swedish Legation in Hungary, and reported to Budapest in July 1944. As a result of his unremitting efforts and ingenuity, the War Refugee Board credited him with protecting from Nazi persecution at least 20,000 Hungarian Jews.

At extreme risk to himself, Wallenberg used both conventional and unconventional methods to buy time for the Jews of Hungary until the advancing Russian army could liberate the country. His main tactic was to issue Swedish "protective" citizenship documents, technically removing anyone holding them from Hungarian jurisdiction. The Nazi collaborator heading the wartime Hungarian regime, Premier Szalasi, decreed in October 1944 that Swedish protective citizenship would not be recognized. But Wallenberg continued to issue the documents and pursue other means, even bribing fascist officials as opportunity presented itself.

In January 1945 the Red Army began to occupy Budapest, starting with the eastern section of the city, Pest. On January 17, Wallenberg went to meet the Soviet commander, Marshal Malinovsky, to transfer his charges from Swedish to Russian protection. He wanted to continue traveling eastward by car to Debrezen in an effort to contact the returning Hungarian government-in-exile so that his mission would not be interrupted by the fighting that would accompany the Russian occupation of Budapest. Raoul Wallenberg has not been seen since that day, 40 years ago. Ironically, this dauntless crusader for human rights has himself become the object of repeated investigations concerning the violation of his own human rights.

In January 1945, the Soviet Foreign Office announced that Wallenberg was under Russian protection. On May 24, 1945, the Swedish Legation in Moscow confirmed to the Swedish Foreign Ministry that Russian

Guy von Dardel
% Onderdonk
815 North Tioga Avenue
Ithaca, New York

President Harry S. Truman
The White House
Washington, D.C.

Dear Mr. President:

I write to you concerning the whereabouts of my brother,
Raoul Wallenberg, a Swedish citizen who went to Hungary in July, 1944
as the representative of President Roosevelt's War Refugee Board and
who has been missing since the Soviet Foreign Office early in 1946
declared him to be under Russian protection.

I appeal to you because I believe that his fate, apart from
being a source of continuous anguish to his family, also touches the
conscience of this great democracy. I ask your aid because my brother's
mercy mission — which included the rescue of 20,000 Hungarian Jews —
was carried out under American auspices, and because two years of effort
through regular diplomatic channels have failed.

The success of Raoul Wallenberg's humanitarian mission from July,
1944 until his disappearance on January 17, 1945 is a matter of public
record. The War Refugee Board officially credits him with saving
20,000 lives; his former American associates in Stockholm as well as
the people of Budapest estimate that perhaps 100,000 men, women and
children owe their survival to him.

The manner in which he carried out his singular assignment has
been described as unparalleled in both courage and resourcefulness.
In the midst of furious battle and barbarous persecution, he literally
snatched thousands of human beings from freight trains bound for
Himmler's extermination camps. He furnished many thousands of otherwise
doomed Hungarian Jews and anti-Nazis with documents of Swedish protective
citizenship. He established an extraterritorial compound in the heart
of Nazi-occupied Budapest and fought off German and Hungarian fascist
marauders who tried to violate this sanctuary.

He set up hospitals, nurseries, schools and public soup kitchens
to care for the hunted and the fear-ridden of Budapest. And when Fascist
Premier Szalasi decreed in October 1945 that Swedish protective channels
would no longer be honored — an edict which spelled death to the surviving
Jews of Budapest — Raoul Wallenberg still found a way. With ingenuity
and daring, he managed to forestall this cruel decree long enough to save
many thousands from the final fires of Auschwitz, Oswiecim and Dachau.

troops indeed had found Wallenberg. The wartime Soviet Minister to Stockholm, Mme. Kollontai, thereupon assured Wallenberg's family that he was alive and well. Shortly thereafter, the Swedish Minister to Moscow asked for an investigation of his countryman's disappearance, and Stalin assured him that he would personally press the matter. The Russians argue that this commitment was fulfilled the next year when the government of Hungary tried, convicted, and executed a Hungarian fascist sympathizer for killing Wallenberg during fighting in Buda, the western sector of Budapest, at the time of the Red Army's occupation of the city. The Soviets have since changed their account and claim that Wallenberg died of a heart attack in 1947 in a Soviet prison.

Yet a large body of evidence suggests that Raoul Wallenberg was arrestd by the NKVD, the Soviet secret police, in January 1945, and has been held in internment camps in the Communist bloc ever since. Frustration with the failure of any investigation to resolve the question of Wallenberg's whereabouts prompted Guy von Dardel, Wallenberg's stepbrother, to write an appeal to President Harry S Truman.

Another strategy to obtain answers about Wallenberg's circumstances was to bring his name before the Nobel Peace Prize Committee. In 1948 an international effort was launched to propose Wallenberg as a nominee for the Nobel Peace Prize to draw attention to his contributions to human rights — and to his plight. In 1984 he was once again actively suggested for the award, in recognition of his gift of life to the Jews of Hungary at the cost of his own freedom.

Although the Swedish Foreign Ministry has pursued the case quietly since Wallenberg's disappearance, and prominent humanitarians — from Albert Einstein to Eleanor Roosevelt — have endeavored to determine his whereabouts, world awareness was not drawn to the case until the early 1980s, after Soviet dissident Aleksandr Solzhenitsyn was awarded the Nobel

Prize. During his visit to Stockholm to receive his award, Solzhenitsyn met with Wallenberg's mother and urged her to insist that the Swedish government take a more public, insistent approach to pressure the Kremlin to account for her son.

In 1985, in the midst of many 40th anniversary remembrances of the close of World War II, commemorative meetings have recalled the unanswered questions about Wallenberg's fate.

The document reproduced here, Guy von Dardel's letter to President Truman, is located in Decimal File 701.5864, General Records of the Department of State, Record Group 59.

Teaching Activities

The following three activities vary according to ability level and interests. Each anticipates a higher level of skills than the preceding activity. They should be presented sequentially, although you may terminate the lesson after any one.

1. *Interpreting the Document.* Present the letter to students and ask them to determine the facts of the situation and then share their answers in class discussion.

a. Why does Guy von Dardel believe that the U.S. government has a responsibility to assist in locating Raoul Wallenberg?

b. According to the letter, what did Raoul Wallenberg accomplish from July 1944 to January 1945? What specific actions did he take in order to accomplish his humanitarian mission?

c. According to von Dardel, what is the position of the Russian government on the Wallenberg case? What major discrepancies between the initial and the final Russian position does he point out?

d. What information does von Dardel have that makes him believe his stepbrother is alive? At the time of his letter, where does von Dardel believe Raoul is located?

e. After examining Wallenberg's background and activities, can you explain why the NKVD might have suspected him of

When the Germans were being driven from Budapest, Raoul remained at his post. On January 17, 1945 he went out to meet Marshal Malinovsky, the Soviet commander, in order to place his charges -- thousands of men, women and children -- under the protection of the Red Army.

Since leaving Budapest under Russian escort for Soviet headquarters, my brother has been missing. Rumors were circulated more than two years ago that he had been killed by Hungarian fascists. But while these rumors have never been supported by a shred of proof, a large body of evidence has come to the attention of the Swedish government which indicates that Raoul Wallenberg has been a Soviet prisoner since January, 1945.

The Soviet government has never retracted the admission by the Russian Foreign Office that Wallenberg was taken under Soviet protection more than two years ago. Nor has Moscow submitted any evidence to support the inspired rumors of his death at fascist hands.

Quite the contrary, the evidence that my brother established contact with the Russian command just before his disappearance has recently been corroborated by Iver Olsen, the former War Refugee Board representative in Stockholm who sent Raoul on his mission to Budapest, and by other reputable witnesses, including members of the Swedish Legation in Budapest. Some of the latter, who were interrogated by Soviet NKVD officers nearly a month after Raoul's disappearance, are firmly convinced that my brother was arrested on the preposterous charge of espionage. This belief is shared by officials of the U.S. State Department and the Swedish Foreign Office.

It is significant, however, that the Soviet government has never admitted holding Wallenberg as a prisoner. On the contrary, Mme. Kollontai, wartime Soviet Minister to Stockholm, gave our family assurance that Raoul was alive and safe. Later, the Soviet military authorities permitted the city of Budapest to hold memorial services for Raoul and to name a street in his honor. With this convenient ceremony, the curtain of oblivion was to be dropped on the actual fate of my brother.

Since that time, however, an ever-larger body of evidence has reached the Swedish government to indicate that Raoul was arrested by the Soviet secret police in January 1945 and is still alive in a Soviet internment camp. The latest report, transmitted to Stockholm only a few weeks ago, places him in Estonia.// Earlier testimony by neutral diplomats and journalists as well as other persons held for some time in Soviet custody, indicates that Raoul was sent to a Soviet internment camp in Czechoslovakia in April 1945; that he was later transferred to Bessarabia and was subsequently sent to a camp in the Ukraine.

espionage?

f. Von Dardel charges that the Soviet military authorities named a street and held memorial services for Raoul so that "the curtain of oblivion" would be dropped on his actual fate. Does memorializing persons or declaring them dead seem to close cases or defuse public concern? Explain.

g. How reliable is von Dardel's letter as a source of accurate information? Consider the circumstances surrounding it, von Dardel's bias, the absence or presence of

Raoul Wallenberg

other information, and your own biases as you evaluate this document's reliability. Pay close attention to von Dardel's chronology of events.

2. *Related Topics and Questions for Research and Reports.* For further study of the issues surrounding this letter, ask students to conduct independent research and make reports on the following topics.

a. Quiet Diplomacy: Ask students to investigate cooperative efforts between the U.S. and foreign governments to resolve human rights violations, for example:

The Algerian-U.S. effort to release hostages in Iran

The Laotian-U.S. effort to determine the fate of Vietnam-era POWs-MIAs

The Colombian-U.S. effort to fight drug trafficking (addiction)

b. Landmark Documents of International Human Rights in the 20th Century: Ask students to write personal definitions of human rights. Recommend that they familiarize themselves with major documents of 20th century human rights including:

The Covenant of the League of Nations
The Geneva Conventions
Franklin D. Roosevelt's Second Bill of Rights
The Universal Declaration of Human Rights of the United Nations
The Helsinki Accords

As a class, develop a definition of what constitutes human rights and what constitutes violations of those rights. Discuss why actions that today are considered violations of human rights were regarded as acceptable behavior by government or society in the past. Focus on U.S. examples, such as slavery, dispossession of the Native Americans, and incarceration of the mentally ill or incompetent.

c. Human Rights Violations: (1) In 1983, the play *Wallenberg: Five Days,* written by Carl Levine, premiered in Denver. If you wish to obtain copies for students to do a dramatic reading, write for further information to Dr. Carl Levine, 817 Balsam Lane, Fort Collins, Colorado 80526. (2) Students may wish to read accounts of violations of human rights in other countries. There are excellent accounts of Russian violations by Aleksandr Solzhenitsyn, for example: *The Gulag Archipelago* (nonfiction), *The Love Girl and the Innocent* (play), and *A Day in the Life of Ivan Denisovich* (novel). It might be illuminating to compare the ideals expressed in articles 125, 127 and 128 of the Soviet Constitution with Solzhenitsyn's testimony. Accounts of violations in other nations include Alan Paton's novel *Cry the Beloved Country,* set in the Union of South Africa, and Jacobo Timerman's *Prisoner Without a Name, Cell Without a Number* (nonfiction), set in Argentina.

3. *Action Strategies.* Students as a group or as individuals may wish to write letters or circulate petitions to aid victims of human rights violations, developed from the following information:

a. A postcard distributed at the premier

The Swedish government has, on a number of occasions, requested the Soviet government for definite information regarding my brother's whereabouts. But since the Soviet Foreign Office announced in January, 1945 that Wallenberg was under Russian protection, Moscow has remained noncommittal.

In view of the manifest inability of ordinary diplomacy to cut through the tangle of red tape and misunderstanding that may still be holding my brother a prisoner — more than two years after the completion of his American-inspired humanitarian mission — I ask your assistance, Mr. President, in obtaining the true facts.

Respectfully yours,

Guy von Dardel

of Levine's play carried the message: I urge the immediate release of Raoul Wallenberg on humanitarian grounds. (Name and address of sender.) Address the postcard to:

Mikhail Gorbachev
The Kremlin
Moscow, RSFSR
U.S.S.R.

b. The U.S. House of Representatives Committee on Human Relations has produced a number of committee reports that might indicate areas of current U.S. concern and strategies of the government and private citizens to promote international human rights.

c. Amnesty International USA has a free packet of materials available to teachers and will send monthly "Urgent Action Appeals" to aid unjustly incarcerated individuals anywhere in the world. Teachers may call 303-440-0913 or send for "The High School Urgent Action File" from:

Urgent Action Network
Box 1270
Nederland, CO 80466

Key Press Release on the Recognition of the State of Israel

Background

In 1917 Chaim Weizmann, scientist, statesperson, and Zionist, persuaded the British government to issue a statement favoring the establishment of a Jewish national home in Palestine. The statement, which became known as the Balfour Declaration, was, in part, payment to the Jews for their support of the British against the Turks during World War I. After the war, the League of Nations ratified the declaration and in 1922 appointed Britain to rule in Palestine.

This course of events caused Jews to be optimistic about the eventual establishment of a homeland. Their optimism inspired the immigration to Palestine of Jews from many countries, particularly from Germany when Nazi persecution of Jews began. The arrival of many Jewish immigrants in the 1930s awakened Arab fears that Palestine would become a national homeland for Jews. By 1936 guerrilla fighting had broken out between the Jews and Arabs. Unable to maintain peace, Britain issued a white paper in 1939 that restricted Jewish immigration into Palestine. The Jews, feeling betrayed, bitterly opposed the policy and looked to the United States for support.

While President Franklin D. Roosevelt appeared to be sympathetic to the Jewish cause, his assurances to the Arabs that the United States would not intervene without consulting both parties caused public uncertainty about his position. When Harry S Truman took office, he made clear that his sympathies were with the Jews and accepted the Balfour Declaration, explaining that it was in keeping with former President Woodrow Wilson's principle of "self-determination." Truman initiated several studies of the Palestine situation that supported his belief that, as a result of the Holocaust, Jews were oppressed and also in need of a homeland. Throughout the Roosevelt and Truman administrations, the Departments of War and State, recognizing the possibility of a Soviet-Arab connection and the potential Arab restriction on oil supplies to this country, advised against U.S. intervention on behalf of the Jews.

Britain and the United States, in a joint effort to examine the dilemma, established the "Anglo-American Committee of Inquiry." In April 1946, the committee submitted recommendations that Palestine not be dominated by either Arabs or Jews. It concluded that attempts to establish nationhood or independence would result in civil strife; that a trusteeship agreement aimed at bringing Jews and Arabs together should be established by the United Nations; that full Jewish immigration be allowed into Palestine; and that two autonomous states be established with a strong central government to control Jerusalem, Bethlehem, and the Negev, the southernmost section of Palestine.

British, Arab, and Jewish reactions to the recommendations were not favorable. Jewish terrorism in Palestine antagonized

3059

OUTGOING TELEGRAM

Department of State
Washington

NO DISTRIBUTION

US URGENT

TO

CERTAIN AMERICAN DIPLOMATIC AND CONSULAR OFFICERS

NIACT

For your secret info and for such precautions as you may consider it necessary to take this Govt may within next few hours recognize provisional Jewish govt as de facto authority of new Jewish state.

Send to following posts:

MISSIONS	CONSULATES
Cairo	Alexandria ✓
Jidda	Port Said ✓
Baghdad	Dhahran
Basra →	Jerusalem
Beirut	Haifa ✓
Damascus	Aden ✓

NEA:LWHenderson:mw

5/14/48

TOP SECRET

1948 MAY 14 PM 5 51 ACCEPTANCE DESK OUT

867N.01/5-1448   A/MUS TOP SECRET

the British, and by February 1947 Arab-Jewish communications had collapsed. Britain, anxious to rid itself of the problem, set the United Nations in motion, formally requesting on April 2, 1947, that the U.N. General Assembly set up the Special Committee on Palestine (UNSCOP). This committee recommended that the British mandate over Palestine be ended and that the territory be partitioned into two states. Jewish reaction was mixed — some wanted control of all of Palestine; others realized that partition spelled hope for their dream of a homeland. The Arabs were not at all agreeable to the UNSCOP plan. In October the Arab League Council directed the governments of its member states to move troops to the Palestine border. Meanwhile, President Truman instructed the State Department to support the U.N. plan, and, reluctantly, it did so. On November 29, 1947, the partition plan was passed in the U.N. General Assembly.

At midnight on May 14, 1948, the Provisional Government of Israel proclaimed the new State of Israel. On that same date the United States, in the person of President Truman, recognized the provisional Jewish government as *de facto* authority of the new Jewish state *(de jure* recognition was extended on January 31). The U.S. delegates to the U.N. and top-ranking State Department officials were angered that Truman released his recognition statement to the press without notifying them first. On May 15, 1948, the first day of Israeli independence and exactly one year after UNSCOP was established, Arab armies invaded Israel and the first Arab-Israeli war began.

The telegram reproduced above is from decimal file 867n.01/5-1448, Records of the Department of State, Record Group 59, National Archives. The press release on p. 471 is from the records of the Truman Library, Independence, Mo. The Library is part of the Presidential Library system of the National Archives and Records Administration.

Suggestions for Teaching
Student Activity

The activity provided is for use with *the telegram.* (You might choose to design another activity for use with the press release.)

While this document does not lend itself to any critical analysis of the Arab-Israeli conflict, we hope that it will provide a starting point from which to consider the conflict.

Note: The document is signed by Secretary of State George C. Marshall.

Loy Henderson, whose name also appears on the document, was director of the Office of Near Eastern and African Affairs, and wrote the document.

NIACT is code for "action communications indicator requiring attention by recipient at any hour of the day or night" and relates to method of distribution.

Discussion questions
1. What kind of document is it?

2. Who wrote it?

3. To whom is it addressed?

4. Does it have any historical significance? Consider the date and message.

5. Why do you suppose the document was at one time classified "top secret"?

6. Write a paragraph describing how you, as a U.S. consul (choose in which country you are stationed), might have reacted to receiving this document.

For Further Research

1. Students should develop a time line of Arab-Israeli conflict from 1948 to the present. They can use the time line to research events that they have noted, drawing parallels, making predictions, etc.

2. Using maps, students should examine changes that have taken place in the area of Palestine over a period of time.

3. Students should research the political

This Government has been informed that a Jewish state has been proclaimed in Palestine, and recognition has been requested by the *provisional* Government thereof.

The United States recognizes the provisional government as the de facto authority of the new ~~Jewish~~ *State of* ~~state.~~ *Israel.*

Harry Truman

Approved.
May 14, 1948.

6:11

aspects of the U.S. position in the Middle East, considering, for example, Truman's position in view of the 1948 presidential election.

Terms to Define
de facto
de jure
consulate
white paper

Cartoon Analysis of Peace Propaganda

We demand the absolute banning of the atom weapon, arm of
terror and mass extermination [*sic*] of populations.
We demand the establishment of strict international control to
ensure the implementation of this banning measure.
We consider that any government which would be first to use the
atom weapon against any country whatsoever would be
committing a crime against humanity and should be dealt with
as a war criminal.
We call on all men of good will throughout the world to sign this
Appeal.

— March 19, 1950

This appeal resulted from a worldwide meeting of the World Congress of Partisans of Peace organized by the Soviets and held in Stockholm, Sweden, in March 1950. After the adoption of this resolution in Stockholm, the Russians set about collecting millions of signatures from citizens around the world. The Stockholm Appeal is represented by the dove in the cartoon reproduced here.

The Stockholm Appeal emerged into a world threatened by atomic destruction. In 1945, with the United States bombing of Hiroshima and Nagasaki, the atomic age had begun. With the end of the war, the United States and, subsequently, the newly formed United Nations sought to secure the atomic genie in a tamper-proof bottle. One of the most significant of these efforts was a United States proposal to the United Nations presented in 1947 by senior statesman Bernard Baruch and often called the "Baruch Plan." This proposal, drafted before the development of Soviet atomic capabilities, recommended international control of atomic material under the United Nations, the "eventual" destruction of "U.S. superiority" in atomic weaponry, and international inspection to ensure compliance. After much debate in the United Nations Security Council, the "Baruch Plan" was rejected by a Soviet veto, but referred to and passed by the General Assembly.

To counter these United Nations efforts to control the development of atomic weapons, the Soviets launched an appeal to the peoples of the world to "ban the bomb," while at the same time developing their own atomic capabilities. The world learned of the Soviets' atomic bomb in September 1949. In contrast to the technical and substantive discussions within the United Nations, the Soviet peace efforts involved general appeals like that in Stockholm in 1950. United States Secretary of State Dean Acheson dismissed these Soviet peace moves as "Trojan Doves."

During World War II, the United States

Cartoon Analysis

	Visuals	Words
Level Three	1. List the objects or people you see in the cartoon.	1. Identify the cartoon caption and/or title. 2. Locate three words or phrases used by the cartoonist to identify objects or people within the cartoon. (Not all cartoons include words.) 3. Record any important dates or numbers that appear in the cartoon.
Level Two	2. Which of the objects on your list are symbols? 3. What do you think each of the symbols means?	4. Which words or phrases in the cartoon appear to be the most significant? Why do you think so? (Not all cartoons include words.) 5. List adjectives that describe the emotions portrayed in the cartoon.
Level One	A. Describe the action taking place in the cartoon. B. In your own words, explain how the words in the cartoon explain or clarify the symbols. C. In your own words, explain the message of the cartoon. D. What special interest groups would agree/disagree with the cartoon's message? Why?	

and the Union of Soviet Socialist Republics had been partners in an effort to defeat the fascist regimes. Between war's end and 1950, however, this relationship was shattered by irreconcilable differences which became very apparent in 1948 with the coup in Prague and the blockade in Berlin and which worsened in 1950 when the U.S.S.R. walked out of the United Nations over the issue of United Nations' recognition of Nationalist China. The partnership broke down completely shortly after the Stockholm Appeal when war erupted in Korea.

The cartoon is No. 306-PS-50-4835 in the Records of the United States Information Agency, Record Group 306. It is reprinted from the *Minneapolis Star and Tribune* of April 17, 1950, with permission of the publishers.

Teaching Activities

1. The "cartoon analysis" chart is designed to help students to analyze almost any political cartoon, whether contemporary or historical. We suggest that you use this worksheet with your students as they seek to interpret this cartoon.

2. Develop a working definition of the word *propaganda* for students. Discuss with students its major techniques (e.g., name calling, glittering generalities). In light of this discussion, consider Secretary of State Acheson's remark that Soviet peace proposals were "Trojan Doves."

3. Cartoonists portray people, nations, and ideas by the use of visual metaphors. For example, United States cartoonists often represent the Soviets with sinister images such as a dark, lurking submarine. Direct students to review political cartoons in their textbook and elsewhere that represent the Russians and note how these symbols have changed.

SNORKEL APPARATUS

RUSSIAN PEACE PROPAGANDA

RUSSIAN INTENTIONS

MINNEAPOLIS TRIBUNE

4. Nuclear freeze propositions have been issues in presidential election campaigns. Direct students to find out each candidate's position on this issue and discuss their findings in class. For information on the nuclear freeze issue, see *Social Education,* November/December 1983.

5. Under Presidents Nixon, Ford, and Carter, U.S.-U.S.S.R. disarmament negotiations were known as S.A.L.T. President Reagan restructured and renamed these discussions S.T.A.R.T. Direct students to investigate the nature of these discussions and their current status.

N.B. To learn more about current United Nations disarmament efforts, contact the United Nations Information Center, 1889 F Street, N.W., Washington, DC 20006. Request its most current "Fact Sheet" on disarmament. Fact Sheet No. 29 contains an excellent bibliography on the subject.

Constitutional Issues: Federalism

Federalism has been an integral part of the American system of government since its inception. Our Constitution divides governmental power between the national government and the state governments, giving substantial functions to each. As Frederick Ogg points out, the relation between these two centers of power is dynamic, not static, and "must be readjusted and reshaped by each generation to meet the changing needs of our society." In response to these changing needs, our federal system has evolved from a relationship of near equality at the formation of the Union to one of national dominance today.

The generation that lived in the years just before the Civil War struggled with this evolution. Their challenge was to balance the power relation between the national government and the states during a time of increasing tension over different economic and social systems in the North and South. In an attempt to protect infant industry in the North, the national government imposed tariffs so high that Southerners were forced to purchase what they considered to be inferior goods from the North.

In 1828 the passage of The Tariff of Abominations, as it was called in the South, provoked a constitutional crisis; South Carolina threatened to secede rather than be bound by a law of the national government that it considered null and void. A combination of compromises and threat of force averted the crisis temporarily, but this crisis of state vs. national supremacy was ultimately joined by the secession of the Confederate States from the Union and the war that followed.

The generation of the 1950s also had to define this relationship between states and national government. Because of the centralization of federal power following two world wars and the social welfare legislation of the New Deal, the national government was left with greatly expanded powers. Against this background were set the tensions created by state segregation laws that violated the rights of black Americans under the Constitution. Unlike the crisis of the 19th century, this crisis was settled by the Supreme Court. Beginning with the *Brown* decision, the Supreme Court struck down all state segregation laws that came before it, effectively dismantling long-established customs of the South. On March 12, 1956, 101 members of Congress signed a "Declaration of Constitutional Principles" in which they decried "the Supreme Court's encroachment on rights reserved to the States and to the people, contrary to established law and to the Constitution."

Many white Southerners had broken with Southern political tradition when they voted for the Republican candidate Dwight Eisenhower in 1952 because they believed he would favor states' rights. The document shown here is from just such a supporter. Documents accompanying this letter reveal that W.D. Lawson was "a very highly regarded cotton merchant" who had served as chair of the Citizens for Eisenhower Movement in Gaston County, N.C., in 1952. In his letter Lawson refers to this crisis in federalism. This document is taken from the Eisenhower Presidential Library, Dwight D. Eisenhower, Records as President (White House Central Files 1953-1961), Official File.

January 21st, 1956

General Lucius D. Clay
Citizens for Eisenhower
45 East 47th Street
New York 17, New York

Dear General Clay:- *yof 138-C-6*

    I am in receipt of your letter of January 17th regarding
the reactivation of "The Citizens for Eisenhower" movement.
It is true that many of us in the South contributed a good deal
of our time and money to the election of President Eisenhower
in 1952. It was our thought by so doing we would revert to our
original constitutional form of government. President Eisenhower
and his Attorney General have pressed for changes in the educational system of our section, which many of us think are as
unconstitutional as anything done under the new deal. I think
I speak for many of President Eisenhower's former followers when
I say that the central government in Washington has no authority
to tell us who shall, or who shall not, attend the schools which
have been erected and whose teachers are paid wholly by the
citizens of this state.

    Being an independent voter, I had hoped that the large vote
cast for President Eisenhower in the South presaged a two party
system for it. The complete disregard of states rights by the
present administration, in my opinion, has killed all chances
of this improvement in our political situation.

    While many of us still hold President Eisenhower in the
highest esteem, and shall vote for him, you may be sure that the
above facts have cooled our enthusiasm considerably. I am sorry
that I cannot associate myself wholeheartedly with another
movement seeking his reelection.

                                Very truly yours,

                                W. D. Lawson

yof 142-A
yof 142-A-4

Teaching Suggestions

Analyzing Tone

1. Share with students the background information. Include background for *Brown* v. *The Board of Education,* federalism, and traditional Southern voting patterns.

2. Ask students to read the letter and answer the following questions.

a. What did Lawson hope would happen when he supported President Eisenhower in 1952?

b. What events had happened to cool his enthusiasm?

c. What might he mean by the following phrases?

- "revert to our original constitutional form of government"
- "pressed for changes in the educational system of our section"
- "disregard of states rights by the present administration . . . has killed all chances for this improvement in our political situation"

Research and Writing

Ask each student to prepare a letter of response to Lawson from President Eisenhower. The letter should reflect Eisenhower's position on school desegregation and deal with Lawson's specific concerns. Ask students first to read about Eisenhower, particularly from biographies of Eisenhower, and attach to their letters a bibliography of the sources they used.

Analyzing Voting Patterns

From the Civil War to World War II the Southern states could be counted on to cast their electoral votes for the Democratic candidate. As the Democratic Party began to champion the cause of civil rights, Southern voting patterns began to change. Ask students to study election maps in their textbooks from 1920 to 1984. Have them make a list of their findings, write them on the board, and write three generalizations about Southern voting patterns from 1920 to 1984 based on their findings.

Forms of Government

1. Listed below are definitions of three forms of constitutional government. Review these with students and explain that different countries use or have used different forms (for example, **unitary:** France, Britain, Israel; **federal:** United States, Australia, Switzerland; **confederation:** United States under the Articles of Confederation).

a. A unitary government is one in which the constitution vests all the power in the central government.

b. A federal government is one in which the constitution divides power between a national government and constituent governments. (In the United States, the constituents are the states.)

c. A confederation is one in which states create by constitutional compact a central government, but do not give it power to regulate the conduct of individual citizens.

2. Divide students into groups of four or five and ask them to create a visual display of one of the three forms of constitutional government. Their display should include the following elements and relationships between elements:

a. central government

b. constituent governments (state governments in the United States)

c. constitution

- source of its power
- how it distributes its power

d. individual citizens and their relationship to central and constituent governments

Rock 'n' Roll Heroes: A Letter to President Eisenhower

Following World War II, the United States experienced three booms that transformed her culture: an economic boom, a technological boom, and a "baby boom." Increased productivity by GIs returning to civilian work triggered a new affluence and a reduced average workweek. This wealth and leisure time, in turn, created a demand for recreational activities. Traditional forms of diversion, such as concerts and theater, could accommodate only a limited number of people. Enterprising businessmen pushed the development of new technologies with applications in entertainment. Columbia Records developed the 33⅓ rpm long-playing (LP) vinyl disc, which was soon followed in the LP field by RCA, which introduced the smaller 45 rpm record. When LPs were introduced in 1948, no company was mass-producing equipment capable of playing them; yet within a few years, high-fidelity and stereophonic sound could be heard on the popular "hi-fi" and "stereo" phonographs. Even more popular than the new sound systems were television sets. In 1947 fewer than 10,000 sets were privately owned, but ten years later, 40 million sets were in use in the United States.

These technological advances brought entertainment to millions. By the 1960s, 179 million Americans were absorbing this mass culture. Significantly, 30 million of them had been born in the previous decade, 1950-60. The "baby boomers," born into a prosperous era, had money to spend and were encouraged by television and radio advertisers to do so. Television also brought the newest in fashion, sports, and music to young viewers across the country. As the oldest of the baby-boom generation reached adolescence, record sales skyrocketed. Since the mid-1950s, the boomer generation has spent billions of dollars on the music of teen romance and youth rebellion that it considers its own — rock 'n' roll.

Rock 'n' roll began as the rhythm and blues music of urban black America. In the years of segregation, R and B, considered unfit for commercial white radio, was played only on black radio stations manned by black disc jockeys, or in segregated theaters. It was rated separately from the rest of popular music. All of this changed in 1951 when Alan Freed of Cleveland decided to share his enthusiasm for Fats Domino, the Drifters, and other black artists. On his radio show, "Moondog's Rock and Roll Party," Freed played recordings by black artists. America's youth liked this new sound and clamored for more. White artists responded to the demand and, in 1954, Bill Haley and the Comets' "Shake, Rattle and Roll" became the first rock 'n' roll record to hit the Top Ten. Soon, each Saturday afternoon, 20 million American teenagers tuned in to Dick Clark's "American Bandstand" television program to see such artists as Chuck Berry and Pat Boone and to learn the latest dance steps.

In 1955 a young truck driver paid $4 to Sun Record Company to cut a personal record as a birthday gift for his mother. Sam Phillips, the owner of Sun Record,

Box 755
Noxon, Mont.

Dear President Eisenhower,

My girlfriend's and I are writting all the way from Montana, We think its bad enough to send Elvis Presley in the Army, but if you cut his side burns off we will just die! you don't no how we fell about him, I really don't see why you have to send him in the Army at all, but we beg you please please don't give him a G. I. hair cut, oh please please don't! If you do we will just about die!

PresLey
PresLey
IS OUR CRY
P-R-E-S-L-E-Y

E. P.
LOVER

Elvis Presley
LOVERS

Linda Kelly
Sherry Bare
Micke Mattson

189

heard the record and immediately signed the Mississippian to a contract. Over the next two years, Elvis Presley's "Hound Dog," "Blue Suede Shoes," and "Heartbreak Hotel" earned him a million dollars. He could not read music and did not compose his own hits, but he had a pleasing voice and, in the opinion of many adolescents, sex appeal. His 1956 appearance on television (above the waist only) drew loud protests (one critic called it "a strip-tease with clothes on") but also brought fame and instant success. By 1959, 21 of Presley's records had sold more than a million copies each. He was not the first entertainer to attract massive adulation (Frank Sinatra had been the bobby-soxers' heartthrob in the 1940s). Although Presley's record sales have fallen before "Beatlemania" and "Jacksonmania," he remains to many "The King" of rock 'n' roll.

In 1958 Presley was inducted into the U.S. Army, where his regular enlisted man's haircut triggered hysteria among many of his youthful admirers. The document reproduced here is a March 1958 letter from three concerned fans to President Eisenhower, from the Dwight D. Eisenhower Presidential Library in Abilene, Kansas.

Teaching Suggestions

1. Introduce the document by placing it in the foregoing context for the students. Discuss the contents of the document and ask students to hypothesize how the letter was treated by the White House. Have students write a letter in response to this request as if Eisenhower were writing it.

2. Ask students to interview adults about their recollections of the early years of rock 'n' roll. Students may want to start with parents and teachers and reach out to local disc jockeys and record store managers.

3. Discuss with students the current registration law. Pose to them the problem of whether artists should be exempt from military service or should be given special assignments if required to serve in the Armed Forces. The format for this discus-

sion might be a debate between spokespersons for each side.

4. Ask students to select a matter of personal concern and write a letter about it to a public official. Work on revisions as needed, then review the final copy when it is turned in with a stamped envelope addressed to the official involved. Mail all letters. Later you may want to have students share and discuss responses to their letters.

5. Assign oral reports with audio and/or visual components under the theme of Heroes of Youth Culture. Subjects might include Frank Sinatra, Elvis Presley, Paul Anka, the Beatles, or Michael Jackson. Students should investigate what their artistic accomplishments have been, why they became popular, what impact they have had on popular culture, and how they might be viewed in the future. Students could be expected to locate samples of these artists' work, to integrate the samples into their presentations, and to analyze the implications and meaning of the samples.

6. Assign students to investigate selected aspects of rock 'n' roll in music history. Students may wish to examine the effects of segregation on music; how traditional gospel, hillbilly, and ballad music have been adapted to rock 'n' roll; or how technology from LP to video has changed popular music. Students may present their research in the form of a paper or oral report.

Note: *Bye-Bye Birdie*, a musical stage show and movie, is the fictionalized account of Presley-mania. Reading the script or attending a film or stage performance would serve as a delightful enrichment activity or culminating exercise for the study of the youth culture of the 1950s.

Bibliography

Berkin, Carol, and Leonard Wood. *Land of Promise*. Glenview, IL: Scott, Foresman and Company, 1983.

Bivins, Betty, Robynn Greer, Bruce Kraig, and Philip Roden, *Life and Liberty*.

Glenview, IL: Scott, Foresman and Company, 1984.

Curti, Merle, and Lewis Todd. *Rise of the American Nation.* New York: Harcourt Brace Jovanovich, 1982.

Haywood, Terry, and Norman Risjord. *People and Our Country.* New York: Holt, Rinehart and Winston, Publishers, 1978.

Rawls, James, and Philip Weeks. *Land of Liberty.* New York: Holt, Rinehart and Winston, Publishers, 1985.

Smith, Lew. *American Dream.* Glenview, IL: Scott, Foresman and Company, 1983.

It's in the Cards: Archives and Baseball

Baseball cards are part of the experience of millions of Americans. They are the physical embodiment of dreams and thus usually represent a solid and positive part of childhood memories. Even if we ourselves have never saved, flipped, or collected cards, we know someone who has or continues to do so. The current card-collecting craze furnishes evidence of its allure for both young and old.

Picture cards supplied with the purchase of merchandise go back at least to the 1880s, when sepia-toned, cardboard-backed photographs of sports stars began to accompany certain tobacco products.

By the 1930s, chewing gum and other manufacturers had also entered the market, but it was not until 1952 that the first really modern baseball cards like the one pictured here were issued. These cards, manufactured by Topps Chewing Gum, Inc., of Brooklyn, New York, were 2½ by 3½ inches and provided color photographs of each major leaguer on one side and full statistical and biographical data on the other.

They proved small enough to fit into a T-shirt pocket or back pocket, large enough to contain entrancing facts, eye-catching enough to provide visual appeal, and sturdy enough to withstand flipping contests and inventory reviews. In short, they were just what kids wanted.

Baseball's Appeal

In the 1950s and 1960s, a number of different developments widened baseball's appeal. Teams expanded, both in number and location of franchises, and an even greater audience was reached when net-works began to televise major league games. The infusion of outstanding black and Latin players raised the caliber of play. Growing numbers of affluent and impressionable youngsters became interested in the game and wanted reminders of the heroes they saw, heard, or read about. Topps was willing to provide those reminders to the baby boomers — along with its bubble gum.

Consequently, within a few years, Topps, using scouts to canvass and sign all likely major league prospects, controlled the bubble gum card industry. Today the company has multibillion-dollar sales, largely from its continued dominance in the sale of baseball cards.

The player depicted in one of Topps' 1959 issues is Saturnino Orestes Arrieta Armas "Minnie" Minoso, a Cuban who played his first professional game as a member of the Negro National League's New York Cuban Giants.

Minnie, as colorful as his many names and — as the document's statistics suggest — capable of generating hits, stolen bases, and runs in profusion, was one of the first truly dark-skinned Latin Americans to play in the big leagues. Before Jackie Robinson integrated the major leagues, only the lightest-hued Latin Americans were admitted to the majors, whatever their abilities.

Playing in a distinguished and often brilliant fashion, Minoso, "the Cuban Comet," performed primarily for the Cleveland Indians and Chicago White Sox until his active playing career ended in 1964. In 1976 and again in 1980, while serving as a coach

minnie minoso

CLEVELAND INDIANS
OUTFIELD

MINNIE AND COLAVITO HERE THE 2ND R.B.I. POWER COMBINATION IN THE A.L. IN 1958

80 MINNIE MINOSO

HT: 5'10" WT: 175 BATS: R
THROWS: R BORN: 11/29/23
HOME: MARIANAO, CUBA

Fleet-footed Minnie swapped White Sox flannels for an Indian uniform last year and had another fine season. He's led the A.L. in steals three times.

YEAR	TEAM	LEA.	G	AB	R	H	2B	3B	HR	RBI	AVG.
1948	Dayton	Cent.	11	40	14	21	7	1	1	8	.525
1949	Cleveland	A. L.	9	16	2	3	0	0	1	1	.188
1949	San Diego	P. C.	137	532	99	158	19	7	22	75	.297
1950	San Diego	P. C.	169	599	130	203	40	10	20	115	.339
1951	Cleve.-Chi.	A. L.	146	530	112	173	34	14	10	76	.326
1952	Chicago	A. L.	147	569	96	160	24	9	13	61	.281
1953	Chicago	A. L.	151	556	104	174	24	8	15	104	.313
1954	Chicago	A. L.	153	568	119	182	29	18	19	116	.320
1955	Chicago	A. L.	139	517	79	149	26	7	10	70	.288
1956	Chicago	A. L.	151	545	106	172	29	11	21	88	.316
1957	Chicago	A. L.	153	568	96	176	36	5	12	103	.310
1958	Cleveland	A. L.	149	556	94	168	25	2	24	80	.302
Major League Totals		9 Yrs.	1198	4425	808	1357	227	74	125	699	.307

State Department Briefing Notebook for President Eisenhower

Jet travel has transformed visits of heads of state to other countries into commonplace events. However, trips like those of President Nixon to China or Egypt's President Sadat to Israel have special significance. Soviet Premier Nikita Khrushchev's visit to the United States in 1959 was both unique for its time and significant because of the tensions between the United States and the Soviet Union in Berlin. The document reproduced here is two pages of a five-page State Department briefing notebook prepared for President Eisenhower to outline the issues to be raised with the Soviet leader, including analysis of the latter's point of view and suggested tactics for the President to use in conveying positions of the United States.

On August 3, 1959, President Eisenhower announced that Nikita Khrushchev would visit the United States in September. In preparation for the Khrushchev visit, Eisenhower took a trip to reassure the leaders of France, Germany, and Great Britain that the Soviet leader's visit would not result in unacceptable commitments. The NATO leaders were especially wary of the Soviets' intentions because of the breakdown of the talks of the foreign ministers in March and the Soviet ultimatum regarding Berlin the preceding year.

In November 1958, the Soviet Union had demanded the departure of the allied forces from Berlin in six months. If the Western powers did not leave, Khrushchev threatened to recognize the government of East Germany, thereby formally partitioning the territory of Germany, and to restrict Western access to Berlin. When the six months had elapsed, the Soviets did not act, but unhappy memories of the Berlin airlift ten years before came into sharp focus. In this tense international climate, Nikita Khrushchev arrived in Washington, DC, to visit the United States for twelve days.

Khrushchev's itinerary was a full one. After his welcome to the United States with the usual formal exchange dinners at the White House, the Communist Party Chairman set off to see this country under the able guidance of the U.S. Ambassador to the United Nations, Henry Cabot Lodge. Khrushchev and his family visited New York City, Los Angeles, San Francisco, Des Moines, and Pittsburgh. As planned, Khrushchev saw a substantial segment of the American people and they saw him. However, the trip was not without its misadventures. In Los Angeles, the Chairman expressed shock at the "immoral" clothing of the dancers in *Can-Can* and rage at being denied a visit to Disneyland for security reasons. Perhaps the most enduring image of Khrushchev was that of the Party Chairman amidst the corn on a farm in Iowa, a scene captured in hundreds of photographs.

On September 27, Khrushchev arrived back in Washington and retired to the presidential retreat at Camp David for talks with President Eisenhower. The State Department memorandum suggested a theme for the discussions:

The major task of modern statesmanship is to find a way to relieve the threat of destruction which weapons of mass destruction have hung over mankind. Khrushchev can make a great contribution to this task and will be so judged by history, not by how much power he can amass and wield. Continued Soviet pressures will, of course, meet our determined resistance and the risk of war will remain and probably increase.

To Eisenhower's delight, Khrushchev agreed, as a result of the talks at Camp David, to relax the Berlin ultimatum. On the Chairman's return to the Soviet Union, simultaneous announcements were made withdrawing the ultimatum entirely. The two superpowers had faced off and withdrawn without serious consequence, and Eisenhower had shown to the allies that he could be a diplomat as well as a general. At home, Eisenhower's popularity rose to its highest point since his re-election three years earlier.

This spirit was not to last, however, for in May 1960 the Soviets announced that they had shot down an American U-2 spy plane and were holding the pilot, Francis Gary Powers. As a result, Eisenhower's trip to the Soviet Union was canceled, and tensions between the nations escalated again.

The document is from the Khrushchev Visit Sept. '59 (2) File, Box 48, International Series, Dwight D. Eisenhower, Papers as President, 1953-61, Dwight David Eisenhower Presidential Library, Abilene, Kansas.

Teaching Activities

1. Introduce the document by placing it in context for the students. Tell them who wrote the memorandum, to whom it was written, when it was written, and for what purpose. Explain "the present situation" referred to in the document. Discuss with students the "dangers" implicit in the situation and the strategies that the memorandum outlined for the President. Students should then restate Khrushchev's probable points in their own words.

2. Many terms mentioned in this document need to be identified for students. Ask the students to locate the following terms in the memorandum: balance of power, Soviet bloc, arms limitation, peaceful co-existence, "Foreign Affairs," bilateral relations, re-militarization, summit conference, and Camp David. Using the resources in the classroom (textbooks and reference books), ask students to explain each term.

3. Discuss with students the elements of competition. You might use sports as a frame of reference, keeping in mind that there are differences as well as similarities in an analogy. Direct students to apply these elements to U.S.-U.S.S.R. relations in the 1950s and early 1960s. They should consider: the goals and objectives, the ground rules, the areas of competition, the strategies, the victories and defeats for both sides, and the consequences of competition. They should discuss how these considerations affect foreign relations.

4. Develop a definition of "agenda" with the students. What is the purpose of an agenda? Who frequently uses an agenda? Why is an agenda useful? Direct students to attend a meeting where an agenda is used. Give students the worksheet to complete.

5. After researching the situations in Berlin and Laos in the late 1950s, students should write a summary of the events preceding Khrushchev's visit to the United States. They should then discuss the United States' commitments to Berlin and Laos mentioned in the document, and the changes in United States policy toward the Communist world as defined by Secretary

S E C R E T

KHV D-0/2

September 11, 1959

U. S. Objectives in Khrushchev Visit and
Suggested Tactics for Conversation with Him

I. **Occasions for Talks**

A. Initial call, afternoon of Khrushchev's arrival
(3:30 - 5:00 p.m.) September 15.

B. Weekend at Camp David, September 25 (6:00 p.m.) to
September 27 (12:00 noon).

C. At larger gatherings: President's dinner, September 15,
and Khrushchev's dinner, September 16.

II. **U. S. Objectives**

Our key purpose should be to impress on Khrushchev the urgent
need of a serious search for ways to reduce the dangers inherent in the present situation and of seeking an acceptable
basis for improved relations.

In pursuing this purpose we should try:

A. To make Khrushchev understand that, if the USSR continues
to act on its view that the balance of power is shifting
to the Soviet bloc and to attempt to enforce its will on
non-Communist countries (Berlin and Laos are current examples), the risks of war will increase as we intend to
honor our commitments. Arms limitation and control will
then become difficult if not impossible and the U.S. will
be forced to intensify its defense preparations.

B. To convince Khrushchev of our sincere interest in arms control but to make it unmistakably clear that adequate inspection and control is the minimum price at which it can
be achieved.

C. To point out the benefits to both sides of better relations but to emphasize that competition in peaceful
fields must be conducted according to accepted ground
rules applicable to both sides.

III. Probable

SECRET

DECLASSIFIED
Authority _STATE DEPT. LTR_
Date _6/10/76_
By _OJH_, NARS Date _6/28/76_

III. Probable Khrushchev Line

Khrushchev will press for "peaceful co-existence." His recent speeches and his article in "Foreign Affairs" as well as the current Soviet line suggest that he will make or imply the following points:

   A. The world must recognize that Soviet power guarantees the permanence of existing Communist regimes. "Peaceful competition" must proceed elsewhere.

   B. Expanded trade is the best road to improved U.S.-Soviet relations.

   C. U. S. bases abroad are the major impediment to agreement on arms control and to better bilateral relations.

   D. "Re-militarization" of Germany is the major threat to peace and to progress on the German question.

   E. A summit conference should be convened to discuss vital issues as decisions can only be reached on that level.

IV. Agenda

   A. Khrushchev's initial call is scheduled for 3:30-5:00 p.m. The President might wish to cut it short and propose a helicopter tour of Washington.

   The primary goal of this conversation would be to make Khrushchev receptive to serious talks at Camp David.

   1. The conversation could open with some informal welcoming remarks and brief general conversation on Khrushchev's tour of the country. We tried to meet his desires and trust he finds the arrangements satisfactory. We would have preferred that it afford greater opportunity to meet broader and more varied sectors of our country and society. We hope he will come to understand the principles and convictions which motivate and guide our people as well as see how widely distributed are the benefits of our productive labors. Our papers, radio and TV are prepared to cover his trip thoroughly, but we hope

that

Worksheet for Activity 4

Date and time of meeting _____

Name of group or committee _____

Items on the agenda _____

_____

_____

_____

_____

_____

Evaluation: In what ways did the agenda seem to you to make the meeting easier?

_____

_____

_____

_____

_____

When would you find an agenda useful in your own activities?

_____

of State John Foster Dulles. Students might mention some additional examples of "honoring our commitments" in the world (e.g., Vietnam, Grenada). As a follow-up to Activity 5, ask the students to look again at page 1 of the document, item II-A. Examine with them the language of the item and the implications of phrases like "to make Khrushchev understand," "the risks of war," "we intend to honor our commitments," and "forced to intensify."

6. In a 1959 article which appeared in *Foreign Affairs,* Khrushchev defined peaceful co-existence as "peaceful competition for the purpose of satisfying man's needs in the best possible way." Divide the class into small groups to make lists of ways countries of such differing systems as capitalism and communism can compete without resorting to arms. Recognize the group with the best list.

7. Ask the librarian or media specialist for photographs, films, or written descriptions of the two world leaders. Using the material available, ask students to (a) study the examples for mannerisms, voice quality, and other clues to personality, (b) carefully read the document again for the tactics outlined for Eisenhower and the positions expected from Khrushchev, and (c) choose a partner and role-play the initial conversation between the two leaders.

Note: Learning Corporation of America has published a film entitled "Khrushchev: The Bear's Embrace" as part of a series, *Leaders of the Twentieth Century: Portraits of Power.* Other useful sources of information for this activity are students' parents and other adults.

No Religious Test: A Letter to Candidate John F. Kennedy

Among the records kept in the historic courthouse of Fairfax County, Virginia, is an oath that officeholders in 1751-52 were required to sign. Public servants declared that there was no transubstantiation "in the sacrament of the eucharist or in the elements of bread and wine at or after the consecration thereof." This religious test thus excluded Roman Catholics from public office in Fairfax County, and its use was the rule rather than the exception in colonial America.

Following the Revolutionary War and the disestablishment of the Church of England in the United States, however, many states adopted measures to promote greater religious toleration. The national government, too, advanced religious freedom, first in the Northwest Ordinance, then in the Constitution, and finally in the First Amendment. Article VI of the U.S. Constitution stipulated "No religious test shall ever be required as a qualification to any office or public trust under the United States." This measure was far too radical for the states, most of which retained in their constitutions religious tests for state office. These persisted as late as 1961, when Maryland's requirement that officeholders declare a belief in God was challenged and found unconstitutional. In *Torasco* v. *Watkins*, 367 U.S. 488, the Court unanimously ruled that the "religious test for public office unconstitutionally invades the appellant's freedom of belief and religion and therefore cannot be enforced against him."

A more insidious evasion of the Constitution's prohibition against religious tests was the informal requirement for public office that candidates belong to a mainstream Protestant sect. Because members of other religions were prevented from seeking and holding office, they were relegated to second-class citizenship, compromising the integrity of the government.

The presidential election of 1928, which was marred by religious bigotry, illustrates this informal test. The Democrats nominated New York Governor Alfred E. Smith, a Roman Catholic of Irish extraction, as their candidate for President. Conservative Protestants turned his religion into a political issue, claiming that Smith, if elected, would be a puppet of the pope. Smith rebutted in a May 1927 article in *Atlantic Monthly*.

What is this conflict about which you talk? It may exist in some lands which do not guarantee religious freedom. But in the wildest dreams of your imagination you cannot conjure up a possible conflict between religious principle and political duty in the United States except on the unthinkable hypothesis that some law were to be passed which violated the common morality of all God-fearing men. And if you can conjure up such a conflict, how would a Protestant resolve it? Obviously by the dictates of his conscience. That is exactly what a Catholic would do. There is no ecclesiastical tribunal

203

which would have the slightest claim upon the obedience of Catholic communicants in the resolution of such a conflict.

Smith's distinguished record as a public servant bore out his assertion that the religious issue was a straw man; but the Republicans did little to dispel the slurs against Smith, and their nominee, Herbert Hoover, won the election in a landslide.

It was not until 1960 that the nation was asked to reconsider its decision of 1928. John F. Kennedy, another Roman Catholic, had swayed voters even in Protestant strongholds such as West Virginia, defeated Protestant candidates, and won the Democratic Party's nomination for the presidency. Nonetheless, his faith was an issue in the campaign. Kennedy's most important speech on religion and public service was made before the Greater Houston Ministerial Association in Houston, Texas, on September 12, 1960. In part, he said, "I am not the Catholic candidate for President. I am the Democratic Party's candidate for President who happens also to be a Catholic. I do not speak for my Church on public matters — and the Church does not speak for me . . . [I]f the time should ever come — and I do not concede any conflict to be even remotely possible — when my office would require me to either violate my conscience or violate the national interest, then I would resign the office; and I hope any conscientious public servant would do the same . . . [I]f this election is decided on the basis that 40 million Americans lost their chance of being President on the day they were baptized, then it is the whole Nation that will be the loser." When Kennedy won the election, it was viewed by many as a victory for religious freedom.

The issue of religious tests did not end in 1960. By the 1980s, Christian evangelicals emerged as a political force. Public response to former ministers' candidacies, including presidential candidates Pat Robertson and Jesse Jackson, has raised new questions about religion and public office.

The featured document comes from the John F. Kennedy Presidential Library. Kennedy received so many letters on religious issues that a staff member was assigned to handle the load. This document is a particularly thoughtful example selected from the many letters sent to the candidate in response to his speech to Houston's ministers. (Document on next two pages.)

Teaching Activities

1. To ensure a close reading of the document, ask students to write responses to these questions:

   a. Who wrote the letter?

   b. To whom was the letter written?

   c. What is the date of the letter?

   d. Why, according to the author, has she written the letter?

   e. What advice does she give Senator Kennedy?

   f. What is the tone or attitude of the letter?

   g. List the major points made in the letter about anti-Catholic feeling.

   h. Do you think the letter would have been helpful to Senator Kennedy? Why or why not?

   Follow up with a class discussion of the questions and responses.

2. Examine Article VI of the Constitution with your students. Ask them to think about examples of religious tests that may have been used in the past. One or two students could research the *Torasco* v. *Watkins* case and report to the class. Ask all students to find other instances when minorities have been officially or informally excluded from participation in the democratic process.

3. Ask students to refer to the Constitution and to list the formal qualifications of the office of president of the United States. Have students brainstorm the informal qualifications of the first 10 presidents. Then consider the first 20 and list the informal qualifications for them. Then consider the first 30 and, finally, take all presidents to the present and list informal qualifications. (The list should shrink over four examinations.) Ask students to hy-

Sept. 16th, 1960

SEP 19 1960 *Rel*

cv 7

Dear Senator Kennedy,

Although a lifelong Democrat, I was only lukewarm about your candidacy until the other night when your appearance before the Texas ministers was shown on television. In the event that you win the election, I hope you are as much a man of honesty and principle as you appeared to be. Also I hope that you were not too much disheartened by what seems to be downright religious prejudice. Besides letting you know that you have made a favorable impression on me, I also write to try to explain to you what may be some of the reasons behind the Texans' seeming stubborness.

As I was born and raised in a protestant family in Missouri, attended a Catholic school where I made the top grades in Cathechism and Bible History, and married into an orthodox Jewish family, I believe I have a well-sampled background from which to consider this question. You probably have not had much experience with the small-town Mid-westerner or Southerner, but perhaps your advisers will include those who understand this point of view.

Can you imagine the thin line of difference between outright religious prejudice, and a reluctance to turn over political control to one of a minority group? I believe the gentlemen in Texas sensed your honesty and have no fear that you yourself would in any way be controlled in office by your religious superiors. These same gentlemen may well include among their friends and fellow club members Catholics of all degrees. It may be that they would not countenance any prejudice in employment, selection for schools, clubs, etc., or any religious requirements, explicit or implied, for any non-political function.

No, this is not exactly the same problem as is usually referred to as religious prejudice. You have to look into the possible local experiences, not maybe as they actually exist, but as they seem to the local person. Their approach and frame of reference is necessarily different from yours. What are the reasons that they hold this reluctance? Well, it seems to an average small-town Mid-western Protestant that he has certain reasons to resent the Catholic church and the way they do business on a local level.

In the first place, he has the uncomfortable feeling that the Catholic Church regards him as inferior in some way to Catholics, -- damned, as it were. This in itself is enough to make the average man furious. The other reasons follow along in the same category. The school that his children go to is not considered good enough for the Catholic children. His boys and girls are not good enough to marry Catholics unless his grandchildren are "swallowed up" by the Church. He hears that in "Catholic" states the laws on birth control and divorce force Protestants to follow the Catholic beliefs in these respects. He may have experienced the fact that the Catholic Church would not join in the All-City endeavors, and since he is probably a great enthusiast for Togetherness, this has left the impression that the Catholic groups are irrevocably on the "other" side.

Advisers: Please refer this letter to Senator Kennedy.

Also, this man has heard of countries in which the Catholic church is in the majority and does not accord to Protestants much in the way of political support. The Protestant American may feel that the Catholic countries run hand in hand with poverty of the masses, superstition, reliance on miracles, over-breeding in the lower classes, gambling, drinking, lack of education, dishonesty among the clergy, etc. I am just trying to give at random some of the evils which, rightly or wrongly, may be linked in this persons mind with the Catholic Church.

I am sure the average man respects you for your religious faith, and he probably has no clear idea of what connection, if any, this has with your holding the Presidency. Sadly enough, many of our voters are probably not capable enough or conscientious enough to think through this matter clearly. He only knows that he is "reluctant". Of course there are those also who are really guilty of outright prejudice; but I am speaking of those who are otherwise free from prejudice and yet hold this political reluctance.

Please do not misunderstand my point. I am **not** trying to state the case for this point of view. I am only trying to help you to see what you have to face in this faceless, nameless body who will not "vote for a Catholic" and who will, on the other hand, not say they won't , for fear of being accused of religious prejudice.

Also, I am trying to soothe, in some small way, that sick feeling that you must have in the pit of your stomach after your exposure to this seeming rotten core of our American public.

Remember that the American people, west of the Appalachians and outside the cities, have strong reasons for not wanting Catholic power and policy to grow. However, also remember that among people of education, intelligence and good will, it is becoming more and more possible to live together and respect all views.

To me, your religious views are of no importance except as they show your honesty, strength of character, unwillingness to compromise for expediency. We desperately need a man of strong moral fiber. Your strong personal ambition and rapid rise make me suspect undue compromise. I hope this isn't true. For the preservation of the world, I hope you will be a strong leader and that God (and Gov. Stevenson) will be at your side.

In dealing with the other peoples of the world, try to under_stand them and their differences as you would have the American people understand you and yours.

God bless you,

Sincerely,

Mrs. Robert Alexander

Mrs. Robert Alexander
4 W 93, apt. 3A
New York, 25, N. Y.

pothesize reasons for former attitudes that Catholics were not suited for civil office. Assign to a pair of students a project for researching the "Catholic issue" in the campaigns of Al Smith and John F. Kennedy. Ask students to account for differences and similarities between the two campaigns.

4. The recent presidential election raised new questions about religion and public office. Divide the class into groups of three to five students, and ask them to draft election guidelines for political campaigns that would allow people, including religious leaders and nonbelievers, to seek public office.

A Literacy Test

As a result of the Civil War, Afro-Americans secured the right to vote through the passage of the Fifteenth Amendment to the Constitution (1870). After the close of the Reconstruction era, however, Southern states instituted various policies to restrict the voting rights of blacks. These restrictions included poll taxes, white primaries, property requirements, literacy tests, and the grandfather clause. Although these qualifications were strictly applied to blacks, ways were provided for most whites to bypass the requirements. In some cases, however, these restrictions also kept poor and illiterate whites from exercising their franchise.

In 1901, the State of Alabama passed a state constitutional amendment by which voters were required to pay a poll tax, and either own property or pass a literacy test. These restrictions assured that in some way many blacks could be kept off voting lists. However, in 1949, a Federal District Court outlawed literacy tests in Alabama. Rising to defend a long-standing practice, a 1951 state statute subsequently instituted local control over voter registration, authorizing local registrars to develop and administer local literacy tests at their discretion. By 1964 the State of Alabama had developed one hundred standard literacy tests, from which local registrars selected one to test a voter's literacy. The literacy test reproduced here, submitted as an exhibit before the Senate in hearings on the 1965 Voting Rights Act, is one of these tests. The passage of the Voting Rights Act (August 6, 1965) thereafter prohibited all such tests and devices as prerequisites for voting.

This document is found in *Proceedings of the Committee on the Judiciary of the United States Senate, Eighty-Ninth Congress, First Session on S. 1564*, March 23-April 5, 1965. U.S. Government Printing Office, Washington, DC, 1965. Hearings held April 2, 1965, p. 762.

Suggestions for Teaching

You may choose to use Activity 1 or Activity 2, or elements of both. The culminating activities are suggested for use with either activity.

1. *The Document as a Reading Tool*

a. Administer the literacy test to the class. Limit the amount of time students have to complete the test.

b. Review students' responses and discuss them with respect to the following:

Have the students ever taken this type of test?

How did the students proceed to take such a test?

c. Review the literacy test with the class by having the students do the following:

• Identify the components of the test. How are they arranged?

• Identify unfamiliar words, phrases, etc.

• Identify elements of the context in which the above appear which may explain their meaning.

• Describe the style of writing of the excerpts and the questions. How are they similar or different? (Consider sentence structure, vocabulary, punctuation, etc.)

• Discuss how this type of review might facilitate taking the test.

2. *The Document in History*

Repeat steps a and b for Activity 1.

Have students review the test by discussing the following:

• Why would such a test be given?

• What level of literacy could be determined by such a test?

• Is it fair, logical, or practical to use excerpts from the Constitution to test literacy? Why or why not?

• What is functional literacy? Would it be a good basis for determining voter qualification?

• Should literacy be a requirement for voting? Why or why not?

EXCERPTS FROM THE CONSTITUTION

Part 1. In case of the removal of the president from office, or of his death, resignation, or inability to discharge the powers and duties of the said office, the same shall devolve on the vice-president, and the congress may by law provide for the case of removal, death, resignation or inability, both of the president and vice-president, declaring what officer shall then act as president, and such officer shall act accordingly, until the disability be removed, or a president shall be elected.

Part 2. In all cases affecting ambassadors, other public ministers and consuls, and those in which a state shall be a party, the supreme court shall have original jurisdiction.

Part 3. In all the other cases before mentioned, the supreme court shall have appellate jurisdiction, both as to law and fact, with such exceptions, and under such regulations as the congress shall make.

Part 4. Neither slavery nor involuntary servitude, except as a punishment for crime whereof the party shall have been duly convicted, shall exist within the United States, or any place subject to their jurisdiction.

INSTRUCTION "C"

(After applicant has read, not aloud, the foregoing excerpts from the Constitution, he will answer the following questions in writing and without assistance:)

1. In case the president is unable to perform the duties of his office, who assumes them? _____

2. "Involuntary servitude" is permitted in the United States upon conviction of a crime. (True or False) _____

3. If a state is a party to a case, the constitution provides that original jurisdiction shall be in _____

4. Congress passes laws regulating cases which are included in those over which the United States Supreme Court has _____ jurisdiction.

I hereby certify that I have received no assistance in the completion of this citizenship and literacy test, that I was allowed the time I desired to complete it, and that I waive any right existing to demand a copy of same. (If for any reason the applicant does not wish to sign this, he must discuss the matter with the board of registrars.)

Signed: _____

(Applicant)

• What was the purpose of voting registration qualifications?

• What voting qualifications exist today?

Culminating Activities

Discuss the background information with students. Assist students in developing a role-play situation based on the background information and the test. Students might begin by setting up a voter registration office, selecting registrar(s) and proctor(s), supplying information related to an election that would have occurred, for example, before 1965. Or have students develop a literacy test to be administered to classmates prior to a real or simulated class election. Have students evaluate the test as a "test" and as a measure of the students' ability to vote intelligently.

"On Your Mark . . . Get Set . . . Go!" — The Space Race

On April 12, 1961, the Soviet Union launched the first manned space vehicle into orbit around the earth. With cosmonaut Yuri A. Gagarin's 108-minute flight, the Soviets captured another first in the space race. The press release featured here is the text of President John F. Kennedy's telegram to Nikita Khrushchev congratulating the Soviets on the first successful manned flight.

In October 1957 the Soviet Union had opened the space race by placing a 184-pound satellite, Sputnik I, in orbit around the earth. Sputnik immediately captured the imagination and interest of the public around the world, but its appearance was no surprise to the international scientific community.

The Soviet's launching of a second satellite within a month nurtured public interest in space exploration. The second satellite weighed over 1,000 pounds and carried Laika, a Husky dog, to measure the effects of weightlessness on a living organism. In January 1958 the U.S. joined the Soviets in space with the successful launching of an 18-pound satellite, Explorer I.

The success of Gagarin's flight accentuated the disparity between U.S. and Soviet commitments to developing space technology. Since World War II, the Soviets had concentrated their technological efforts on developing massive booster rockets to launch large payloads outside the earth's atmosphere. The United States, in contrast, did not unify its research and development efforts in space technology until President Eisenhower created the National Aeronautics and Space Administration in 1958. In his April 12, 1961, news conference, President Kennedy responded to reporters' inquiries on the subject of Soviet leadership in the space race in this way:

> . . . a dictatorship enjoys advantages in this kind of competition over a short period by its ability to mobilize its resources for a specific purpose. We have made some exceptional scientific advances in the last decade, and some of them—they are not as spectacular as the man-in-space, or as the first Sputnik, but they are important.[1]

In less than a year, U.S. astronaut John H. Glenn, Jr., would orbit the earth three times, becoming the first American to do so.

In a special message on national goals delivered to Congress in May 1961, President Kennedy acknowledged the Soviet challenge in space and declared that landing a man on the moon was a national goal to be met by the end of the decade. Astronaut Neil Armstrong would step onto the moon July 20, 1969, five months before President Kennedy's deadline. At the opening of the 1970s, the space race score between the United States and the Soviet Union appeared even.

[1] J. F. Kennedy, *Public Papers of the President of the United States,* 1961 (Washington, DC: U.S. Government Printing Office, 1962), p. 261.

IMMEDIATE RELEASE   April 12, 1961

Office of the White House Press Secretary
- -

THE WHITE HOUSE

FOLLOWING IS THE TEXT OF THE
PRESIDENT'S TELEGRAM TO THE
CHAIRMAN OF THE COUNCIL OF
MINISTERS, UNION OF SOVIET
SOCIALIST REPUBLICS, N.S.
KHRUSHCHEV:

12 April 1961

The people of the United States share with the people of the Soviet
Union their satisfaction for the safe flight of the astronaut in man's
first venture into space. We congratulate you and the Soviet scien-
tists and engineers who made this feat possible. It is my sincere
desire that in the continuing quest for knowledge of outer space our
nations can work together to obtain the greatest benefit to mankind.

John F. Kennedy

# # # # # # #

U.S.-U.S.S.R. Cooperation

In his telegram to Khrushchev, President Kennedy referred to cooperation between the two nations. This proposition would become reality in two areas — space law and a joint space mission. In 1966 the United States and the Soviet Union signed an agreement to protect the free use of outer space by all nations and to prohibit its military use. This accord was the basis for an international treaty approved by the United Nations General Assembly and ratified by 62 nations in 1967. In 1971 the United States and the Soviet Union began a cooperative space project, which resulted in July 1975 in the launching of U.S. and U.S.S.R. space vehicles that docked in outer space. The Apollo-Soyuz mission brought together three U.S. astronauts and two Soviet cosmonauts, who conducted joint scientific experiments in space. Eighteen years after opening the space race, the fierce competitors came together as teammates.

The document featured here is from "Space — Man in Space, 1961": Subject Files, 1958-1961; Records of the Office of Science and Technology, Record Group 359.

Teaching Activities

I. Library Scavenger Hunt

Use the document to help students explore the resources of the school or public library. Direct students to find the answers to these questions raised by the document. The answers to most of these questions are available in reference books located in your school or public library.

1. What was the name of the astronaut mentioned in the document?

2. What was the name of his spacecraft?

3. Locate the birthplace of the Russian astronaut on a map of the Soviet Union.

4. How many republics make up the Union of Soviet Socialist Republics?

5. Who was the White House Press Secre-tary in April 1961?

6. How long had N.S. Khrushchev been Chairman of the Council of Ministers when he received this telegram?

7. What other events occurred on April 12, 1961?

8. Who was the first U.S. astronaut to orbit the earth?

9. How many years before you were born did the first American orbit the earth?

10. In 1961, what was the name of the government agency that directed U.S. space projects?

Answers:

1. Yuri A. Gagarin; 2. Vostok; 3. Gzhatsk in Smolensk; 4. 15; 5. Pierre Salinger; 6. 4 years; 7. variable answer; 8. John H. Glenn, Jr.; 9. variable answers; 10. National Aeronautics and Space Administration (NASA).

II. Issues for Discussion

Consider some of these questions with your students.

1. How did the U.S.-U.S.S.R. space race begin and where is the competition today?

2. The U.S. and U.S.S.R. have not worked together to explore outer space. Develop a list of the reasons why not and an alternate list of potential benefits from such cooperation. Does one list seem more compelling than the other? Why?

3. Do you think space exploration is worth its cost to the U.S. economy?

4. Develop a list of the benefits of space technology to your everyday life.

5. In your lifetime, what has been the most exciting event in space exploration to you? Why?

President Kennedy's Address to the Nation on the James Meredith Case

He was not allowed to attend a major southern university. He was constantly threatened and verbally abused. He was even accused of stealing.

James H. Meredith was black. On January 21, 1961, one day after President John F. Kennedy was inaugurated, Meredith applied for admission to the University of Mississippi. Having attended Jackson State University, the University of Maryland, Washburn University, and the University of Kansas with a record of excellent grades, Meredith felt confident of his decision to apply. However, academic achievement was not his primary reason for applying. The University of Mississippi did not admit blacks. James Meredith wanted to change that.

Meredith wrote a letter requesting information on admission to the registrar's office at the university. He also wrote to the four other universities he had attended, asking that his transcripts be sent to the University of Mississippi. He followed all admission procedures very carefully. On February 21, he enclosed in a second letter a $10 deposit for a room in the men's dormitory. Despite his efforts, the University of Mississippi rejected his application after Meredith informed them in his letter of February 21 that he was black.

The registrar at "Ole Miss," Robert B.

Ellis, wrote Meredith that his application was received after the deadline for registration and was therefore not acceptable. Meredith's room deposit was returned.

Meredith fought back. He again sent the $10 deposit to Ellis, on May 21, requesting that it be used for his stay during the next summer session. However, on May 25, Ellis wrote to inform Meredith that his undergraduate credits could not be transferred from Jackson State because that school was not a member of the Southern Association of Colleges and Secondary Schools. Ellis added that the application did not meet other requirements, but he failed to say what they were. He also said that Meredith's file had been closed. On May 31, 1961, Meredith responded by filing suit in the U.S. district court against the University of Mississippi, claiming that he had been denied admission because of his race.

The trial lasted a year. The credibility of the case rested solely on Meredith's testimony. Beginning with the deposition, Meredith faced questions, many of which had nothing to do with his application for admission to the university. The questions were aimed at intimidating him and falsifying his story. They asked where his wife was from, who had married them, what type of car he had driven to the hearing, if he had credit cards or paid cash for every-

Good evening, my fellow citizens:

The orders of the Court in the case of Meredith vs. Fair are beginning to be carried out. Mr. James Meredith is now in residence on the campus of the University of Mississippi. ~~He will~~

~~be enrolled tomorrow as an under~~

~~graduate student.~~ This has been accomplished thus far without the use of National Guard or other troops -- and it is to be hoped that the law enforcement officers *with the assistance of marshals* of the State of Mississippi will ~~be~~ continue to be sufficient in the future. All students, members of the faculty and public officials in both Mississippi and the

thing. They even asked him to spell the words "notary public." For blacks in southern courtrooms at that time, questions such as these were known as "the treatment." Finally, the court ruled against Meredith, asserting that he had not met all the procedures required for admission, including obtaining letters of recommendation from alumni. Meredith had failed to satisfy the court that his admission to the University of Mississippi was denied on the grounds that he was black.

Meredith appealed this decision to the U.S. Court of Appeals for the Fifth Circuit. His case finally received full attention from the court, the State of Mississippi, and the United States public. On June 25, 1962, more than a year after he had initially applied to the university, the U.S. Fifth Circuit Court handed down its decision. James Meredith was to be allowed to attend the University of Mississippi. The court stated in its decision that Mississippi schools practiced a segregationist policy and further explicitly recognized the difficulty for a black student to meet the requirement of obtaining letters of recommendation from alumni, since there were no black alumni of the university nor any white alumni likely to be willing to write them. The court also said that the requirement for such letters was adopted by the university only a few months after the historic Supreme Court decision in *Brown* v. *The Board of Education of Topeka, Kansas.*

Meredith's legal victory was challenged. Mississippi Governor Ross Barnett proclaimed on September 13, 1962, that the State of Mississippi would not conform to the federal court decision. The state would defy the court order to admit James Meredith to the state university. Governor Barnett declared: "The operation of the public school system is one of the powers which was not delegated to the Federal Government but which was reserved to the respective states pursuant to the terms of the Tenth Amendment." He went on to say that the federal government had used the judicial system illegally to take away the reserved powers of the State of Missis-

sippi. Governor Barnett declared that Mississippi was "no longer subject to the laws of the United States."

All three branches of the state government of Mississippi were determined to take as many actions as possible to obstruct execution of the federal court's decision allowing a black to enroll in a white university. Meredith was tried, convicted, and sentenced to a year in jail on charges of false voter registration. A few days later, the Mississippi legislature held an emergency midnight session to pass a law stating that a person could not enroll in the university if he or she were involved in a criminal proceeding, or if he or she were convicted of a crime with a minimum sentence of a fine of $300 or a year in jail. The governor was appointed registrar of the university effective September 20, the day Meredith first arrived on campus.

The U.S. Government would not tolerate the defiance of the State of Mississippi. On September 30, 1962, the President of the United States issued an Executive Order stating that justice was not going to be obstructed by any person or state. President Kennedy knew that above all, a president has the responsibility to enforce the law and maintain order throughout the country. On October 1 the president communicated his order on the Meredith case in a radio and television address. In this speech, Kennedy reaffirmed the supremacy of the federal courts over the state courts in settling constitutional issues. Reproduced here are the first three pages of the president's speech. The entire document is kept at the John F. Kennedy Presidential Library, a part of the National Archives located in Boston, Massachusetts.

James Meredith, in pursuing the constitutional procedure to enact change within our system, had effected a revival of a question as old as the Constitution itself: Are the State governments the ultimate authority in this country or is the federal government? John Kennedy responded in no uncertain terms, the Constitution is the supreme law of the land and the federal

nation, ~~it is to be hoped~~, ~~can now~~ return
to their normal activities with full
confidence in the integrity of American
law.

This is as it should be. For our
nation is founded on the principle that
observance of the law is the eternal
safeguard of liberty -- and defiance of
the law is the surest path to tyranny.
The law which we obey includes the final
rulings of our courts as well as the
enactments of our legislative bodies.
Even among law-abiding men, few laws
are universally loved -- but they are
uniformly respected and not resisted.

3

Americans are free, in short, to disagree with the law -- but not to disobey it. For in a government of laws, and not of men, no man -- however prominent or powerful -- and no mob -- however unruly or boisterous -- is entitled to defy a court of law. If this country should ever reach the point where any man or group of men, by force or threat of force, could long defy the commands of our courts and Constitution, then no law would stand free from doubt, no judge would be sure of his writ and no citizen would be safe from his neighbors.

courts are its final interpreters.

Teaching Activities

1. Divide the class into three groups. Give each group one of the questions listed below.

    a. How does President Kennedy's speech reveal his responsibilities as president?

    b. What constitutional issues are addressed in his speech?

    c. What persuasive techniques does Kennedy employ in this speech to the American people?

Allow time for the students to exchange their ideas and consult their textbooks for more ideas. Write all ideas on the board or on chart paper for the students to see. Conduct a classroom discussion summarizing the role of the president, the principles of law and order, the balance between federal and state power, and the techniques of an effective speech.

2. James Meredith said, "The very existence of the human being makes everything possible." Discuss with your class the meaning of this statement. Ask your students to list some examples of situations in which an individual human being cannot make a change. How could such situations be eliminated? What could individuals do to eliminate them? Explain why more people do not try to change social situations that they feel are unfair or unacceptable.

3. Ask students to play the role of James Meredith in 1962. Have them write a letter home to his parents describing his life on campus and the surrounding social climate.

4. Ask students to compare and contrast the University of Mississippi in the 1960s with the university today. Research the opportunities available to blacks and minorities on the campus today. Evaluate the impact that Meredith had on the opportunities presently available. Have students present their findings in an essay.

5. Suggest that each student find two other individuals in history who shared James Meredith's belief that one person could enact change within a society and prepare a brief report to present informally to the rest of the class. Ask reporters to capsulize the attitudes and values of their two selected figures in two or three words. Write these words on the board. Direct students to make a composite of an individual of conscience based on the entire list of words.

Abington v. Schempp: A Study in the Establishment Clause

A little more than 25 years ago, the Supreme Court heard a series of First Amendment cases related to school prayer and Bible reading. In a concurring opinion in one of these cases, Justice William J. Brennan declared that "the Court's historic duty to expound the meaning of the Constitution has encountered few issues more intricate or more demanding than that of the relationship between religion and the public schools." Nevertheless, a succession of cases affecting religion and public schools are appealed to the Court, heard by the justices, and decided year after year.

Our students need a historical framework of First Amendment freedom-of-religion cases in order to understand recent decisions made by the courts. Beginning with the first major case involving the establishment clause of the First Amendment brought before the Supreme Court in 1947, *Everson* v. *Board of Education,* the justices have used a broad construction of the clause. Justice Hugo Black's opinion in that case clearly describes this construction:

The 'establishment of religion' clause of the First Amendment means at least this: Neither a state nor the Federal Government can set up a church. Neither can pass laws which aid one religion, aid all religions, or prefer one religion over another. Neither can force nor influence a person to go to or to remain away from church against his will or force him to profess a belief or disbelief in any religion. No person can be punished for entertaining or professing religious beliefs or disbeliefs, for church attendance or non-attendance. No tax in any amount, large or small, can be levied to support any religious activities or institutions, whatever they may be called, or whatever form they may adopt to teach or practice religion. Neither a state nor the Federal Government can, openly or secretly, participate in the affairs of any religious organizations or groups and vice versa. In the words of Jefferson, the clause against establishment of religion by law was intended to erect 'a wall of separation between church and State.'

In the Everson case, the Court nevertheless upheld the State of New Jersey parochial school busing plan on the basis that the assistance was to the child, not to a religion. In 1948 and 1952, the Court heard two cases involving released time for religious instruction. In the first case, *McCollum* v. *Board of Education,* the Illinois program was declared unconstitutional because the instruction was given within the school building. On the other hand, in the second case, *Zorach* v. *Clauson,* the New York program was upheld as constitutional because the instruction was outside the state-owned school facility. Thus the Court established a test to determine the extent to which the public school may accommodate religious education during the school day, a distinction used by the Court

SUPREME COURT OF THE UNITED STATES

Nos. 142 and 119.—October Term, 1962.

School District of Abington Township, Pennsylvania, et al., Appellants, 142　　　　　*v.* Edward Lewis Schempp et al.	On Appeal From the United States District Court for the Eastern District of Pennsylvania.
William J. Murray III, etc., et al., Petitioners, 119　　　　　*v.* John N. Curlett, President, et al., Individually, and Constituting the Board of School Commissioners of Baltimore City.	On Writ of Certiorari to the Court of Appeals of Maryland.

[June 17, 1963.]

Mr. Justice Clark delivered the opinion of the Court.

Once again we are called upon to consider the scope of the provision of the First Amendment to the United States Constitution which declares that "Congress shall make no law respecting an establishment of religion or prohibiting the free exercise thereof . . . ." These companion cases present the issues in the context of state action requiring that schools begin each day with readings from the Bible. While raising the basic questions under slightly different factual situations, the cases permit of joint treatment. In light of the history of the First Amendment and of our cases interpreting and applying its requirements, we hold that the practices at issue and the laws requiring them are unconstitutional under the Establishment Clause, as applied to the states through the Fourteenth Amendment.

later in the Schempp decision.

A cluster of Bible-reading and prayer cases was decided in 1962 and 1963. The New York Regents' prayer written for that state's public schools was ruled in violation of the First Amendment in *Engle* v. *Vitale,* June 1962. Then in the October 1962 term, the Court struck down a Pennsylvania law requiring the daily reading without comment of ten verses from the Bible followed by a recitation of the Lord's Prayer. The opinion for the second case, *Abington Township, Pennsylvania* v. *Schempp,* and its companion case in Maryland, *Murray* v. *Curlett,* was written by Justice Tom C. Clark. The Court's conclusion, as enunciated by Justice Clark, was based on the facts that the exercises were required, the students recited the exercises in unison, the exercises were held in public buildings, and the exercises were supervised by state-paid teachers.

In none of these cases, however, did the Supreme Court rule voluntary prayer unconstitutional. Furthermore, the Court did not rule against teaching *about* religion in public schools. Concerning this, Justice Clark wrote, "it might well be said that one's education is not complete without a study of comparative religion or the history of religion and its relationship to the advancement of civilization." A number of educational organizations, including NCSS, have developed guidelines for teaching about religions in the public school curriculum. For a copy of the NCSS position statement and guidelines, write to NCSS headquarters.

The issue of Bible reading and prayer in the public schools is reflected more immediately by a proposed constitutional amendment permitting organized prayer in the public schools, the recent court cases in New Jersey *(Karcher* v. *May)* and Alabama *(Wallace* v. *Jaffree),* and the continuing confusion over the meaning of the establishment clause.

The document reproduced here is a portion of Justice Clark's opinion of the

Court in the Schempp case. Located in the National Archives, the opinion is part of the Records of the U.S. Supreme Court, Record Group 267, Appellate Case Files, No. 142, O.T. 1962.

Additional religious freedom documents along with teaching suggestions may be found in a National Archives documentary teaching package entitled *The Constitution: Evolution of a Government.* For more information, contact the Education Branch, National Archives and Records Administration, Washington, DC 20408; or call 202-523-3347.

Teaching Suggestions

1. Prepare a worksheet listing the following items for analyzing the document: type of document, author of the opinion, to whom the document was written, audience for whom it was written, what cases were decided, justification for hearing both cases as one, decisions rendered, constitutional basis for considering the case, summary statements of reasons for decision, and three unfamiliar legal terms used in the document and their definitions. Photocopy a worksheet and a copy of all three pages of the document for each student and ask students to complete the worksheet while carefully reading the document.

2. Direct students to find out the story of the Schempp case. Give the students a chance to tell the story aloud in class with as many students as possible adding details. Ask the students to summarize the story along with the finding of the Court in the case and then conduct an opinion poll among other students and teachers in the school and youths and adults in their neighborhoods and communities to discover the current attitudes toward prayer in the public schools. Compare results of the polls in class.

3. Working with your students, compile a list on the chalkboard or the overhead projector of arguments that could have been used on both sides of the Schempp case. Divide the class into groups of five or six students. Ask students to discuss the argu-

ABINGTON SCHOOL DISTRICT *v.* SCHEMPP. 21

with the contention that the Bible is here used either as an instrument for nonreligious moral inspiration or as a reference for the teaching of secular subjects.

The conclusion follows that in both cases the laws require religious exercises and such exercises are being conducted in direct violation of the rights of the appellees and petitioners.[9] Nor are these required exercises mitigated by the fact that individual students may absent themselves upon parental request, for that fact furnishes no defense to a claim of unconstitutionality under the Establishment Clause. See *Engel* v. *Vitale, supra,* at 430. Further, it is no defense to urge that the religious practices here may be relatively minor encroachments on the First Amendment. The breach of neutrality that is today a trickling stream may all too soon become a raging torrent and, in the words of Madison, "it is proper to take alarm at the first experiment on our liberties." Memorial and Remonstrance Against Religious Assessments, quoted in *Everson, supra,* at 65.

It is insisted that unless these religious exercises are permitted a "religion of secularism" is established in the

---

[9] It goes without saying that the laws and practices involved here can be challenged only by persons having standing to complain. But the requirements for standing to challenge state action under the Establishment Clause, unlike those relating to the Free Exercise Clause, do not include proof that particular religious freedoms are infringed. *McGowan* v. *Maryland, supra,* at 429–430. The parties here are school children and their parents, who are directly affected by the laws and practices against which their complaints are directed. These interests surely suffice to give the parties standing to complain. See *Engle* v. *Vitale, supra.* Cf. *McCollum* v. *Board of Education, supra; Everson* v. *Board of Education, supra.* Compare *Doremus* v. *Board of Education,* 342 U. S. 429 (1952), which involved the same substantive issues presented here. The appeal was there dismissed upon the graduation of the school child involved and because of the appellants' failure to establish standing as taxpayers.

22   ABINGTON SCHOOL DISTRICT *v.* SCHEMPP.

schools. We agree of course that the State may not establish a "religion of secularism" in the sense of affirmatively opposing or showing hostility to religion, thus "preferring those who believe in no religion over those who do believe." *Zorach* v. *Clauson, supra,* at 314. We do not agree, however, that this decision in any sense has that effect. In addition, it might well be said that one's education is not complete without a study of comparative religion or the history of religion and its relationship to the advancement of civilization. It certainly may be said that the Bible is worthy of study for its literary and historic qualities. Nothing we have said here indicates that such study of the Bible or of religion, when presented objectively as part of a secular program of education, may not be effected consistent with the First Amendment. But the exercises here do not fall into those categories. They are religious exercises, required by the States in violation of the command of the First Amendment that the Government maintain strict neutrality, neither aiding nor opposing religion.

Finally, we cannot accept that the concept of neutrality, which does not permit a State to require a religious exercise even with the consent of the majority of those affected, collides with the majority's right to free exercise of religion.[10] While the Free Exercise Clause clearly prohibits the use of state action to deny the rights of free exercise to *anyone,* it has never meant that a majority could use the machinery of the State to practice its beliefs. Such a contention was effectively answered by Mr.

---

[10] We are not of course presented with and therefore do not pass upon a situation such as military service, where the Government regulates the temporal and geographic environment of individuals to a point that, unless it permits voluntary religious services to be conducted with the use of government facilities, military personnel would be unable to engage in the practice of their faiths.

ABINGTON SCHOOL DISTRICT *v.* SCHEMPP. 23

Justice Jackson for the Court in *West Virginia Board of Education* v. *Barnette*, 319 U. S. 624, 638 (1943):

> "The very purpose of a Bill of Rights was to withdraw certain subjects from the vicissitudes of political controversy, to place them beyond the reach of majorities and officials and to establish them as legal principles to be applied by the courts. One's right to . . . freedom of worship . . . and other fundamental rights may not be submitted to vote; they depend on the outcome of no elections."

The place of religion in our society is an exalted one, achieved through a long tradition of reliance on the home, the church and the inviolable citadel of the individual heart and mind. We have come to recognize through bitter experience that it is not within the power of government to invade that citadel, whether its purpose or effect be to aid or oppose, to advance or retard. In the relationship between man and religion, the State is firmly committed to a position of neutrality. Though the application of that rule requires interpretation of a delicate sort, the rule itself is clearly and concisely stated in the words of the First Amendment. Applying that rule to the facts of these cases, we affirm the judgment in No. 142. In No. 119, the judgment is reversed and the cause remanded to the Maryland Court of Appeals for further proceedings consistent with this opinion.

It is so ordered.

ments thoroughly and then take a position, pro or con. Encourage each group to reach a consensus rather than take a vote. A recorder from each group should report to the class the group's position and the reasons for taking that position.

4. Use the document and the note to the teacher to help students make a list of establishment clause court cases from Everson to the most recent. Prepare a data-retrieval chart that includes the following items of information to be gathered for each of the cases: date, original jurisdiction of case, principal figures in the dispute, circumstances surrounding the issue, decision reached by the Court, basis of the decision, and changes in legal interpretation of the issue. After assembling the information, the students could chart a time line in the classroom tracing the history of the interpretation of the establishment clause and indicating the changes in interpretation during the past 40 years.

5. Beginning with the statements made by Justice Clark in the document, conduct a class discussion on the Court's position on teaching about religion in the public schools. Instruct students to gather information from a variety of sources on what is the legal, ethical, appropriate, and responsible place of religion during the school day and on the school campus.

6. For further study, you might direct students to research additional religious freedom issues related to education raised in court cases, such as released time, equal access to public facilities, teaching of evolution versus creationism, tuition tax credits to parents of students in private sectarian schools, and public financial grants to religious bodies.

Close Encounters with the Fourth Dimension

Nearly 40 years ago, the current age of interplanetary flights, or unidentified flying objects (UFOs), dawned upon the public with the inexplicable experiences of airplane pilot Kenneth Arnold. On June 24, 1947, over Washington state, pilot Arnold reported having sighted from his cockpit 9,200 feet above ground a group of bright objects traveling at speeds unachieved by man, which he described as shaped like saucers. Though Arnold's experience with UFOs was not the first, his report attracted great press attention and, later, official military interest.

1947 marked the beginning of the U.S. Air Force's official investigations into UFO reports. The Air Force effort, centered at Wright-Patterson Air Force Base in Dayton, Ohio, was known variously as Project Sign, Project Grudge, and, finally, Project Blue Book. The first two projects were secret and short-lived. Project Blue Book, however, lasted from 1948 to 1969.

For the purposes of its investigations, the Air Force defined a UFO as "any aerial object or phenomenon which the observer is unable to identify." Its interest in UFOs grew out of both security and scientific concerns. Between 1947 and 1966, the Air Force investigated 11,108 reports of UFOs. Upon investigation, only 676 remained "unidentified." Most of the sightings were explained by the Air Force as astronomical phenomena, aircraft, or balloons.

The document reproduced here is typi-cal of those sighting reports. In 1962, Project Blue Book received 474 reports of UFOs, though only 15 remained "unidentified" after Air Force investigations. The file of the Greenwich sighting includes this notation by an Air Force staff member: "Description of the obj. [object] & flight conform to that normally expected of an a/c [aircraft]."

Since 1969, the government has had no official investigation procedures for UFO sightings. The Air Force's Project Blue Book files are now in the National Archives. The National Aeronautics and Space Administration, the agency that now does most space research, simply tells interested callers that the government no longer collects data on UFO sightings.

The document reproduced here is from case files, September 6-15, 1962, Project Blue Book, Records of the Headquarters United States Air Force, Record Group 341. The names and addresses of the two UFO reporters have been deleted to protect their privacy.

Teaching Activities

1. Before discussing the letter in class, review its basic elements with students: Who? What? When? Where? Why?

2. Ask each student to react to the letter either verbally or in writing. Ask students to justify their reactions with specific details from the letter. Finally, ask each student to pose two questions that the writer

National Aeronautics and Space Administration   ██████████ Lane
Research Department (UFO Studies)   Greenwich, Conn.
Washington, D. C.   September 17, 1962

Dear Sirs:

I would like to report an unidentified flying object observed by myself and a friend on September 15, 1962, 11:20-11:30 P. M., from a dock at the end of Steamboat Road in Greenwich, Connecticut. ████████████ of Brookside Park, Greenwich, and I were at that time sitting in his car, overlooking Long Island Sound from the gener. area of the Indian Harbor Yacht Club. Beginning at 11:00 P. M. we had observed the moon, stars and clouds visible from the dock overlooking the bay.

At about 11:20 we both noticed a very brightly glowing object, fairly well above the Eastern horizon. We noticed that the light came from at least two sources, each close enough to the other to effect a blending of the light rays. Almost as soon as this glow caught our attention, the light suddenly was extinguished, and the object then became invisible to us. But very soon the lights glowed on again.

The object moved Westward - toward us. I got out of the car, and walked to the Eastern extremity of the dock, in order to achieve as good a view of the object, as it approached, as possible. Larry remained in the car.

It did not pass directly overhead, but turned Southward (████ ̶n̶o̶t̶e̶d̶ said that it ̶h̶a̶d̶ ̶b̶e̶e̶n̶ a 90-degree turn) Before and during its change of course I noted that it emitted a very faint sound, similar to high-altitude aircraft. The sound seemed to follow the object itself at a considerable distance behind. A third source of light became evident. Apparently the object had three large lights - two in front, and one in the rear - that created a triangular effect. As it turned, I observed the back, or under- side of the object, and was amazed to see an apparent row of much smaller lights, presumably on the "wings" (if there were any). Some of these numerous lights were red in color. Whether any were green in color, I can't ascertain. While the object headed West, all of the lights blinked on and off, fairly rhythmically. At 11:30 these lights were still seen, but more faintly with each minute, as the object continued to head South- ward. It's course at that point seemed more undulating than straight.

Could you please inform me whether you or any other agency dealing with UFO have received similar reports made Sept. 15, 1962, and if objects matching or similar to the above description have been reported at any time? Whatever acknowledgement and materials you could mail to me on the subject would be much appreciated.

The only measure by which I could guess the altitude of the object was the barely discernable sound it caused, which suggested that it traveled at a very high altitude, and was of immense size.

We wondered whether the Air Force or NASA was testing a new, secret aircraft, and if publicity about it would cause embarrassment to those responsible for security tests.

It is the opinion of both ████ and myself that the object behaved so much unlike conventional aircraft, that it is doubtful whether the object was conceived anywhere on this planet.

I would very much like to hear your opinion on the matter. If it would be in your interests, perhaps you could help me do a research paper on UFO for Columbia University.

                             Respectfully yours,

of the letter leaves unanswered.

3. In class define *reliability*. Discuss with students the reliability of this letter as a historical source.

4. Students, especially middle-school students, enjoy discussions of unusual phenomena — Big Foot, unicorns, and the prospects of interplanetary visitors. Their interest in these subjects is an opportunity to refine their skills as judges of evidence and developers of logical arguments. Divide the class into two groups. Assign Group 1 to collect evidence to support the UFO report and direct Group 2 to collect evidence to counter the claims of the observers. Enjoy the lively discussion.

5. In 1949, when George Orwell's *1984* was published, interplanetary travel seemed a cockamamie idea. Today, with the space shuttle gliding in and out of the Earth's atmosphere, the idea of travel to other planets seems much less fantastic. Discuss with students their "wildest dreams" of the future. Ask students to consider what changes they foresee in schools, transportation, government, and entertainment by 2034. Classify their predictions to discern where they envision the greatest changes.

6. History is replete with examples of individuals whose observations led them to espouse ideas contrary to prevailing thought; Jesus, Galileo, Joan of Arc, Gandhi, George Orwell, and many others, including our UFO observers. Obviously their points of observation (scientific, societal, and so forth) differ, but they shared one common problem. Discuss with students the proposition that gaining acceptance of an unusual idea involves at least three processes: establishing credibility, convincing skeptics on the rational level, and touching the emotions of the skeptics so that they also accept the phenomenon at a nonrational level.

Tonkin Gulf: A Study in Historical Interpretation

In August 1964 President Lyndon Johnson announced that U.S. ships had been attacked by the North Vietnamese in the Gulf of Tonkin. Johnson dispatched U.S. planes against the attackers and asked Congress to pass a resolution to support his actions. The resolution, featured here, became the subject of great political controversy in the course of the undeclared war that followed.

The details of the events preceding passage of the resolution remain clouded. Your textbook most likely chronicles the Gulf of Tonkin incident as the Johnson administration described it, but consensus about what actually happened remains elusive. This lack of consensus provides you with an excellent opportunity to discuss the process of historical interpretation with your students.

Questions still arising from the Tonkin Gulf incident are these: Did North Vietnamese torpedo boats attack the U.S. destroyers *Maddox* and *Turner Joy* in the Gulf of Tonkin in August 1964 once? or twice? or not at all? Were the American ships attacked because they were on reconnaissance for South Vietnamese forces raiding the North Vietnamese coast? How did the hotly contested 1964 presidential election campaign influence President Johnson's quick response to the attack? Did the mounting instability of the South Vietnamese government affect the U.S. reaction to the Tonkin Gulf incident? Did members of the Johnson administration mislead Congress to gain approval to send U.S. ground forces into South Vietnam? Why didn't President Johnson ask for a declaration of war against North Vietnam?

To aid you in your class discussions of the resolution, you will find here a brief description of the events surrounding U.S. involvement in Vietnam and the passage of the resolution. This description reflects generally accepted scholarship, but of course the events are subject to alternative interpretations.

The United States in Vietnam

In the 1880s, Vietnam became a colony of France. During World War II, the Viet Minh (the Revolutionary League for the Independence of Vietnam) emerged, intent on national independence. With the defeat of Japan by the Allies, France reasserted her sovereignty in Vietnam and drove the Viet Minh underground. The leader of the Viet Minh, Ho Chi Minh, sought and received support for his guerrilla activities from the emerging communist regime in China. As a counter to Ho Chi Minh's "Democratic Republic of Vietnam," France granted independence to the "State of Viet-Nam" within the French Union in 1949. The United States formally recognized the government of Emperor Bao-Dai in 1950, but extensive U.S. military and economic aid could not prevent a stunning French defeat by the Viet Minh at the battle of Dien Bien Phu in May 1954.

Simultaneously with the fall of Dien Bien Phu, a 14-nation conference seeking

PUBLIC LAW 88-408

Eighty-eighth Congress of the United States of America

AT THE SECOND SESSION

Begun and held at the City of Washington on Tuesday, the seventh day of January,
one thousand nine hundred and sixty-four

Joint Resolution

To promote the maintenance of international peace and security in southeast Asia.

Whereas naval units of the Communist regime in Vietnam, in violation of the principles of the Charter of the United Nations and of international law, have deliberately and repeatedly attacked United States naval vessels lawfully present in international waters, and have thereby created a serious threat to international peace; and

Whereas these attacks are part of a deliberate and systematic campaign of aggression that the Communist regime in North Vietnam has been waging against its neighbors and the nations joined with them in the collective defense of their freedom; and

Whereas the United States is assisting the peoples of southeast Asia to protect their freedom and has no territorial, military or political ambitions in that area, but desires only that these peoples should be left in peace to work out their own destinies in their own way: Now, therefore, be it

Resolved by the Senate and House of Representatives of the United States of America in Congress assembled, That the Congress approves and supports the determination of the President, as Commander in Chief, to take all necessary measures to repel any armed attack against the forces of the United States and to prevent further aggression.

Sec. 2. The United States regards as vital to its national interest and to world peace the maintenance of international peace and security in southeast Asia. Consonant with the Constitution of the United States and the Charter of the United Nations and in accordance with its obligations under the Southeast Asia Collective Defense Treaty, the United States is, therefore, prepared, as the President determines, to take all necessary steps, including the use of armed force, to assist any member or protocol state of the Southeast Asia Collective Defense Treaty requesting assistance in defense of its freedom.

Sec. 3. This resolution shall expire when the President shall determine that the peace and security of the area is reasonably assured by international conditions created by action of the United Nations or otherwise, except that it may be terminated earlier by concurrent resolution of the Congress.

Speaker of the House of Representatives.

(Acting) *President pro tempore of the Senate.*

APPROVED

AUG 10 1964

an end to the war in Korea was meeting in Geneva. At the request of France, this conference also sought to prevent further fighting in Vietnam between the victorious Viet Minh and a noncommunist nationalist government that succeeded the French-controlled administration. In an informal agreement — the Geneva Accords — the conference provisionally divided the territory of Vietnam into two parts at the 17th parallel until July 1956, when an internationally supervised election would determine the government of all of Vietnam.

In September 1954, a protocol to the Southeast Asia Treaty Organization (SEATO) protected South Vietnam, as well as Laos and Cambodia, from outside invasion or subversion just as the treaty itself did for its regular signatories (United States, Great Britain, France, Australia, New Zealand, the Philippines, Thailand, and Pakistan). The SEATO agreement, like NATO for Europe and, later, CENTO for the Middle East, institutionalized Secretary of State John Foster Dulles' "containment" policy, which was designed to resist Sino-Soviet expansion on a global scale. By extending the protection of a multinational treaty to South Vietnam, the SEATO protocol gave the area international status. The national elections scheduled for 1956 never took place.

By 1960, Ho's revolutionary tactics and President Ngo Dinh Diem's unpopular policies finally culminated in the open conflict that the 1954 Geneva conference had tried to avoid. In 1961 President John F. Kennedy committed the first U.S. military advisers to Diem, thereafter increasing their numbers to establish a U.S. "presence" that would bolster morale in South Vietnam. In November 1963, just before Kennedy's assassination, the already shaky government of President Diem collapsed under a military coup.

Lyndon Johnson assumed the direction of U.S. policy at a time of great instability in South Vietnam. That country would see seven governments in the year 1964. Johnson faced not only changing governments in South Vietnam, but also a strident presidential election against conservative Republican Barry Goldwater at home. On August 4, 1964, President Johnson shocked the nation when he announced in a late evening television address that:

> ... renewed hostile actions against United States ships on the high seas in the Gulf of Tonkin have today required me to order the military forces of the United States to take action in reply. The initial attack on the destroyer *Maddox,* on August 2, was repeated today by a number of hostile vessels attacking two U.S. destroyers with torpedoes. The destroyers and supporting aircraft acted at once on the orders I gave after the initial act of aggression. We believe at least two of the attacking boats were sunk. There were no U.S. losses.... Air action is now in execution against gunboats and certain supporting facilities in North Viet-Nam which have been used in these hostile operations. In the larger sense this new act of aggression, aimed directly at our own forces, again brings home to all of us in the United States the importance of the struggle for peace and security in southeast Asia. Aggression by terror against the peaceful villagers of South Viet-Nam has now been joined by open aggression on the high seas against the United States of America.[1]

The President went on to say that he would ask the Congress for a formal resolution in support of his actions. Congress passed the Tonkin Gulf Resolution on August 7 with only two senators dissenting (Wayne Morse and Ernest Gruening). Johnson, and later, President Richard Nixon relied on the resolution as the legal basis for their military policies in Vietnam. But as public resistance to the war heightened, the resolution was repealed by Congress in January 1971. The Tonkin Gulf Resolution is Public Law 88-408, 88th Congress; General Records of the United

---

[1] L. B. Johnson, *Public Papers of the President of the United States.* Book II (Washington, DC: U.S. Government Printing Office, 1965), p. 927.

States Government, Record Group 11.

Teaching Activities

1. Analyzing the Tonkin Gulf Resolution

a. Identify terms — joint resolution, 88th Congress, Vietnam, Charter of the United Nations, international waters, commander in chief, Southeast Asia Collective Defense Treaty, protocol state, Speaker of the House of Representatives, Acting President pro tempore of the Senate.

b. Review with students each element of the resolution to assure that they comprehend its meaning. What questions does each raise?

c. Discuss with students the general sense of the resolution.

2. Interpreting the Tonkin Gulf Resolution

a. Why did President Johnson seek congressional support for his actions in Vietnam when Presidents Eisenhower and Kennedy had not?

b. On August 7, the day the resolution was passed by the Senate, Senator Wayne Morse, rejecting the resolution, said: "... we are in effect giving the President of the United States warmaking powers in the absence of a declaration of war. I believe that to be a historic mistake." Discuss this point of view with students.

c. For what other reasons did the resolution eventually become so controversial?

d. In recent years, U.S. Presidents have committed military forces to fight in foreign countries without a formal declaration of war by Congress. Discuss with students the arguments for and against this change in governmental responsibilities. Consider the constitutional, political, and military implications.

3. Understanding the Tonkin Gulf incident in the context of the war in Vietnam — student activities

a. Using several sources, develop a time line of the August 1964 events in the Gulf of Tonkin. Compare the facts to see if students can reach agreement as to what happened.

b. Encourage students to talk with several adults about their recollections of the Tonkin Gulf incident and their attitudes toward U.S. involvement in Vietnam during the 1960s. Try to reach a cross-section of adults; e.g., a Vietnam War veteran, an anti-war demonstrator, a newspaper person, a World War II veteran, a draftee. Direct students to ask the adult if his or her attitudes toward U.S. conduct in the war changed and if so, when and why. Develop a list of the attitudes reflected by these adults and consider what accounts for the differences among them. Ask several of these people to visit your class and share with students their recollections of the war.

c. It has been said that television news of Vietnam shaped American perceptions of war in a way not experienced in previous wars. As students interview adults who experienced the war, direct them to test this assertion.

d. Consider with students how the U.S. involvement in Vietnam has affected American attitudes toward the draft, toward conventional war, and toward nuclear war.

Constitutional Issues: Watergate and the Constitution

When Richard Nixon resigned in 1974 in the wake of the Watergate scandal, it was only the second time in our history that impeachment of a president had been considered. Nearly every action taken with regard to the case had some constitutional significance. The document shown here deals with a specific question: Should the Watergate Special Prosecutor seek an indictment of the former president?

It is two pages of a three-page memorandum written for the Watergate Special Prosecutor in August 1974, after Richard Nixon resigned the presidency and before President Ford pardoned him. (The third page adds one more item to the pro-indictment list and adds another category, "delay decision.")

The Office of the Special Prosecutor was created by Executive Order in May 1973 and twice faced the question of whether to seek an indictment of Richard Nixon. The first time was in March 1974, when the grand jury handed down indictments of seven White House aides for perjury and obstruction of justice.

President Nixon was named an "unindicted coconspirator" at that time because Watergate Special Prosecutor Leon Jaworski advised the grand jury that in his opinion a sitting president could not be indicted. In his view, the House Judiciary Committee was the appropriate body under the Constitution for examining evidence relating to the president.

The House Judiciary Committee pursued its constitutional mandate and drew up five articles of impeachment, three of which they approved in the summer of 1974. When the president was forced by the Supreme Court in August 1974 to surrender tape recordings that revealed his knowledge of the cover-up, even his staunchest supporters in the House admitted that they would have to vote in favor of impeachment. On August 9, 1974, President Richard Nixon resigned the presidency and became citizen Richard Nixon.

Thus, for the second time the Watergate Special Prosecutor's Office faced the question of whether or not to seek an indictment. Article I, section 3, clause 7 of the Constitution provides that a person removed from office by impeachment and conviction "shall nevertheless be liable to indictment, trial, judgement and punishment according to the law." But there are no guidelines in the Constitution about a president who has resigned. The memorandum shown here is typical of others in this file. It outlines reasons for and against pursuing an indictment against Richard Nixon. It is taken from Records Relating to Richard M. Nixon, Records of the Watergate Special Prosecution Force, Record Group 460.

Teaching Suggestions

The activities below assume that students are familiar with the Watergate scandal. Textbooks may vary in the extent of

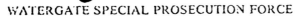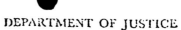

WATERGATE SPECIAL PROSECUTION FORCE   DEPARTMENT OF JUSTICE

Memorandum

TO   : Leon Jaworski   DATE: August 9, 1974
        Special Prosecutor

FROM : Carl B. Feldbaum
        Peter M. Kreindler

SUBJECT: Factors to be Considered in Deciding Whether to
         Prosecute Richard M. Nixon for Obstruction of
         Justice

        In our view there is clear evidence that Richard M. Nixon
participated in a conspiracy to obstruct justice by concealing
the identity of those responsible for the Watergate break-in
and other criminal offenses. There is a presumption (which in
the past we have operated upon) that Richard M. Nixon, like
every citizen, is subject to the rule of law. Accordingly,
one begins with the premise that if there is sufficient evidence, Mr. Nixon should be indicted and prosecuted. The
question then becomes whether the presumption for proceeding
is outweighed by the factors mandating against indictment and
prosecution.

        The factors which mandate against indictment and prose-
cution are:

    1. His resignation has been sufficient punishment.

    2. He has been subject to an impeachment inquiry
        with resulting articles of impeachment which
        the House Judiciary Committee unanimously
        endorsed as to Article I (the Watergate
        cover-up).

    3. Prosecution might aggravate political
        divisions in the country.

    4. As a political matter, the times call for
        conciliation rather than recrimination.

    5. There would be considerable difficulty in
        achieving a fair trial because of massive
        pre-trial publicity.

The factors which mandate in favor of indictment and prosecution are:

1. The principle of equal justice under law requires that every person, no matter what his past position or office, answer to the criminal justice system for his past offenses. This is a particularly weighty factor if Mr. Nixon's aides and associates, who acted upon his orders and what they conceived to be his interests, are to be prosecuted for the same offenses.

2. The country will be further divided by Mr. Nixon unless there is a final disposition of charges of criminality outstanding against him so as to forestall the belief that he was driven from his office by erosion of his political base. This final disposition may be necessary to preserve the integrity of the criminal justice system and the legislative process, which together marshalled the substantial evidence of Mr. Nixon's guilt.

3. Article I, Section 3, clause 7 of the Constitution provides that a person removed from office by impeachment and conviction "shall nevertheless be liable and subject to Indictment, Trial, Judgment, and Punishment, according to Law." The Framers contemplated that a person removed from office because of abuse of his public trust still would have to answer to the criminal justice system for criminal offenses.

4. It cannot be sufficient retribution for criminal offenses merely to surrender the public office and trust which has been demonstrably abused. A person should not be permitted to trade in the abused office in return for immunity.

5. The modern nature of the Presidency necessitates massive public exposure of the President's actions through the media. A bar to prosecution on the grounds of such publicity effectively would immunize all future Presidents for their actions, however criminal. Moreover, the courts may be the appropriate forum to resolve questions of pre-trial publicity in the context of an adversary proceeding.

their coverage, so you may want to supplement the textbook with a chronology of events. (See *Social Education,* "Document of the Month," May 1982, for suggested readings and a timeline of events.)

1. Before distributing the document, ask students whether or not they would have been in favor of prosecuting the former president in August 1974 and why. List their reasons on the board. Duplicate and distribute copies of the document and ask them to choose the argument on each side that seems most persuasive to them. Ask for volunteers to stage a class debate on the question: Should the Watergate Special Prosecutor seek an indictment of Richard Nixon?

2. The framers of the Constitution purposely created a system of government in which the three branches would be in a state of tension when in disagreement. This tension has often been criticized for paralyzing the processes of government. However, it is generally agreed that these very tensions, together with the vigorous efforts of a free press, worked to reveal the full extent of the Watergate scandal. In order to illustrate this, ask students to match the unit of each branch of government with the event for which it was responsible.

The Legislative Branch
___ 1. Senate Select Committee on Presidential Campaign Activities
___ 2. House Judiciary Committee

The Executive Branch
___ 3. President
___ 4. Office of the Watergate Special Prosecutor

The Judicial Branch
___ 5. U.S. Supreme Court
___ 6. U.S. District Court of the District of Columbia
   a. imposed heavy sentences on the Watergate burglars, hoping they would talk
   b. claimed executive privilege
   c. investigations here revealed existence of White House taping sytem
   d. requested a trial subpoena for 64

White House tapes for evidence in the Watergate cover-up trial
   e. adopted three articles of impeachment
   f. ruled that executive privilege does not extend to criminal proceedings and that the president must turn over the tapes

KEY: 1. **c,** 2. **e,** 3. **b,** 4. **d,** 5. **f,** 6. **a.**

3. Ask students to look up each of the following sections of the Constitution and explain how it relates to the story of Watergate. Also ask them to indicate which of these constitutional references are referred to in the document shown here.
   a. Article I, section 2, clause 5
   b. Article I, section 3, clause 6
   c. Article I, section 3, clause 7
   d. Article II, section 1, clause 8
   e. Article II, section 2, clause 4
   f. Amendment I

President Nixon's Letter of Resignation

Where were you on December 7, 1941, or on November 22, 1963, and how did the events for which we remember these dates affect your personal and public life? Keeping in mind that today's high school seniors have no memory of the events of the summer of 1974, you may wish to use Richard Nixon's letter to Secretary of State Henry Kissinger, in which he resigned from the office of President of the United States, as a springboard to discussions of such questions with your students.

To refresh your memory of the events surrounding this letter, we present a selective chronology, beginning with the "bugging" of the Democratic National Committee headquarters in the Watergate building in May 1972 and ending with President Gerald Ford's pardon of the former President in September 1974.

How do we place these events, which became known collectively as "Watergate," in historical context; and what is their significance to our history? Elizabeth Drew, in her fascinating *Washington Journal, the Events of 1973-1974*, comments on this question in her August 8, 1974, entry:

There is already some talk about what "the historians will say" — the historians, those unknown people who in the future will have the franchise to interpret what is going on now. We tend to assume that out of their years of accumulation of fact they will sift the truth — a truer truth than any we can hope to grasp. They will have many more facts, and they will have what is called "perspective" (which means they will not be trapped in the biases of our day and can freely write in the biases of *their* day — can find what they are looking for). But I wonder if they will really understand what it was like. Will they know how it felt to go through what we have gone through? Will they know how it felt to be stunned — again and again — as we learned what had been done by people in power? Will they know how it felt to be shocked, ashamed, amused by the revelations — will they understand the difficulty of sorting out the madcap from the macabre? (What *was* one really to think about someone in the pay of the White House putting on a wig and travelling across the country to visit a sick, disgraced lobbyist?) Can they conceivably understand how it felt as we watched, on our television screen, our President say, "I am not a crook"? Will they be able to understand why, almost two years ago, some very sensible people wondered whether it was the last election? Will they understand how it felt — as it did last fall at the time the President fired Special Prosecutor Cox, and on several later occasions—when it seemed that there were no checks on power? Will they understand how degrading it was to watch a President being run to ground? Will they know how it was to feel in the thrall of this strange man, who seemed to answer only to himself? Knowing the conclusion, as they will, will they understand how difficult, frightening, and fumbling the struggle really was?[1]

President Nixon addressed his letter of resignation to Secretary of State Kissinger

---

[1] 1974, Elizabeth Drew, *Washington Journal* (Random House). Originally in *The New Yorker.*

THE WHITE HOUSE

WASHINGTON

August 9, 1974

Dear Mr. Secretary:

I hereby resign the Office of President of the
United States.

Sincerely,

Richard Nixon

11.35 AM

HK

The Honorable Henry A. Kissinger
The Secretary of State
Washington, D.C.   20520

THE CHRONOLOGY

May 28, 1972 Electronic surveillance ("bugging") equipment is installed at Democratic National Committee headquarters in the Watergate building.

June 17, 1972 Five men are arrested while attempting to repair the surveillance equipment at Democratic National Committee headquarters.

August 30, 1972 President Nixon announces that John Dean has completed investigation into the Watergate buggings and that no one from the White House is involved.

September 15, 1972 Bernard Barker, Virgilio Gonzalez, E. Howard Hunt, G. Gordon Liddy, Eugenio Martinez, James W. McCord, Jr., and Frank Sturgis are indicted for their roles in the June break-in.

January 8, 1973 Watergate break-in trial opens. Hunt pleads guilty (January 11); Barker, Sturgis, Martinez, and Gonzalez plead guilty (January 15); Liddy and McCord are convicted on all counts of break-in indictment (January 30).

February 7, 1973 U.S. Senate creates Select Committee on Presidential Campaign Activities.

April 17, 1973 President Nixon announces that members of the White House staff will appear before the Senate Committee and promises major new developments in investigation and real progress toward finding truth.

April 23, 1973 White House issues statement denying President had prior knowledge of Watergate affair.

April 30, 1973 White House staff members H.R. Haldeman, John D. Ehrlichman, and John Dean resign.

May 17, 1973 Senate Committee begins public hearings.

May 25, 1973 Archibald Cox sworn in as Special Prosecutor.

July 7, 1973 President Nixon informs Senate Committee that he will not appear to testify nor grant access to Presidential files.

July 16, 1973 Alexander Butterfield informs Senate Committee of the presence of a White House taping system.

July 23, 1973 Senate Committee and Special Prosecutor Cox subpoena White House tapes and documents to investigate cover-up.

July 25, 1973 President Nixon refuses to comply with Cox subpoena.

August 9, 1973 Senate Committee files suit against President Nixon for failure to comply with subpoena.

October 19, 1973 President Nixon offers Stennis a compromise on the tapes; that is, Senator John Stennis (D-Miss.) would review tapes and present the Special Prosecutor with summaries.

October 20, 1973 Archibald Cox refuses to accept the Stennis compromise. President Nixon orders Attorney General Elliot Richardson to fire Cox, but Richardson refuses and resigns in protest. Acting Attorney General Robert Bork fires Cox. These events come to be known as the "Saturday Night Massacre."

October 23, 1973 President Nixon agrees to hand over tapes to comply with subpoena.

November 1, 1973 Leon Jaworski named Special Prosecutor.

November 21, 1973 Senate Committee announces discovery of 18½-minute gap on tape of Nixon-Haldeman conversation of June 20, 1972.

February 6, 1974 House of Representatives authorizes House Judiciary Committee to investigate whether grounds exist for impeachment of President Nixon.

April 16, 1974 Special Prosecutor issues subpoena for 64 White House tapes.

April 30, 1974 President Nixon submits tape transcripts to House Judiciary Committee.

July 24, 1974 Supreme Court unanimously upholds Special Prosecutor's subpoena for tapes for Watergate trial.

July 27, 1974 House Judiciary Committee adopts article I of impeachment resolution, charging President with obstruction of investigation of Watergate break-in.

July 29, 1974 House Judiciary Committee adopts article II of impeachment resolution, charging President with misuse of powers and violation of his oath of office.

July 30, 1974 House Judiciary Committee adopts article III of impeachment resolution, charging the President with failure to comply with House subpoenas.

August 9, 1974 President Richard Nixon resigns.

September 8, 1974 President Gerald Ford pardons former President Nixon.

on the basis of a 1792 act of Congress that established procedures for the resignation of federal officers. While the 25th Amendment to the Constitution established the line of succession, the 1792 act set up the process. The letter is from Letters of Resignation and Declination of Federal Office, General Records of the Department of State, Record Group 59.

Teaching Activities

Discussion Questions

The depth of your discussions will vary according to the background of your students. To improve the discussions, we list below several secondary readings appropriate for students. Caution students that, as with all evidence, the authors of these books represent a certain point of view. Have students consider these issues:

1. What do you remember of the events of Watergate? How were these events significant to you? How did they affect your family?

2. Do you think President Nixon should have resigned? Explain your answer.

3. If President Nixon had included in his letter his reasons for resigning, what do you think he might have said?

4. President Nixon's resignation was a landmark event in our political history. What other events in your lifetime would you describe as landmarks?

5. What is impeachment? What are the roles of the House of Representatives and the Senate in the impeachment process?

6. Review and discuss the details of the 25th Amendment to the Constitution. Compare and contrast the procedures for changing leadership in a parliamentary system of government with our procedures.

Student Readings

For all students:
Bernstein, Carl, and Bob Woodward. *All the President's Men.* New York: Simon & Schuster, 1974.

Woodward, Bob, and Carl Bernstein. *The Final Days.* New York: Simon & Schuster, 1976.

For advanced students:
Dean, John W. *Blind Ambition: The White House Years.* New York: Simon & Schuster, 1976.
Drew, Elizabeth. *Washington Journal, the Events of 1973-1974.* New York: Random House, 1974.
Frost, David. *I Gave Them a Sword: Behind the Scenes of the Nixon Interviews.* New York: William Morrow and Company, 1978.